The Age of Aging

How Demographics are Changing the Global Economy and Our World

The Age of Aging

How Demographics are Changing the Global Economy and Our World

George Magnus

To Paul,

Thanks for coming to the Chatham House talk, and I hope you enjoy the book. Best Wishes

George Magnus

John Wiley & Sons (Asia) Pte. Ltd.

Other Wiley Editorial Offices

John Wiley & Sons, Inc., 111 River Street, Hoboken, NJ 07030, USA
John Wiley & Sons, Ltd., The Atrium, Southern Gate, Chichester,
    West Sussex P019 8SQ, UK
John Wiley & Sons (Canada), Ltd., 5353 Dundas Street West, Suite 400, Toronto,
    Ontario M9B 6H8, Canada
John Wiley & Sons Australia Ltd., 42 McDougall Street, Milton, Queensland 4064,
    Australia
Wiley-VCH, Boschstrasse 12, D-69469 Weinheim, Germany

Library of Congress Cataloging-in-Publication Data

IBSN: 978-0-470-82291-3

Typeset in 10.5/14 point, Melior by C&M Digitals (P) Ltd.
Printed in Singapore by Saik Wah Press Pte. Ltd.
10 9 8 7 6 5 4 3 2 1

Contents

To Lesley, Daniel, Jonathan, Rachel and Ben

Acknowledgments

Demographic change is having a steadily greater impact on our lives, business and public policy. I am fortunate to have had the opportunity to consider it in some detail. In 2005 and 2006, I wrote two major research reports for UBS clients on some of the major economic and market consequences of demographic change and population aging. The research and thought that went into these reports encouraged me to look at the subject matter in a more holistic way, resulting in this book. I am grateful to UBS and to the company's research management for the working arrangements that allowed me the opportunity to do so, and for its support.

Several economist colleagues at UBS, past and present, were persuaded to look over parts of or the entire book and revert with comments and opinions. So, thanks to Jonathan Anderson, Paul Donovan, Ian Douglas, Sanjay Mathur and Simon Ogus. I would also like to thank Larry Kummer, who not only read parts of the book and challenged some of my prejudices, but also supplied me with a flow of articles, blogs and references to material I might otherwise have failed to notice.

Economists write a lot, but all too often, what they write, however good or profound, can be obscure and shrouded in complex language and jargon. Ideas are great but communicating them effectively is important. I would like to thank Gwen Robinson for helping me to communicate better many ideas and much analysis, which might otherwise have been opaque or inefficiently expressed. I would also like to note the editing of Graham Watts, whose rigorous work was executed with total professionalism and commanded my thorough admiration.

There are others who played meaningful roles in the production of this book and to whom thanks are also due. Sophie Constable produced formatted documents, complete with graphs and tables, from my raw documents and hieroglyphics. I received much in the way of encouragement and advice, in particular from Loretta Napoleoni, who brought an author's perspectives to me, and Alistair Michie, who encouraged me with robust business and political ideas, as well as some particular insights about China.

Finally, I am indebted to my wife, Lesley for her unflinching support and direct assistance in my endeavors. Thanking one's wife or partner is, of course, standard acknowledgement material but I know now that it is definitely neither gratuitous nor pro forma. Aside from reading and editing, it is a very special thank you for compassion, understanding, and encouragement. I also want to thank my children, Daniel, Jonathan, Rachel and Ben for being an inspiration in a way they cannot possibly have been conscious about: their very being drove me to consider the future in ways that will definitely affect them for a lot longer than it will me and my generation.

Why demographics matter

People have always been fascinated by or fearful of population developments. Nowadays, many of us fear overpopulation. We fret about congestion in countries and communities and, for both good and bad reasons, we are becoming more vocal about immigration. In some countries, especially in Africa, we see poverty, famine, and disease on a scale that shocks. Not least, we peer anxiously at a new phenomenon: rapidly aging populations. Demographic change is now one of our main preoccupations. What will our world look like, and how will it function in the next 25 or 50 years as it supports a further three billion people, mostly in developing countries, and as the populations of several richer societies decline? And how will our societies adapt and change as, in some Western countries, the over-65s become the fastest growing age group, outnumbering children?

Demography is defined as "the branch of knowledge that deals with human populations, especially the statistical analysis of births, deaths, migrations, disease etc., as illustrating the condition of life in communities."[1] Voluminous books and research papers have been published on these topics and on the biggest issue of demographic change: population aging. Interest in gerontology, the study of the process of aging, has been around for centuries—and is even more relevant now against a backdrop of increases in both average life expectancy and the maximum age to which any one person might expect to live. This book, though, is not about gerontology but rather about the economic, social, and sometimes political consequences of a world in which different populations are aging at different rates. For the most part, aging research is highly academic, sometimes requiring an understanding of algebra and econometrics, or is specifically about the thorny and complex issues of retirement pension and personal finance planning. At the other extreme, there is a lot of news coverage of sensitive subjects such as immigration or of dire warnings of economic and social collapse.

What I try to do here is bridge the gap and look at the spectrum of demographic challenges we all face in ways that I hope people, with and without specialist knowledge will find illuminating and revealing, if sometimes provocative. Much of the book is about the economic and social characteristics and implications of demographic change but, inevitably, there are frequent forays into the political, both national and international, including ways in which public policy, the law, and human behavior could or should change. However, those looking for clear and self-evident solutions to such issues will be disappointed. There is no template, no precedent, and no proven theory to help us anticipate the consequences of population change and aging. Instead, I look to frame the challenges and the resulting issues, rather than lay out a blueprint for policymakers. Similarly, when it comes to some of the more overtly social and political matters related to global demographic change, I look to explore some of the things that societies are going to have to think about and address, including many that are taboo, rather than offer any particular legislative agenda.

The last decade has witnessed the strongest economic growth around the world—for over 40 years—and a rapid acceleration in the pace of globalization and technological change. Yet it has also emphasized or aggravated, especially in the West, a range of fears and insecurities about income inequalities, threats to jobs, immigration, the affordability of pensions, large and unstable financial imbalances in the global economy, and environmental degradation. If it's an unfortunate truth that the poor are always in need of help, and often without a strong political voice, the same cannot be said of the middle classes in Western societies. It is in the middle classes in America and Europe that the greatest increase in discontent and in economic insecurity can be detected. While this may be hard for the baby boomers to cope with, their young adult children and grandchildren are finding it even tougher.

In the coming decades we will battle with these issues, rather than bask in the afterglow of the breakneck speed of global economic growth of recent years, not least because the United States and other advanced economies began to succumb in 2007 to a serious banking crisis and possibly a sustained economic downswing. Aging societies, the characteristics of which will become increasingly evident from 2008, will become a challenge of growing importance.

Some of the issues of aging societies were taken up in a German TV drama-documentary in 2007. Germany's population is one of the world's oldest and fastest aging, and the program set out to consider the implications of aging (*2030—Aufstand der Alten* (Uprising of the Elderly)). The three-part thriller, set in the year 2030, started with an aggrieved pensioner kidnapping the head of a healthcare company that had, with government backing, stolen money from retirees under the false promise of a happy and comfortable life in a retirement resort. The plot thickens, and a reporter uncovers a commando group that plans to dispose of the elderly to camps in Africa. Such aging angst, albeit presented in this perhaps tongue-in-cheek way, reflects an increasing consciousness about the implications of aging societies, not only in the West but, in due course, around the world.

The footprints of aging are everywhere. Now that the euphoria of triumphalist capitalism, stirred by the fall of the Berlin wall in 1989, has passed many have begun to believe that free market capitalism cannot address the needs of the politically vocal middle classes, let alone the poor, and certainly not in aging societies. New forms of social or welfare capitalism will be required to accommodate the shift toward a grayer world—as well as to manage the implications of climate change, globalization, and other social issues.

The coming significant and prolonged changes in the size and the characteristics of the population and the labor force could undermine economic growth. Aging societies will have to figure how to get more age-related spending from the welfare state and how to pay for it. Aging societies will experience changes that affect asset prices, wages, and profits. They may see the gradual disappearance of involuntary unemployment—but at the same time those in work may face rising pressures to save through higher taxes and social charges. Such societies will require additional efforts to invest in education and training, not only to allow workers to stay ahead in a globalized world but also to boost the productivity of the fewer people of working age.

Many of the premises on which modern welfare programs were established have changed or soon will. Retirement pensions, for example, were designed to allow people to stop working and enjoy their last few years in relative comfort while making way for new, younger workers. Today, although pensioner poverty is becoming a growing problem and longer life expectancy means more disability, retirement is for many an extended period of state-supported or company-financed leisure, which was never anticipated. Now Western countries have to think about how all of this is going to be paid for as the numbers of younger contributors to state pension and healthcare schemes decline or grow much more slowly.

To address these challenges over the next decade or two, it is probable that the role and influence of the state, and what is demanded of it, will expand. Demographic change involves public policy areas that span health, education, social and labor market institutions, immigration, openness of the economy to trade and investment, retirement pension systems, and national savings and taxation systems. Free market solutions and ways of addressing these issues are available of course, but it is unlikely that we will be willing to depend on market-based outcomes as our societies age. In the late nineteenth century, and again in the twentieth, people needed or wanted to accord the state a bigger role to introduce and develop social welfare systems to tend to larger and younger populations. Today, its role may have to be expanded again as populations become older and possibly smaller at the same time.

Developing countries will also have to face these questions, if not now then with added force in a decade or two. China, in particular, will have to balance rising economic aspirations and growing social and environmental problems with the structure of central political control. What Beijing calls attempts to "coordinate market mechanisms" may be a unique way of combining such control with the operation of at least some market forces. It remains to be seen, however, whether this model can provide growth and stability, greater equality, environmental improvement, and financial security for its growing bands of childless over-65s.

The demography dial

Our world is home to 6.5 billion people, and current projections are that it will grow to about 9.2 billion by 2050. Although the growth rate of the world's population is expected to slow from roughly 1.2 percent per year now to less than 0.5 percent by 2050, nearly all our new citizens are going to be born, and grow up, in developing countries. In the developed or advanced world, many countries will experience the curious phenomenon of population decline. In Japan, this process has already begun.

More of us will be living in towns and cities. This is not a new trend, as on average about half of us are urban creatures today, but by 2030 this proportion will be over 60 percent. In advanced societies, and in Latin America, the urban population is expected to rise from an already high 70–80 percent to about 85–90 percent. In other developing countries in Asia and Africa, the urban population is expected to rise from 40 percent today to nearly 55 percent. As this occurs, there will be a near 50 percent increase in the average number of people occupying each square kilometer of land.

That means more people in more crowded cities, with the biggest changes happening in the developing world. These are the things at the core of excited, and sometimes emotional, debates concerning climate change, the adequate availability of resources—including crude oil and water—immigration and domestic and international security.

The biggest change, and one that mankind has never experienced before, is advanced population aging. The median age of the world's population—where half are older and half are younger—is 28 years. By 2050, it will have become 38 years.

In Europe it will be 47, in China 45, and in North America and Asia about 41. This aging process is the result of two mega-trends. The first is a low or declining fertility rate at, or below, the so-called replacement rate of 2.1 children per woman. Most countries in the West, except for the United States, have fertility rates below this level, as indeed does China. In other words, women are generally having fewer or no children, and family size is shrinking. The second is rising longevity—or the tendency to live much longer thanks to improvements in health, diet, preventive care, and so on.

It follows that over the next few decades, many countries are going to be characterized by a rising proportion of old people and very old people (aged over 80) and by a slower growing, or shrinking, proportion of young people. It is fair to ask what "old" means in the first half of the twenty-first century, especially in societies dominated by service industries and information and communications technology. Are we "too old" to do meaningful work at 63 or 67 or 74? Clearly not, but I shall argue that attitudes to work, and to older people capable of work, are going to become much more important—and certainly more so than the stereotypes that come to mind so easily.

The number of people aged over 60 is expected to reach one billion by 2020 and almost two billion by 2050, some 22 percent of the world's population. In Japan, this age group is expected to double to about 38 percent of the population, only a few percentage points higher than it is expected to be in China. In Europe and America it will account for about 28 percent and 21 percent respectively. And those aged over 80 are expected to account for about 4 percent of the world's population, four times as big as now. For the first time, the number of over-65s will exceed those aged less than five years. This is the first time there has been such a shift in age structure, and with it will come new economic, social, and political issues we've never had to tackle before. In some countries, notably Japan but quite soon in western Europe and even in China, this means that there aren't going to be enough children growing up to become workers and employees to support a rapidly growing elderly population.

As I shall point out later, these changes in age structure are going to lead to significant changes in dependency, which in turn will have enormous economic and financial consequences. Dependency ratios are defined as the number of old or very young people as a percentage of the working age population, that is those aged 15–64. Most developing countries will still have falling dependency ratios for the next 20 years because youth dependency is falling, and old-age dependency isn't rising especially fast yet. Western countries, on the other hand, have completed the decline in youth dependency and now face a rapid increase in old-age dependency.

It is small wonder, then, that there is now an extensive debate going on about the economic and social effects and characteristics of aging societies, covering the affordability and financing of pensions and healthcare, the statutory retirement age, immigration, labor, and possibly skill shortages, and the implications for tax, social, employment, and education policies. In addition, noncommunicable diseases will become more of a burden, family structures will change, the way we retire from work will shift toward greater self-provision, our health and pension systems will come under greater strain, and new roles for government and government policy will have to be formulated.

It is not possible to predict today what life will look like in the next 50 years—any more than our parents or grandparents could. Imagine if surveys from 1908 or 1958 had asked people what they thought the world would be like in 2008. The answers would probably be laughable today. In terms of demographic change alone, experts have underestimated life expectancy, overestimated mortality, and been surprised by the downswing in fertility rates. And they can't really predict immigration trends. That said, population growth and aging are slow-moving developments that should be among the more predictable. Unlike unfolding globalization, the complexities of the Middle East, and the rise of China, demographic shifts tend to be more stable. Unlike the human responsibility for climate change, where we may have to wait 30 years to find out which side of the scientific debate was right, demographic change is transparent and clearly for us to manage. By understanding and examining the scale and implications of demographic change, we can prepare. By preparing, we can try to mitigate some of the repercussions, for a while at least, and, who knows, even come up with innovative solutions that can sustain our spirit. There's no guarantee we will succeed before some sort of crisis erupts, or maybe even at all. So, let us explore the Age of Aging and see what is in store for us, our children, and theirs.

Endnote

1   *The Oxford English Dictionary.*

Chapter 1

Introducing a new age

> *The day is coming when great nations will find their numbers dwindling from census to census.*
> —Don Juan in George Bernard Shaw, *Man and Superman*, Act 3, 1903.

The distinguished economist, author, and public servant J.K. Galbraith, who died in 2006 at the ripe old age of 97, referred some 10 years earlier to the "still" syndrome. He was reflecting on the way the elderly are reminded constantly about the inevitability of decline. The "still" syndrome, he said, was adopted by the young to assail the old as in "Are you still working?" or "Are you still taking exercise?" or ". . . still writing," ". . . still drinking?" and so on. His advice was to have a retort ready to call attention to the speaker's departure from grace and decency. His was to say, "I see that you are *still* rather immature." He urged old people to devise an equally adverse, even insulting, response and voice it relentlessly.[1]

You can see Galbraith's point. I do not wish to become embroiled in an argument about "agism," but the fact that we can live and work longer than our parents and grandparents and that it looks like our children will do even better, reflects great improvements in health, education, technology, and economic growth. It is the consequences of that success that I propose to look at here. For, while we might like the idea of living healthier and longer lives, population aging brings with it very real economic and social problems.

In the very long run, the issue of population aging will probably fade. The baby boomers will move on to the great retirement home in the sky, and the global trend toward lower fertility rates will result in the restoration of better demographic balance. For the time being, however, we will have to face up to the problems created by such age and gender imbalances, and the divide between the old-age bulge of developed countries and the youth bulge of developing ones. Some communities and countries will deal with these challenges more successfully or with less disruption than others.

In some ways, you could see aging and population trends as more evidence of the West's steady decline. While there may be some truth in this, the global and complex nature of population aging also means we must look at aging through different spectacles.

For the West the challenges that lie ahead will be formidable. They aren't quite the same as those discussed in *Decline of the West*, a cyclical theory of the rise and fall of civilizations as foreseen by the controversial historian and philosopher Oswald Spengler in 1918.[2] His rather prejudiced views—he believed in German hegemony in Europe and was seen by the Nazis as a sort of intellectual heavyweight—were set against a background of what he called the prospect of "appalling depopulation." Today, it is population aging rather than depopulation that concerns us, along with the economic and social changes associated with a shift of power to the younger countries in the developing world, typified by China and India. These things are already influencing our perceptions of economic and financial security. As if this were not enough, younger people in Western societies will probably have to deal with a generational shift in feelings of prosperity and well-being. What seemed to come easily to the baby boomers will be less accessible to their children and grandchildren. How well Western societies and institutions cope with these changes is of great importance.

From a philosophical point of view, the quote from George Bernard Shaw's play at the start of this chapter may be of interest. Drawn from a dream sequence, in which Don Juan and the Devil debate the relative benefits of Hell over its dull alternative, the passage also discusses love and gender roles, marriage, procreation, and the enjoyment of life.

Everyone is affected everywhere

Baby boomers will remember the term "swinging sixties" with nostalgia and some affection. Notwithstanding the restrictions in the 1960s on what you could do in public, this era of "sex, drugs, and rock 'n' roll" was essentially a public celebration of a golden age for youth and of rising political and social consciousness. Young people aspired to freedoms, rights, and means of expression that were revolutionary in the context of the environment in which they had grown up, even if not in the traditional context of the violent overthrow of government. In fact, the sixties may have been anything but swinging in some respects, but the impact of the boomers on social organization, political processes, and economic outcomes was unquestionably significant. What mattered was not so much the demand for change, but that it occurred in the context of an enormous increase in the proportion of young people in the population.

Time and age, though, have moved on and in many countries, for the first time ever, there are already more people of pensionable age than there are children under 16 years—and the difference is going to increase over the next 20 to 30 years. It is both apt and increasingly urgent, therefore, to focus attention on the different prospects and lifestyles faced by different generations.

If you were born before the end of the Second World War, the chances are you are retired or soon will be. You may worry about many things in your life, but financial security is probably not one of them, and your state and/or employee pension is most likely secure.[3] If you were born after the Second World War but before say 1963, you are now on the cusp of retirement or within 10 or 20 years of it. Most of you should not have to worry too much about financial security, but some at the younger end of this age group are almost certainly going to confront the implications of population aging head-on.

Those who are Generation X, born between the mid-1960s and 1979, or Generation Y, born between 1980 and the fall of the Berlin Wall in 1989, or belong to the subsequent Internet Generation, are a large part of the focus of this book. They form what has been called the "boomerangst" generation. Although this term normally refers to the fears and concerns of the boomers themselves, it is also apt to apply it to their children and grandchildren. Indeed, it is a direct allusion to both some behavioral characteristics of younger people today and some of the financial and social issues with which they are growing up. For it is on their shoulders that the worrying burden and task of managing and coping with population aging will fall.

Although it is the macroeconomic implications of these changes that I examine in this book, there are many personal issues that people will have to confront that will affect both themselves and their elders. By way of background, consider just three: First, younger people today have higher divorce and separation rates. Nonmarried women are less likely than non-married men to have adequate financial security for retirement, but the latter have bigger problems in forming and maintaining social networks. Second, childless couples and single-parent families comprise a growing social class, and care for separated or single middle-aged women, as they age, becomes a more pressing issue when they do not have adult children to help. And third, support for the growing band of older citizens will become crucial. More and more over-65s will be living alone and belong to families that will be "long" in terms of generations and "narrow" in terms of the number of children, siblings, and cousins.

It would be wrong to think that these demographic issues are unique to the West. Many developing countries, while younger than Western societies, are aging faster, and most will confront similar problems from about 2030–35. Yet, for now at least, they lack the West's wealth, social infrastructure, and financial security systems. Some developing countries, notably China and South Africa, will confront their aging issues—for quite different reasons—much earlier than most. For South Africa, the main problem is the devastating effect of HIV/AIDS on the mortality of younger, working-age people. In China's case, it is because of the impact of the one-child policy, as well as other more common causes of declining fertility rates and rising life expectancy. China's population aged under 50 and, by implication, much of its labor force, starts to contract around the same time as in Germany, in 2009–10. Despite our fascination and, for some, fear at the speed with which say, China and India, are becoming major world powers, it is possible that they too face a parallel to the West's "decline." Later, I shall explain that the reason for this slightly chilling warning lies in the interplay between aging populations on the one hand and a growing gender gap characterized by an excessive male:female ratio on the other.

Moreover, just because one country or region seems to be more youthful than another, you cannot assume that its economic prowess and potential is greater. Age—or youth—is important but always in context. For example, the so-called Tiger countries (South Korea, Taiwan, Hong Kong, and Singapore) were, in 1970, virtually indistinguishable from the main South American countries with identical age structures and median ages. Between 1970 and 2007 their populations of working age grew at almost identical rates. But over this period, income per head, which was about the same for both geographic regions in 1970, quadrupled in the case of South Korea and Taiwan, and rose sixfold for Hong Kong and Singapore, while barely doubling in South American countries. Demographic factors alone cannot explain this discrepancy, but the organization and marshalling of human (and other) resources by government, and agencies of the state, were unquestionably crucial to the Tigers' success.

In considering the prospects for aging societies, therefore, it is important to understand not only the basic demographics of countries and regions but also a range of other economic, social, and political conditions and policies that could affect those population trends in a more or less positive way.

Although much of this book is about the macroeconomics of demographic change, there are no equations, and the concepts are pretty simple to understand. But demography reaches far into the microeconomics of how and why we spend and save, how we interact with work, family, and each other, and how we plan for retirement and old age, as well as into areas such as globalization, immigration, and international security.

Mostly, we just don't think, or perhaps don't like to think, about aging. Our consumer culture is dominated by images of youth, energy, dynamism, and sex. As population aging advances, however, it is inevitable that the youth intensity of this culture will change and with it our collective interest in the implications of older societies. Even now, rare as it is to hear demographics discussed at the pub or at a social event, popular interest is increasing: the affordability of pensions, for example, is now a widespread concern. We are at the start of a unique development in history and shall soon see how Western societies and some of the major "emerging" nations will cope. The West will have to figure how to manage and prosper with not having enough children to become tomorrow's workers and breadwinners. Developing countries will have to create societies that offer employment and hope to their young before aging starts to manifest itself in about 2030–35.

The demographic debate laid bare

The book is divided into 10 further chapters. The first three discuss population issues from a historical and contemporary perspective. From Thomas Malthus, through Karl Marx and Charles Darwin to the baby boomers, the Club of Rome, and climate change, demographic developments have been and remain important even as the pendulum of public debate has swayed back and forth over time. What is new today are the large changes in age structure, brought about by rising life expectancy and falling fertility rates, and the silent but significant shifts in old-age and youth dependency.

Therefore, I consider the main characteristics of an aging world, and what their implications are, and ask how some of the economic consequences could be addressed. For the most part, these possible solutions fall into four categories: raising the participation in the workforce of people who could work more or longer but don't; raising productivity growth so that those at work contribute more to society and the economy; sustaining or increasing high levels of immigration so as to make good possible labor and skill shortages; and paying attention to the inadequacy of savings, which, in many countries, threatens to cause financial problems when resources have to be transferred between generations to ensure adequate financial security for today's and tomorrow's retirees.

Differing prospects for richer and poorer nations

The next three chapters look at population and aging issues in more detail, first in the United States, Japan, and western Europe and then in emerging and developing countries. Japan is our laboratory for aging issues, and so developments there may hold lessons for the rest of us. Some are relevant, some not, but Japan's relative slippage from the center of global affairs may have something to do with its rapid aging, especially in the company of large and populous neighbors. America's circumstances are altogether different—as are those of some other, mainly Anglo-Saxon, countries.

In America, the aging of society is a slower process, and the country's population is still expected to rise by 100 million over the next 40 years or so. But it is a country, a superpower, that is being stretched, not only militarily but also financially. It is already the world's biggest debtor nation, presiding over a reserve currency that may be in slow decline. The key demographic issue for the United States, however, is the affordability and financing of not only pensions but notably healthcare. The European Union includes countries that are aging more rapidly, notably Italy and Germany, and some in which depopulation is already occurring, or soon will. Financing of pensions and improving the way labor markets work are already important policy issues for EU leaders and will dominate the national and EU policy agenda in the next decades.

The bigger and more macroeconomic implications of aging societies in the West follow, and I ask whether aging could damage our wealth. What should we expect will happen to inflation and interest rates as demographic change unfolds? What could happen in the equity markets and to the returns needed to accumulate adequate pension assets? And—hottest potato of the lot—what does demographic change imply for house prices?

Emerging and developing countries are of particular interest for a variety of reasons, not least because the bulk of the rise in the world's population in the next 40 years is expected to occur in sub-Saharan Africa and in the arc of countries from Algeria to Afghanistan. The more pronounced characteristics of aging societies won't become apparent to these countries until the 2030s. Until then, they will have strong demographic advantages, which give them the potential to wield both economic and political power. I shall discuss specifically the particular issues that await China, India, Russia, sub-Saharan Africa, and the Middle East and North Africa.

Demographics and other global trends

The last three chapters consider the significance of demographic change in areas that are often overlooked in discussions about population and aging. Globalization defines the way in which countries and populations interact. It is neither static nor stable, however, and it is certainly vulnerable to reverses—or destruction, as occurred between 1914 and 1945. So how might aging societies evolve if the rising hostility to globalization in richer economies continues?

Immigration is an important way in which countries with advanced aging characteristics can supplement future labor or skill shortages. It is also an intensely political and emotional issue, and you can have some serious reservations about the practicality and usefulness of high or higher immigration in aging societies without being opposed to immigration. It is important to look at it in some detail and at the economic arguments advanced in its favor as a solution to the problems of aging societies.

Following on from immigration, religion and international security are hardly softer topics, but it is appropriate to consider some issues associated with both. So I look at whether the higher fertility rates associated with people with high levels of religious belief or practice mean that Western societies, for example, are, in effect, at the cusp of reversing decades or even centuries of secularization. There is also the contrast between the youth bulge in developing countries, some of which are, or aspire to be, powers, and the old-age bulge in the West, and how it provides a fitting backdrop to ponder the implications for global security.

Last, in the epilogue, I consider some big questions that might be faced by the baby-boomers' children and grandchildren, the "boomerangst" generation. And in a postscript on population forecasting, I detail some of the main aspects of this particular branch of futurology.

Endnotes

1 Encyclopaedia Britannica Online, "John Kenneth Galbraith's Notes on Ageing: The Still Syndrome," http://www.britannica.com/eb/article-218599.
2 Oswald Spengler, *Decline of the West*, originally written in German, published in English, (Oxford: Oxford University Press, 1991).
3 Many people have been shocked by events that have compromised or even destroyed what they thought to be secure pensions. One of the more celebrated examples concerned the thousands of employees who worked for a Houston-based energy company called Enron that went bankrupt after an accounting scandal in 2001. Because the employees were obliged to hold their pension assets in the company's stock, the price of which collapsed, their pensions became worthless. There are many other examples of the dilution or destruction of pension plans as a result of corporate bankruptcy or takeovers but also because of changes to pension plans and eligibility.

Chapter 2

Population issues from Jesus Christ to aging and climate change

> More generally ... population and environmental problems created by nonsustainable resource use will ultimately get solved one way or another: if not by pleasant means of our own choice, then by unpleasant and unchosen means, such as the ones that Malthus initially envisioned.
> —Jared Diamond, *Collapse*.[1]

Around the time of the birth of Jesus Christ, and through the duration of the Roman Empire, the world's population was probably no larger than 200 million. According to Angus Maddison, Professor at the Faculty of Economics, University of Groningen,[2] Netherlands, world population was still less than 270 million in 1000. By 1700, however, the total had grown to about 600 million and by 1820, may have just surpassed one billion. Yet, it had taken two centuries to double. It took just over one century to double again to 2.3 billion in 1940. In 1960, world population was around 3 billion. Today, half a century later, it has more than doubled again to about 6.5 billion, and the United Nations expects it to reach 8.2 billion in 2030 and just over 9 billion by 2050 (see Figure 2.1).

Despite the fact that population has risen especially sharply only for the last 100 years, social commentators, philosophers, and economists have been looking throughout history at population trends. Edward Gibbon, in his renowned *The History of*

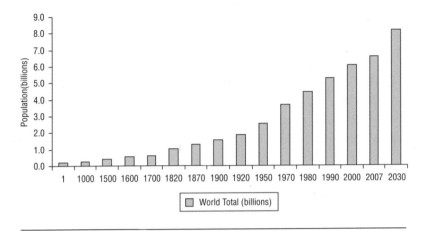

Figure 2.1   World population

Source: Angus Maddison, Groningen Growth and Development Center.

---

the Decline and Fall of the Roman Empire,[3] suggested that the
Roman Empire collapsed because it eventually fell victim to barbarian invasions on its periphery, which succeeded because of a
loss of civic virtue among citizens in its center. Roman citizens,
Gibbon argued, had become lazy, even "outsourcing" their duties
to barbarian mercenaries, who became so numerous that they
eventually overwhelmed the empire.

Gibbon's account of social decay in Rome contrasts with what
many see as the idealism, belief system, extended family focus,
and higher fertility on the part of Christians. And in turn, said
Gibbon, the characteristics and philosophy of Christians sapped
the enthusiasm of Roman citizens to fight and sacrifice for the
empire. Not a few observers have wondered if the West is today's
"Rome" but I shall come to that later.

In terms of population size, then, not much happened for the
best part of a millennium and a half—well, not much by the standards of what happened in the second millennium. Population
growth was slow and often interrupted by famine and disease,
notably the Black Death, or Black Plague, in the mid-fourteenth
century, which is estimated to have wiped out anywhere
between a third and two-thirds of Europe's population. The
acceleration in population growth began after 1750 in England
and then, with gusto, in mainland Europe after 1800.

Population take-off, Malthus, and Marx

Numerous theories have been proposed as to why this happened when it did. The Industrial Revolution is credited with being the main catalyst. It brought new technology, better diets and medical care, and, eventually, prosperity. But this standard explanation isn't the whole story. Other noneconomic factors were important in stimulating population growth. These included a decline in the age of marriage in step with an increased tendency toward marriage, and a rising incidence (if not acceptability) of illegitimate children. The development of factory and urban life, meanwhile, made it possible for people to marry and start families, in stark contrast to rural and feudal lifestyles, where marriage and family were linked to the ownership and inheritance of land—or at least rights to live and work on land. This, in turn, tended to favor middle-aged adults.

In any event, just as England's population expansion was getting under way, the first major critique and warnings about population growth were articulated by Thomas Malthus, an English economist and demographer, known widely for his view that world resources, notably food, would not be able to keep pace with world population. He explained and argued his point in *An Essay on the Principle of Population*, published in 1798. He thought that a crunch point would arrive by the mid-nineteenth century and that only war, pestilence, famine, and disease would ultimately check population growth. Here is an example of his thinking:

> The power of population is so superior to the power of the earth to produce subsistence for man that premature death must in some shape or other visit the human race. The vices of mankind are active and able ministers of depopulation. They are the precursors in the great army of destruction, and often finish the dreadful work themselves. But should they fail in this war of extermination, sickly seasons, epidemics, pestilence, and plague advance in terrific array, and sweep off their thousands and tens of thousands. Should success be still incomplete, gigantic inevitable famine stalks in the rear and with one mighty blow levels the population with the food of the world.[4]

The reality, as is well known, was rather different, and Malthus's basic message has come to be seen as deeply flawed. But his sorry reputation in this regard is a little harsh. He did acknowledge that man was specifically different from other animals because of his "means of support" and the power he had to increase those means. He also made clear that population growth was strongly influenced by people's decisions about sex, work, and children. But what mattered most was that excessive population growth would be checked by natural causes. These, in turn, would have significant effects on society, for example, by increasing misery, poverty, and vice. Much of his thinking on these matters had a critical effect on the way subsequent philosophers approached such topics as evolution, society, and capitalism.

Charles Darwin was an admirer of Malthus, and he developed the concept of the struggle for existence in his famous *On the Origin of Species*, published in 1859. Since then, Malthus seems to have been put out to grass, although, as I shall show, "Malthusian" warnings about the negative aspects of population growth have re-emerged in the twenty-first century.

Karl Marx disagreed with Malthus, branding him and his followers bourgeois reactionaries. Marx accused them of condemning the poor to eternal misery and denying any possibility of changing the world. To Marx, people—labor, to be precise—were the source of all value. Population growth, by definition was a good thing because it would raise labor supply. The issue for Marx was which social class would own the means of "production, distribution, and exchange" and to what ends that ownership should be put. Marx said Malthus had muddled up cause and effect. It wasn't the pressure of population growth on the (limited) means of production that mattered but the opposite. It was the particular (capitalist) means of production that put pressure on population growth. In other words, the misery and destitution Malthus believed would result from excessive population growth, Marx saw as the consequence of unjust or class-ridden institutions, themselves spawned by capitalism.

By the time the first era of major globalization arrived in the last quarter of the nineteenth century,[5] angst about population growth had waned. The world was preoccupied with fast economic growth, the expansion of cities, advances in public health and social welfare, the wealth generated by industrialization and new technologies, and the opening up of new markets and countries. Yet, there were many lingering and unresolved problems of poverty, unemployment, malnutrition, and disease. High mortality rates in childbirth and limited life expectancy were the rule. Mankind's social and economic conditions were central to Marx's teachings, which were taken up not only by the new working class movements in industrial countries but also, contrary to predictions and with far greater success, in predominantly agrarian societies, notably Russia and China.

Fertility debate gathers significance

By the early part of the twentieth century, discussion about population took on a new dimension, at least in the West. Falling birth rates were becoming an issue, despite the fact that the global fertility rate was still over five children per woman of childbearing age. In America, almost seven decades before the introduction of modern contraception (which was then illegal), native-born American women, that is, women born in the United States as opposed to migrant women, were looking after much smaller families. On average, they had 3.5 children or roughly half as many as in 1800. And in urban areas, the fertility rate was still lower— below three in some cities. This prompted President Theodore Roosevelt to say, in front of the National Congress of Mothers in 1905, that if family size continued to decline and there were only two children per family, the "nation ... would very deservedly be on the point of extinction."[6] Old age, of course, was certainly a distant or unlikely prospect for most people, in the United States in 1900 with average life expectancy for white and black Americans at 47 and 33 years, respectively.

Japan, however, known nowadays for its exceptionally low birth rate, looked quite different in the late nineteenth and early twentieth centuries. By 1902, when Japan signed a naval alliance with the United Kingdom—which the former saw as recognition of its growing size and influence in the world— its population was about 49 million. This compared with

37 million three decades earlier. During these years, there was a significant increase in Japanese emigration to such places as Hawaii, the western United States, and Brazil. In 1905, Japan defeated Russia in Manchuria (a province of northeastern China)—the first time since the Middle Ages that non-Europeans had defeated a European power in a major war—and Japanese influence, backed by a military presence, began to grow.[7] Japan sought to colonize the region, and the Japanese state sponsored the emigration there of impoverished family farmers from central and northern Japan. In some ways, the expansionary impulses of Japan between the two world wars were not unlike those of Nazi Germany, which looked eastwards for its *Lebensraum* (or living space).

This is unimaginably different from today, given the substantial and sustained aging—and population decline—under way in Japan. Nevertheless, some historians look back on Japan's success in 1905 as the opening gambit, as it were, in a long, drawn-out struggle for world power between the West and the East, now of course with China in the hot seat.

In Europe, meanwhile, both Hitler and Mussolini encouraged women to have more babies and bigger families both to ward off the birth rate declines, seen as the prelude to imperial decay, and to establish numerical superiority over "inferior" peoples and races. In a radio address on Mother's Day in 1935, Hitler's interior minister Wilhelm Frick referred to Germany's falling birth rate since 1900 but asserted that racial factors lay behind the fact that "honest families in all social classes" were having fewer children while "those less worthwhile" were becoming more numerous.[8] German mothers with more than three children were honored with a Mother's Cross from 1938 as the Nazis used economic incentives and ideology to get them to have more children. Family policy, in fact, remained taboo in Germany long after the Second World War and until relatively recently.

Under rather different circumstances, Winston Churchill told British citizens in a radio address in March 1943, that "one of the most somber anxieties ... is the dwindling birth rate" and went on to encourage the country to have larger families if Britain was to survive as a great power and leader in the world.[9] Churchill's words and language were, of course, ever-powerful but it is doubtful even he could have been responsible for, or even then have been aware, that British mums and dads had started a trend, dating from a year or two earlier, that was to define the postwar decades and change the world: having the (additional) children who were to become the baby boomers. And the British weren't alone.

At the end of the Second World War, in 1945, General Charles de Gaulle, head of the newly-formed postwar government of France, called upon French citizens to produce "*en dix ans, douze millions de beaux bébés pour la France*"—12 million beautiful babies for France over the next ten years.[10] De Gaulle perhaps saw the role of women in the immediate aftermath of war to be reproduction rather than production, based on the reasonable belief that conception and consumption were two sides of the same coin. France must have listened, because between 1946 and 1956, 9.2 million babies were born, and by 1960 France had delivered de Gaulle's 12 million babies.

From the 1950s onwards, a "happy" view about population growth and larger families took hold. Economists and demographers said that population growth and bigger families actually boosted economic growth and development by encouraging advances in technology and more flexible institutions. Maybe they were bound to say that as the fertility rate had already risen to four children in the United States by 1957 and a little later, in 1964, in western Europe. The proof, of course, came as levels of prosperity increased steadily after the Second World War.

In the United Kingdom, the prime minister, Harold Macmillan, told a rally of his Conservative Party in Bedford in 1957, "We have never had it so good," and the optimism of the 1960s that followed became legendary. Population trends at the time were clearly associated with economic and social progress, such as the Green Revolution. New high-yield crops that increased food supply dramatically were seen, in part, as the result of the pressure of strong population growth, especially in poorer countries.

Today of course it is possible to look back and see how those birth rates of the 1940s to the 1960s have long been overtaken by more or less inexorable decline and by smaller families. Why has this pronounced slump in fertility happened—and not just in rich countries?

More to the point, maybe, does it matter? Many commentators and lobby organizations think that stable, or even declining, populations are a long overdue and welcome development in what they see as an overpopulated planet, with an excessive dependence on economic growth that, they say, is sapping the vitality of our ecosystems and supplies of natural resources. Well, yes, it does matter, and it would be dangerous to fall into the no-growth trap, advanced by these neo-Malthusians. The reality is that birth rates have fallen well below the replacement rate of the population in many rich, and some poor, countries at a time when the age structure is shifting steadily toward older groups. With that comes the threat of economic decline and rising social tension.

It is legitimate to warn of the social and environmental costs of overpopulation and poorly managed economic growth and to pursue improved means of population control to help strike a balance between demographic change and economic prosperity. However, to do this by suppressing birth rates still further rather than by harnessing human knowledge, technology and institutions is shortsighted. It is also prejudicial to the aspirations of people for better living standards and a fairer distribution of the fruits of economic growth. As I shall make clear, aging citizens are not the only concern of aging societies. We shall need to pay as much attention to the sustainability of replacement level fertility rates, to youth, and to the quality and quantity of tomorrow's working-age people.

Falling fertility, family structures, and modern times

You have to see declining birth rates as global and historical. They may have fallen especially sharply since the 1960s but, leaving aside the baby boomers, the trend toward lower fertility has been occurring for a very long time. To explain why, you can choose from a range of factors including social, emotional, religious, medical, and cultural. More recently, you would have to recognize the significance of the pill. But my discipline guides me to look also for economic reasons.

Rising income and improved well-being are often cited as reasons for the expansion of family size. But that wouldn't explain why the baby-boomers' parents were so prolific during, and soon after, the Second World War. Nevertheless, there is probably an important economic aspect to fertility trends that is related to a decision we rarely actually make formally. What I mean by this is that couples seldom sit down to discuss a rather important aspect of having children: cost. By "cost" I do not just mean the future cost of clothing, education, musical instruments, student travel, and so on. It is a broader concept that incorporates choices on costs and benefits that we make all the time, even if implicitly.

To understand this, think how family life has changed over the last 100 years and tended to lower fertility. With the introduction of social security and insurance systems, the benefit of having many children for support declined, and this would have contributed toward lower fertility. Compulsory education and a rising tendency for young people to enter university raised the cost of having children and had the same effect of lowering fertility. Perhaps the biggest social change of the last 50 years, though, has been the opening of employment and income opportunities to women—in which arguably the pill played a role. With these, the "cost" of having children has also risen in that having children or more children often involves giving up access to a more lucrative career or stream of income. It is what economists call the "opportunity cost" of children or, put another way, the income or lifestyle we give up to stay at home and look after children.

Somewhat perversely, perhaps, technology may have had the opposite effect on fertility. The spread of technological advances into the home, especially during and after the Second World War, would presumably have had a thoroughly favorable cost impact on the decision to have children or more children. In other words, the reduction in the number of hours and the amount of effort put in to running a household would have lowered the cost (broadly defined) and made it more viable to have children.

In effect, major homebuilding programs in the twentieth century were the start, but what followed was revolutionary: take your pick from widespread access to cheap energy and tap water, availability of central heating or air conditioning, the mass diffusion of household appliances and the commercialization of both frozen and fast food. It has been estimated that the total time allocated to housework and childcare fell from roughly 58 hours a week in 1900 to 40 hours by the mid-1970s.[11]

At that time, and subsequently, a global theme that was decidedly antinatalist developed. Private foundations, aid agencies and multilateral institutions, such as the United Nations and the World Bank, argued that rapid population growth was having distinctly negative effects on low-income countries, including economic deprivation and social strife. Maybe the antinatalist consensus of the 1970s and 1980s was simply a response to the earlier acceleration in population growth. In a way, it didn't matter that much because by the time this consensus was being formed, fertility rates had already started declining again.

Many factors have contributed to this decline. The common ones include better female access to education, expanded adult education, cheap and readily accessible birth control methods, and declining child mortality rates in urban areas. And in most parts of the developing world, these factors—aided and abetted by other measures of economic and social advance—will probably continue to depress or cap low fertility rates. For richer societies and communities, modern technology—the Internet and modern communications systems in particular—could strongly influence the way we think about children and family. It may liberate people to work more, shop, research, learn, and blog from home, changing the economic function of "home" and thereby working against higher birth rates and larger families. Equally, however, higher productivity in the home, improved access to childcare, and the introduction of robotics into the home over the next decade could make it all the more realistic to balance work and leisure with rearing more children.

A British economist, John Maynard Keynes—some would say the godfather of modern economic thinking—is renowned for his macroeconomic theories and analysis as they apply to modern economies; but more than that he had opinions on most issues, including on population. He was one of very few thinkers to take comfort in the progress mankind had made. In 1930, he wrote an essay called "Economic Possibilities for Our Grandchildren."[12] Remember that this was before the economic slump of the 1930s and its political aftermath, but, he wrote, the "economic problem" may not be the permanent problem of the human race. He thought that within 100 years—or, at the time of my writing, in 22 years—man might be able to face his real problem: namely how to use freedom from pressing economic worries, how to occupy leisure time, and how to live wisely and agreeably. This would only happen, he said, if there were no significant wars or increase in population. This blissful state of affairs would presumably be one in which more people might have more children. You'd have to be an unashamed optimist, however, to believe that this nirvana will arrive in the next 20 years or so. New perils are lurking—and not only those of war.

Climate change, food, oil, and water join the fray

In 1972, a pessimistic report was published. The Club of Rome, a nonprofit making global think tank of economists, scientists, and businessmen, issued a report called *The Limits To Growth*[13] in which the authors tried to model the consequences for the planet of the interactions between Earth and human systems in an echo of what Malthus had tried to show about 200 years earlier. The study concluded that in less than 100 years, society would run out of so-called nonrenewable resources, that our economic systems would collapse, and that the world would experience massive unemployment, falling food production, and population declines as mortality rose. The authors also said that even if the problems of resources and pollution could be solved, food availability would eventually puncture the growth of population. They concluded that the only solution would be to place immediate limits on population and pollution and slow down or arrest economic growth.

The report was viewed for the following 30 years or so as little more than another Malthusian alarm bell—lots of noise but no substance. And notwithstanding the oil and Middle East crises in the 1970s and early 1980s, the world economy managed to get through that period and embark on an unprecedented phase of economic expansion from 1982 to 2007. True, there have been a couple of rather mild recessions (1990–91 and 2001–02) and recurring bouts of financial turbulence. By and large, however, the record of the last 25 years is one of sustained, and often strong, economic expansion, the integration of many developing economies into the global economy, rising incomes per head, the eradication in many parts of the world of famine, and, until very recently, virtually no sign of resource shortages. Happy days.

If only. Today, the Club of Rome view looks like a premature but perfectly reasonable shot across the bows. Many now believe there are simply too many people on the planet for everyone to share in better living standards, environmental protection, clean air, adequate water, and food.

Consider this quote from the Optimum Population Trust,[14] a UK think tank focused on the impact of population changes on the environment:

A population almost the size of Germany's is being added to the planet each year, with the equivalent of one new city added every single day. Every year about 56.4 million people die, but they are more than replaced by the annual 137 million births—a natural increase of 81 million human beings, all of whom add to the numbers causing environmental degradation to their only habitat—Earth.

For the record, 81 million people is about 9,200 extra people each hour or 221,000 a day.

This is modern Malthus. It is no longer just about the pressure of population growth on food supplies but its overall impact on the environment generally and therefore on our ability to sustain life, certainly in some parts of the world. Warnings are coming thick and fast these days that the rising demands of population growth on the earth's ecosystems will lead ultimately to the gradual or sudden collapse of the world's natural food chain, resources, and weather systems.

Concerns about climate change, greenhouse gas (GHG) emissions, and pollution, are proliferating. Some climate change experts say that global population growth, the rapid expansion of the world economy in the last 50 years, and the demand for urban lifestyles, energy for industry and households, and modern, cheap transportation have all contributed to global warming. They also warn that growth in world population in the last 50 years has gone hand in hand with more rapid increases in carbon dioxide and other GHG emissions and in global temperatures. In February 2007, the fourth report of the Intergovernmental Panel on Climate Change (IPCC) took this discussion further than ever in a blunt assessment of the role played by mankind in global warming and, therefore, by implication, the degree to which population growth is to blame. The IPCC said the evidence for global warming was unequivocal, that it was "almost certainly" man-made and that ultimately it would make not just parts of Asia and South America uninhabitable, but also most of southern Europe.[15]

At its core, this argument is about the costs to the planet of economic and population growth, but it is sensitive for many reasons, not the least of which is that the bulk of the world's economic and population growth is occurring in developing countries. Despite the fact that richer and more industrial countries emit more carbon than developing countries, the next 20 years will see the latter group account for virtually all the world's population growth, the vast majority of the growth in the world's labor force, and a near 10 percent increase in its share of world output. This kind of performance will see the developing world then close the gap on the richer countries in terms of both income levels but also carbon emissions and environmental damage.

The issue of mankind's responsibility is relevant to population and society in more than the obvious ways. For those who know little about or do not fully comprehend the science of climate change, it is difficult to properly judge the natural or anthropogenic arguments. But it is clear that carbon dioxide emissions, sea levels, and global temperatures are rising, that the ice caps are melting and that the volatility and extremes of weather patterns are becoming more pronounced. If we are convinced that mankind has been a major reason, as the IPCC argues, then of course this would have critical consequences for the role and scope of government regulation and legislation in a wide range of human activities over the next several decades. From our perspective here, these activities might well extend to family planning and size, contraception, abortion and fertility, community planning, immigration, education policy, and so on. Whether or not you believe in the man-made characteristics of climate change, however, environmental degradation is a concern for everyone. Left unchecked, the perils of global warming could have devastating effects on communities and on countries. Scientists warn that rising sea levels will increase coastal flooding and erosion, and pollute groundwater supplies. Rising temperatures will reduce coastal cropland and living space, and create more heat stress. More destructive and more frequent hazardous weather patterns will create threats to public health through droughts, storms, and the proliferation of tropical diseases such as malaria and dengue fever. Changing rain and snow patterns, meanwhile, will probably add to pressure on population growth in regions of existing water stress.

It is not only health and life and death that come into sharper focus from extremes of climate change. There is a likely new phenomenon—the environmental refugee. I look later at immigration and how it has become such an important and politically sensitive issue. But for the most part, immigration concerns economic migrants or political refugees. Environmental refugees have not, as yet, become a major force in the world, but they are bound to do so in the future. As they do, new pressures on social and political structures will appear.

Green political movements argue that long-range strategies to address the threat of climate change are unlikely to succeed without careful attention being paid to demographic trends, but this is a highly charged political issue. Who is going to pay careful attention to whose demographic trends? Countries as diverse as Japan,

Germany, and Russia are already seeing their populations decline. They are facing the consequences of population aging and youth depopulation in the next 20 years. At the other extreme, India, most of the countries in sub-Saharan Africa, and the Middle East are all experiencing or craving fast economic growth and have rising populations and a growing proportion of 15- to 40-year-olds. The demographic trends of this latter group of countries have direct economic consequences that favor, or lead to, higher rates of economic growth.

As these population developments unfold, so too could friction and conflict over the environment, energy, food, and water supplies. There are, therefore, growing calls for multilateral institutions to be strengthened and charged with the deployment of technologies and resources to address the consequences of population and economic growth on the environment.

Food and oil supplies

While recurring famine in developed and most developing countries, fortunately, is not an issue anymore, it remains a massive problem for too many poor countries and people, especially in Africa. Regular famines and horrific images of refugee camps, disease, and death crush any belief that the problems of population growth and poverty have been resolved. The picture looks almost classically Malthusian: rapid population growth and limited food availability and or famine, but this is the twenty-first, not the eighteenth or nineteenth century. Despite the best efforts of global charities and celebrities to boost publicity and raise money to help famine victims, the problem simply won't go away.

Generally speaking, though, while food supplies in most of the world are adequate, there have been sharp increases recently in the cost of grains and other foods working their way into the cost of living. This is partly the result of changing consumption patterns in emerging markets, where incomes are gradually increasing and diets are changing from staple to more protein-oriented foods. The United Nations estimates that nearly 30 percent more beef, 50 percent more pig meat, and 25 percent more poultry will be consumed in developing countries by 2016, along with 70 percent more skimmed milk powder and sugar.

In addition, poor harvests in Australia and China in 2007 added to food price pressures while soaring oil prices in 2006–08 resulted in a significant switch by farmers growing sugar cane, maize, and rapeseed oil for food to growing them to convert to biofuel. In the United States, a third of the maize crop was used to produce ethanol for fuel last year, a 48 percent rise compared with 2005.

So was Malthus right for Africa but not for the rest of us? To focus on the lack of food supply misses the point. After all, famine relief in one year might save a lot of people from death or disease temporarily but won't protect them in the future. The main issue is not food supply itself but the lack of means and structures to grow, export, and buy food. If poor countries enjoyed stronger support or protection in the global economy and could develop their agricultural and raw material sectors to create more jobs, incomes, and appropriate institutions, perhaps these recurrent problems would diminish.

The new but fast growing concern about resources and population, in both rich and poor countries, is about the adequacy of crude oil supplies, the lifeblood of the modern economy. The issue, known as "Peak Oil," is about just how much more capacity the world has to boost traditional supplies of crude oil. Traditional in this sense, or conventional, means oil that can be extracted at a relatively low cost, compared for example with oil that can be extracted from shale, tar sands, and deep in the ocean. The argument is essentially that the world's largest oil fields, those producing more than one million barrels a day, have already been discovered and that the discovery of oil in new fields is not keeping pace with the rate of growth of global oil consumption. US oil production, for example, has been falling gradually since the 1970s, the UK's North Sea oil production is declining, and many other oil producing countries such as those in the Middle East, Russia, and Mexico are no longer able to increase oil production. Even Saudi Arabia, believed to have the largest oil reserves, seems to have been unable—certainly unwilling—to raise its oil production to a significant extent.

Those who hold this view say the world may be close to, or within five years of, reaching the point where oil production from conventional oil wells starts to level off and then decline. This discussion is really about the geology of oil and the exhaustion of oil fields, rather than economics or population specifically.[16] That said, supply is always a problem if demand is growing too quickly. In 2008, the nominal price of crude oil reached an all time high of over US$140 per barrel (also a record level in real terms, in which general inflation is taken into account) amid numerous political fears, including long-running ones in the Middle East and newer ones about tensions between the United States and Iran over Tehran's nuclear policies. At the same time, however, under the influence of vigorous demand for oil and other raw materials from China and India, it was evident that for the first time global demand for crude oil, at about 83 million barrels per day, could only just be matched by available supply.

While oil prices will always rise and fall with changes in the strength of the global economy, the longer-term outlook hinges on how much extra oil can be produced. In 2006–08, the discovery of a number of "large" oil finds was publicized, including off the coast of Brazil, in the Gulf of Mexico, and in China. Obviously, it will take some time before these finds translate into production, and it is not possible to know to what extent these might satisfy growing demand. Moreover, some industry experts assert that the commercial exploitation of Canadian and Venezuelan tar and shale deposits will eventually make up for any shortages of conventional oil. But whether or not this is the case, it will take many years and a lot of money before we know for sure. In the meantime, strong population-driven energy demand in both emerging and developing countries and high levels of energy consumption in advanced countries will probably drive a rise in oil demand that often will not be met without further significant price increases.

There are some bleak conclusions about what this might mean for our economies and communities. Typically, high or sharp increases in oil prices have been associated with slow economies and rising unemployment. On the other hand, resisting or trying to offset high oil prices is also not such a good idea. High prices are exactly what are needed to help restrain energy consumption, encourage conservation, and encourage new, efficient ways of harnessing and using alternative energy sources.

Water shortages too?

Compared with the 1970s, global population has roughly doubled, but water consumption has gone up about five times. Agriculture accounts for about 70 percent of water use globally and for even higher usage in several developing countries. As we think about what the future holds, we should note again that world population is predicted to grow by 50 percent to over 9 billion by 2050 and that three of the world's biggest grain producers—China, India, and the United States—will confront increasingly severe water imbalances. China, which has more than 20 percent of the world's population (largely in the north) and has only 7 percent of the world's water supply (largely in the south), is already struggling with such problems.

According to the World Bank, over 1 billion people do not have access to safe drinking water, over 2.5 billion lack basic sanitation, and in sub-Saharan Africa, two in five people don't have access to clean water. Waterborne illnesses, sourced to unsanitary supplies, are reckoned to cause 5 million deaths each year, half of them in children aged under five. By 2025, it is estimated that some 3.5 billion people will live in places where water is scarce or becoming scarce.

It is not just population growth, pollution, industry, and energy sector demands and poor urban planning that are putting pressure on water supplies. Climate change is expected to have a profound effect as a result of global warming, a gradually more arid world, melting glaciers, changes in weather patterns, and rising sea levels. The Stern Review on the economics of climate change, conducted for the U.K. government in 2006, says, for example, that, "people will feel the impact of climate change most strongly through changes in the distribution of water round the world and its seasonal and annual variability."[17] The US National Center for Atmospheric Research, meanwhile, has estimated that the percentage of the earth's land surface affected by drought more than doubled between 1970 and 2000 and argues that rising temperatures will only exacerbate this alarming trend.[18]

The Middle East and North Africa already use more water each year than they get from rainfall and river flows, so they are depleting groundwater resources. The World Bank says that by 2050, population growth and climate change could together cut available water supply per person by half. It also reckons that more than a billion people in South Asia could be hit by drought and floods as a result of the melting of the Himalayan glaciers. According to the environmental group, World Wide Fund for Nature (WWF), 14 African countries already face water stress, and a further 11 are expected to join them by 2025, at which point about half the African continent's expected population of 1.45 billion will face water stress or scarcity.[19]

Climate change then is expected to put millions more at risk from floods, landslides, and rising sea levels. Among a long list of repercussions and implications, unstable, insecure, or reduced water supplies pose serious threats to food production and security, and could help spread diseases such as malaria, dengue fever, yellow fever, cholera, and typhoid. These in turn would drive the growth of environmental refugees and migration. So, on top of worrying about the impact of population growth and economic development on supplies of food and crude oil, policymakers and governments must also devote more attention to how these problems—along with climate change—will affect water supply and usage.

What happened to the dominant species?

Thomas Malthus underestimated the ingenuity of human beings to cope with growing population and deliver rising living standards. The baby-boomer generation and their children have grown up in a period of unprecedented economic expansion and rising prosperity at the same time as some rather exceptional changes in global population. These changes, specifically the fact that in the poorer countries' population is still growing, and in the richer ones only the proportion of older people is, are now seen by many to threaten economic growth and prosperity. In later chapters I consider in detail the implications of this skewed distribution of global population. But it is tempting to dismiss these concerns with the question: Why shouldn't our capacity to adapt and adjust remain our best hope to deal with population change and its effects in the next decades?

Those who wish to answer this question cannot just sit back and wait for innovation. They will have to grapple with many issues that we have looked at so far only by way of introduction. First, total population growth is still seen by many as a problem in an already heavily populated planet, especially as it will be concentrated in the developing world. Second, it is associated increasingly with environmental degradation and threats to oil and water supplies. Third, with low or declining fertility and life expectancy continuing to rise, the age structure of the population is shifting in ways never experienced before. Declining or stagnant numbers of younger people will have to support a growing proportion of old and very old people.

There are, thus, implications for our economies and communities and how governments will respond. How too will our societies and institutions evolve, and what sorts of challenges or opportunities will population aging present? Who will fund pensions in the future and how? As I address these questions, bear in mind also that there will be political implications as well from a growing band of "gray" voters and from the tension between older Western and younger emerging countries. A new vista on population issues is in the process of opening up, and it is to these issues that I now turn.

Endnotes

1 Jared Diamond, *Collapse: How Societies Choose to Fail or Succeed*, (London: Penguin Books, 2006).
2 See for example http://www.ggdc.net/maddison/.
3 Edward Gibbon, *The History of the Decline and Fall of the Roman Empire*, abr. ed. with an introduction by David P. Womersley (London: Penguin Books, 2000).
4 http://www.econlib.org/library/Malthus/malPop3.html.

5   *Globalization* is a widely used and much abused word. Since we shall have
    a few occasions to use it, it might help to define it. It is, strictly speaking, a
    process in which distance is destroyed as both the time for, and cost of,
    interaction is reduced. In our globalization, the principal factors have been
    the Internet, information and communications technologies, and advances
    in faster and low-cost transportation. These have enabled and encouraged
    a vigorous increase in economic and social integration across national
    boundaries that can be measured by increases in world trade and invest-
    ment and international migration. Although economic integration has
    occurred steadily throughout history, the first great leap of globalization, so
    to speak, occurred in Victorian times from the 1820s until 1914, especially
    after 1870. The main factors then were the development of steam power,
    public projects such as the opening of the Suez Canal, the development of
    the telegraph, and telephone and electric power generation.

6   Theodore Roosevelt, "On American Motherhood," speech before the
    National Congress of Mothers, Washington, DC, March 13, 1905.

7   Against a background of growing unrest and opposition from
    Chinese nationalists, Japan created an incident in 1931 as an excuse
    to take over the whole province.

8   Sebastian Herold, Germany's Population Problems No Longer
    Taboo," *Deutsche Welle*, December 27, 2005, http:/www.dw3d.de/
    dw/article/0,2144,1836769,00.html.

9   Quoted in Hans J. Morgenthau, *Politics Among Nations: The Struggle
    for Power and Peace*, Brief Ed. revised by Kenneth W. Thompson
    (New York: McGraw-Hill, 1993), p. 143.

10 Quoted in Claire Duchen, "A new woman for a new France:" in *Clio*
    1/1995, Resistances et Libérations France 1940–45, at http://clio.
    revues.org/document520.html.

11 J. Greenwood, A. Seshadri, and M. Yorukoglu, "Engines of
    Liberation," *Review of Economic Studies*, 72, No. 1 (2005).

12 John Mayaard Keynes, *Essays in Persuasion* (New York: W.W. Norton &
    Co, 1963).

13 Donella H. Meadows et al., *The Limits to Growth* (Universe Books, 1972).

14 http://www.optimumpopulation.org/index.html.

15 IPCC, *Climate Change 2007: Mitigation of Climate Change*
    (Cambridge and New York: Cambridge University Press, 2007).

16 See, for example, Matthew R. Simmons, *Twilight In The Desert*
    (Hoboken, NJ: John Wiley and Sons, 2005).

17 Nicholas Stern, *The Economics of Climate Change: The Stern Review*
    (Cambridge: Cambridge University Press, 2007) Part II, 3.2, p. 62.

18 The University Corporation for Atmospheric Research, "Drought's
    Growing Reach: NCAR Points to Global Warming as Key Factor,"
    www.ucar.edu/news/releases/2005/drought_research.shtml.

19 World Wide Fund for Nature, "The Facts on Water in Africa,"
    http://assets.panda.org/downloads/waterinafricaeng.pdf.

Chapter 3

The age of aging

> *Youth is full of sport, age's breath is short; youth is nimble, age is lame; Youth is hot and bold, age is weak and cold; Youth is wild, and age is tame.*
> —William Shakespeare, *The Passionate Pilgrim.*

The British Nobel Prize–winning economist J.R. Hicks asserted nearly 70 years ago that "the whole Industrial Revolution of the last two hundred years has been nothing else but a vast secular boom, largely induced by the unparalleled rise in population."[1] If he was right, then some of us are in trouble because population growth is not only slowing in most places but, in several countries in the West, about to reverse.

The expected expansion in global population, 3 billion in the next forty years, actually represents a slowing from the 2 billion people who joined the ranks of Earth's citizens between 1980 and 2005. The actual growth rate of world population has already slowed from 2 percent per annum in the late 1960s to just over 1 percent currently. Present predictions suggest that the growth rate will have fallen to 0.7 percent by 2030 and 0.4 percent by 2050. These predictions assume that fertility rates will continue to decline, especially in the poorest of the less developed countries, thanks to the steady spread and adoption of family planning methods. If this were not to happen, though, the world's population would expand by an additional 2.7 billion people to reach about 11.9 billion by 2050. That is 25 percent bigger for the world as a whole, compared with the central prediction, and about 30 percent bigger for the developing countries.

So, two major issues stand out. First, if we are concerned about population growth on what seems our increasingly crowded planet, real effort has to be applied to the nurturing of smaller, economically viable and stable families across vast tracts of the developing world. Second, the richer countries (and several not so rich countries) of the world will, in any event, have vastly different concerns, namely how to adjust to stagnant or declining populations with rapidly rising age structures.

Global population changes

The structure of the world's population today, and projected to 2050, can be seen in Figures 3.1 and 3.2. North America includes the United States and Canada. Europe's population share has been split between western and eastern European nations, the latter including Russia. Asia's has been divided between the bulk of the continent, Japan and western Asia, including Turkey and the Middle East. Latin America includes the Caribbean islands. Oceania includes Australia, New Zealand, and the Pacific islands.

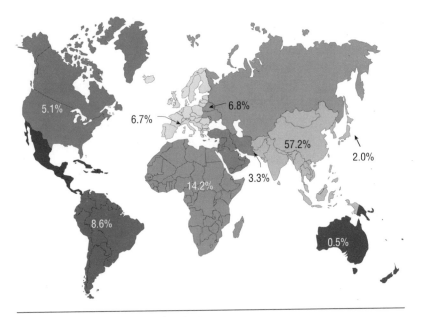

Figure 3.1   World population distribution 2005
Source: United Nations Population Division.

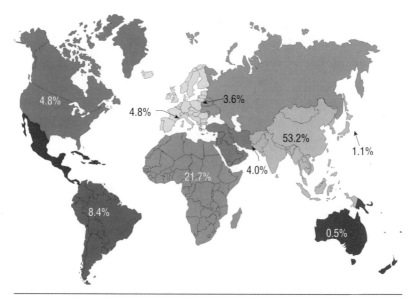

Figure 3.2 World population distribution 2050
Source: United Nations Population Division.

Among the big losers by 2050 (see Figure 3.3), on what we might call the demographics death row, will be Japan, whose numbers will shrink by about 26 million to 102 million. Europe's population is expected to decline by 67 million to 664 million, but this is due overwhelmingly to the decrease of population numbers in Russia and eastern Europe. In fact the latest United Nations population estimates are slightly higher for western Europe than they were two years ago. Population is now predicted to rise by about 10 million until 2025 and then start to fall, so that by 2050, it will be comparable to today. In the 15 countries that comprised the European Union before its expansion that began in May 2004, population is predicted to rise from 390 million to 401 million by 2025 but then to slip back to 397 million by 2050. This is largely down to the increase of 20 million in the United Kingdom, France, and Spain offsetting the 12 million fall in Germany and Italy.

Of the top 25 population shrinkers by 2050, 18 are to be found behind what used to be called the Iron Curtain. Ukraine and Bulgaria are expected to be about 43 percent and 34 percent

Figure 3.3   World Population change 2005-50
Source: United Nations Population Division.

smaller, respectively. Russia's population will drop by over 30 million or about 22 percent. The populations of the countries in eastern Europe that have joined the European Union and those of the Baltic republics and the Balkans will experience falls of between 10 and 30 percent. The other big decliners are Japan, Italy, Germany, Greece, and Portugal.

The population of the United States in 2025 is forecast to rise by about 49 million from today's level of about 305 million and by 2050 it is expected to have reached 402 million. These numbers indicate a growth rate now of about 0.9 percent per year falling away to about 0.4 percent by the middle of the century. In fact, only a dozen of the 29 wealthier nations belonging to the Organization for Economic Cooperation and Development (OECD) are expected to have either slowly growing, or at least stable, populations: Aside from the United States, the list includes the United Kingdom, Australia, Canada, New Zealand, the Ireland, the Netherlands, Scandinavia (Denmark, Sweden and Norway), Mexico, and Turkey.

In the rest of the world, the fastest growing populations are likely to be in sub-Saharan Africa, Middle East and North

Africa where 2 percent population growth is liable to persist for a while before declining to 1 percent by mid-century. The biggest single contributor to the 2.5 billion gain in world population by 2050 will be India, whose population will grow by almost 500 million. India's population of 1.17 billion today will then overtake that of China, whose population of 1.33 billion today will expand by only 80 million.[2] But Indonesia, Iran, Brazil, Turkey, and many other developing countries will all be prominent contributors to population growth.

Your world party guest list

Let us look at the change in world population distribution another way. Suppose you organized a major event every 50 years and invited 100 guests according to the makeup of the world's population. You had always had several guests from China, India, and the United States. In fact in 1950, they would have supplied 43 of your guests, with Russians and Japanese making up another seven. By the time you had checked off three-quarters of your guests, about 12 would have come from Europe (Germany, the United Kingdom, Italy, France, Ukraine, Spain, and Poland), and there would have been only one representative from Africa, a Nigerian.

Hold the event today, and 60 percent of them would come today from just 10 countries. Almost 40 would come from India and China and about 20 from just eight other countries, namely the United States, Indonesia, Brazil, Pakistan, Bangladesh, Nigeria, Russia, and Japan. In fact, once you had counted off three-quarters of your guests, you would find only four west Europeans, one each from Germany, the United Kingdom, France, and Italy.

In 2050, your event would welcome some familiar guests and some new ones, but several wouldn't have received another invitation. Thirty-three would come from India and China and 25 from 10 countries—the United States, Indonesia, Pakistan, Nigeria, Brazil, Bangladesh, the Democratic Republic of Congo, Ethiopia, the Philippines, and Mexico. Again, looking at three-quarters of your list, your European guests would be still fewer, with just 2.3 from Germany, the United Kingdom, and France.

In 1950, only China, India, the United States, and the Soviet Union had populations over 100 million. Today 11 countries do so, and by 2050 there will be 19, with Vietnam having joined this group, and Iran, Turkey, and Uganda knocking on the door. Today Pakistan and Bangladesh each have more people than Germany and France combined. By 2050, the United Kingdom will be 20 percent smaller than Tanzania and 10 percent smaller than Afghanistan; Germany will be three-quarters the size of Turkey. Vietnam will be bigger than both Russia and Japan.

North America, South America and the Caribbean, and Asia are going to expand at similar rates. Oceania, albeit with a miniscule share of world population, will grow just a little faster. Europe's population will drop by 10 percent (but this masks a 25 percent fall in Russia and eastern Europe and a roughly stable population in the rest of Europe). Even here there will be differences, with a 10 percent rise in the United Kingdom and gains in Scandinavia, while Japan, Germany, and Italy will experience drops of 12 percent, 10 percent, and 7 percent, respectively. Africa's population is expected to more than double, while the populations of Turkey and the Middle East are expected to rise by four-fifths.

Three stages of ages

The phase of population change upon which we have embarked can be seen as the third, probably the last, in a cycle that goes back about 200 years or more (see Table 3.1). According to the demographer Ronald Lee, the first major phase of population change began in Europe around the turn of the nineteenth century when mortality rates began to decline.[3] This downtrend in both rich and poor countries was thought to be a spent force a few years ago, but the United Nations and others have since noted that, contrary to expectations, mortality rates have continued to fall.

Table 3.1   Global Population Trends 1700–2100

Year	Life Expectancy (Years at birth)	Total Fertility Rate (Births per woman)	Population Size Billions	Population Growth Rate (% /year)	Population <15 (% of total population)	Population >65 (% of total population)
1700	27	6	0.68	0.5	36	4
1800	27	6	0.98	0.51	36	4
1900	30	5.2	1.65	0.56	35	4
1950	47	5	2.52	1.8	34	5
2000	65	2.7	6.07	1.22	30	7
2050	74	2	8.92	0.33	20	16
2100	81	2	9.46	0.04	18	21

Source: Ronald Lee: "The Demographic Transition: Three Centuries of Fundamental Change."

As a result, life expectancy rates in advanced and developing countries may not only rise further, but a lot further than we envisage today. Some experts think life expectancy could rise to as much as 100 years or more by the end of this century. Others caution that new diseases, a flu pandemic, greater HIV/AIDS incidence, drug-resistant strains of certain diseases such as malaria and tuberculosis, and the incidence of obesity and diabetes could all reverse life expectancy gains. It is already happening in Russia, eastern Europe, and sub-Saharan Africa, and in certain population groups in other countries. While these factors certainly limit or reverse life expectancy for many, the fundamental trend toward rising longevity in the world is not in danger, at least as far as we can predict. In any event, medical research and measures to encourage healthier lifestyles will presumably continue to act as strong counterweights.

It is important to see aging as a global phenomenon. Life expectancy in advanced and poorer societies was markedly different in 1950. In rich countries average life expectancy was about 66 years. This was about 60 percent longer than it was in developing countries and almost twice as long as for citizens of the very poorest countries in the world.

Today, the gap has closed a bit. In rich countries, life expectancy is now about 77 years on average (72.9 years for men and 80.2 years for women). In developing countries, life expectancy is now 63.7 years for men and almost 67 for women whereas in the poorest of these countries, it is 53.4 years and 55.8 years, respectively. It is predicted that by 2050, life expectancy for men and women in rich countries might have risen to 79 and 85 years, respectively. In developing countries, life expectancy is expected to rise to 72 for men and 76 for women. In the poorest economies, life expectancy is also expected to rise to 65 and 69 years, respectively.

Because of poor health standards or disease, not all regions enjoy or can look forward to steady gains in life expectancy. In southern Africa, where the incidence of HIV/AIDS is the highest in the world, life expectancy has collapsed in the last 10–15 years from 61 years to 49 years and is not expected to get back to that higher level until at least 2045–50. In Russia, male life expectancy is now less than 59 years, compared with 64.5 years in the late 1960s, and is slightly lower than India's 61.7 years. Again HIV/AIDS, a high incidence of tuberculosis, alcohol-related illness, and other failures of public health have been blamed.

The second phase of the demographic cycle was the more abrupt decline in fertility, which started in Europe in about 1890. As already noted, there was a reversal in this trend after the Second World War, though it has of course resumed. As recently as 1970, women in developing countries were still having 6 children or more on average, but this has since fallen to less than 3 (4.63 in the poorest countries).

There are 62 countries, host to 45 percent of the world's population, that have fertility rates at or below the replacement rate of 2.1. Of these, 24 comprise the industrial countries plus China, Taiwan, and South Korea. Most of East Asia has subreplacement fertility rates and many in South and Central America do too. In the Arab and Muslim world, Algeria, Tunisia, Lebanon, and Turkey have subreplacement fertility rates. Iran has the same rate as the United States (2.04); but Iraq and Afghanistan have fertility rates of 4.3 and 7.1, respectively. The United Nations' central projection suggests the fertility rate in advanced economies will rise a little from 1.6 today to 1.85 by 2050 but that the global fertility rate will continue to fall from 2.55 to 2 by 2050.

The lowest fertility rates in the world right now belong to Macao and Hong Kong (both Special Administrative Regions of China), Belarus, South Korea, Ukraine, Poland, Bosnia and Herzegovina, the Czech Republic, Slovenia, and Singapore. These countries have fertility rates of between 0.91 and 1.26 which is 50 percent or less of the global average. The highest rates, on the other hand, are almost all in Africa, headed by Niger and Guinea-Bissau and in Afghanistan where fertility rates of over six to seven children are common. As stated earlier, though, the presumption that fertility rates in these latter countries will halve or more by 2050 rests on the successful take-up of family planning and birth control and, of course, on a multitude of social and economic improvements that tend to be associated with smaller and more stable family size.

The key features of today's low or falling fertility rates are: (a) that it is pretty much universal and (b) that, for the first time, it's mostly voluntary. The global nature of low fertility speaks to the combination of several common factors such as faster economic growth, improvements in female literacy and job opportunities and the greater availability of safe, cheap, and legal methods of birth control. Western societies aside, these conditions apply equally in the Roman Catholic countries of Latin America, mostly Muslim ones in the Middle East, including Sunni Turkey, Shi'ite Iran, Algeria, Lebanon, and Tunisia, and in Asian societies, including China, South Korea, and Singapore. As fertility rates converge over time at low levels, the fastest-aging societies are not Japan and Italy but Singapore, China, and South Korea.

The voluntary nature of low fertility is an interesting social phenomenon. For people in developing countries who benefit from being drawn out of poverty and from better access to healthcare and social protection, the fall in fertility rates from high levels is to be expected. For people in rich economies, the efforts to make work and parenting more compatible have clearly resulted in a desire to have fewer children, aided and abetted, of course, by better education and career opportunities for women, maternity (and now in many countries, paternity) leave, and the growth in childcare facilities provided by national or local governments, companies, or private individuals.

The third and contemporary phase is the result of these two megatrends of rising life expectancy and falling fertility. Though these trends have been evolving for a long time, today's environment is different. When mortality rates first started to decline, the effect was to rejuvenate the population because the largest drop in mortality tended to affect children. Then, as the decline in fertility rates became more marked and longevity rose, younger societies became more productive because of the effect generated by smaller numbers of children per family and growing numbers of people in the labor force, typically the 15- to 64-year-old-age group.

But now, advanced societies have moved beyond the point of either rejuvenation or greater productive potential. Rising life expectancy will result in growing numbers of old and very old people, while low or falling fertility will reduce the growth and or size of the population of working age. This unique and rapid change in age structure will involve declining child dependency and rising old-age dependency.

Aging and dependency

Half of the 2.5 billion increase in the world's population in the next 40 years will be made up of people over the age of 60. In 2050, they will number roughly 2 billion—that's three times as many as today's 673 million. As a proportion of world population, the over-60s will double, accounting for 22 percent, compared with 10 percent today and 8 percent in 1950 (see Figure 3.4). About four-fifths of the over-60s will be living in less developed countries compared with three-fifths today.

Further, the very oldest members of society, the over-80s, are expected to increase from 88 million to over 400 million by 2050. Less developed countries are home to 50 percent of the over-80s today, but this share will rise to 71 percent. The

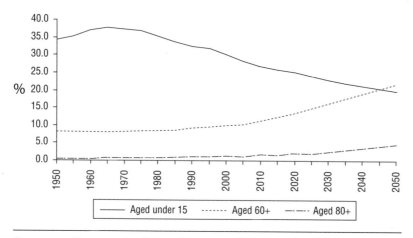

Figure 3.4   More over-60s than under-15s (% of world population)
Source: United Nations Population Division.

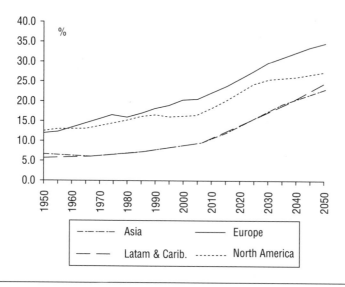

Figure 3.5   Over-60s (% of population)
Source: United Nations Population Division.

biggest concentration of over-80s is in Asia, which today has 39 million (44 percent) of the world's oldest citizens, but by 2050 Asia's eldest will number about 238 million (60 percent of the world's total).

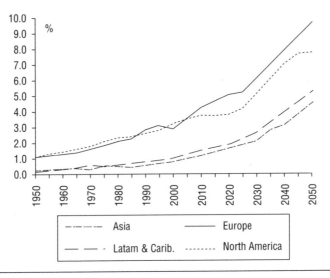

Figure 3.6   Over-80s (% of population)
Source: United Nations Population Division.

By contrast, although the number of under-15s in the world will drop only slightly from 1.84 billion to 1.82 billion, they will decline as a share of total population from 28 percent to about 20 percent. In fact, their numbers will drop by about 0.3–0.5 percent per year in Europe, Latin America, and Asia. Africa's under-15s will grow by just under 1 percent per year, while America's and Australia's will rise by about 0.2 percent per year.

Let us use the world maps again to highlight the major changes in the population of older members of society in some main countries and regions.

The current position (see Figure 3.7) is that the highest proportions of over-60s can be found in Japan and Europe at anything between a fifth and a quarter. The United States and Australia are relatively youthful, by comparison, with roughly 17 percent of their populations aged under 60. On this basis, Turkey, Mexico, Latin America, China, and South Korea remain young by comparison.

By 2050 (see Figure 3.8), South Korea will have caught up with Japan to have among the highest proportion of over-60s, at more than 40 percent. China will have a higher proportion of

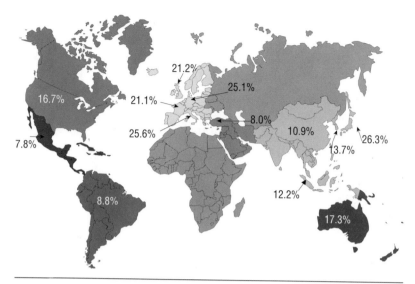

Figure 3.7   Over-60s in 2005

Source: United Nations Population Division.

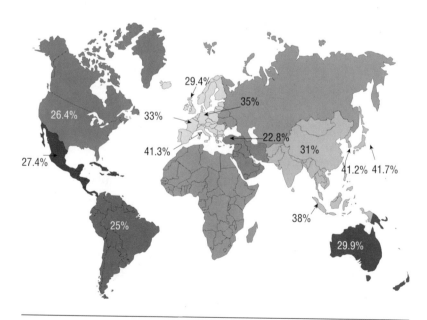

Figure 3.8   Over-60s in 2050

Source: United Nations Population Division.

over-60s than the United Kingdom, at almost a third, and Spain, Italy, and Germany will have the highest share of over-60s in western Europe but appreciably lower than those in eastern Europe and the Balkans. Latin America, (including Mexico) and Turkey will be catching up or overtaking the United States with a quarter or more of the population aged over 60. Africa, by contrast, though having doubled its elderly population share will still only have 10 percent of its population aged over 60.

What about the workers?

So far, we have looked at the changes taking place in the numbers and proportions of the very young (those aged under 15) and the older groups in society (those aged over 60 or 65). Now let us turn to those economically active persons, aged 15 to 64, so that we can see how the dependency of both young and old on the working-age population is going to change. Though the over-60s tend to be classified nowadays as the "older population," it still seems appropriate to use a slightly wider age group, 15–64 years, as the benchmark for the working-age population and for the dependency of children and older people. In fact, in years to come, custom may demand that we widen the age band even further if it becomes common for people to work until they are, for example, 67 or even older.

Let us look at a few examples of past and prospective changes in the 15–64 age group. It is mainly from this group that we source our leaders, innovators, captains of industry, employees, the armed forces and most of what we consume, invest, and pay in taxes. It's fair to point out that the faster this age group expands, the stronger is the potential for high economic growth and rising living standards, but the opposite is true as well, and many of us will have to deal with the consequences of stagnation or shrinkage in the number of people of working age, unless we can compensate for this some other way. The next chapter will discuss ways in which this can be addressed, at least for a while, but success could prove volatile and elusive.

The first three examples, shown below, are the United States (Figure 3.9), Japan (Figure 3.10), and western Europe (Figure 3.11).

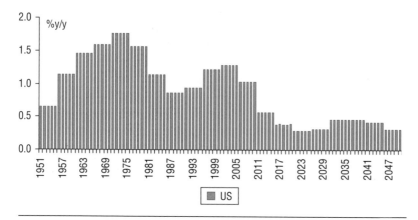

Figure 3.9   America's working-age population will grow slowly

Source: United Nations/Haver Analytics.

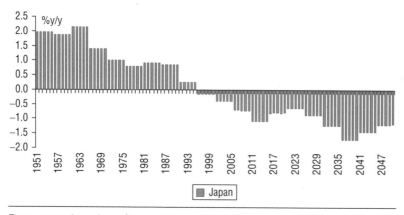

Figure 3.10   Japan's working-age population is falling

Source: United Nations/Haver Analytics.

The charts show the annual change in the numbers of working-age people from 1950 to 2050. In all three cases, growth rates were quite high in the 1950s and 1960s and, in the case of the United States, again in the 1990s, but the overall trend has been, and will be, toward slower growth. In the United States, the working-age population is predicted to grow at a rate of between 0.25 and 0.5 percent per year from 2010 onwards, and, as things stand, America's workforce will grow but only slowly.

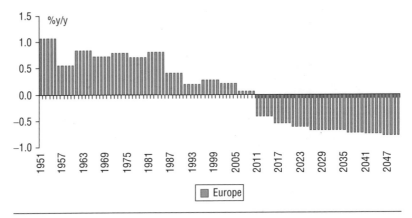

Figure 3.11   Western Europe's working-age population is close to a slump

Source: United Nations/Haver Analytics.

In Japan, by contrast, the working-age population is already declining and, in fact, started to do so in the 1990s. From now on and until 2050, it is expected to fall every year by between 0.5 and 1.5 percent per year.

In western Europe, the working-age population is currently almost at a standstill but from about 2009–10, it is predicted to start falling and then to continue to do so by 0.5–1 percent per year for the next 40 years.

Apart from the most developed countries, some developing countries will also soon run into an extended period during which the population of working age is expected to decline. Foremost among these are China, Russia, South Africa, and a little later, South Korea (see Figure 3.12–3.15).

But for the most part, developing countries will not have to cope with a halt in the growth of working-age people until 2030–40 (see Figure 3.16). In the meantime, they should be able to enjoy the economic benefits, which an expanding labor force will bring.

Dependency ratios for the old and the young are not comparable

According to Ronald Lee's data shown in Table 3.1 on page 39, the total dependency ratio (young and old as a share of the total

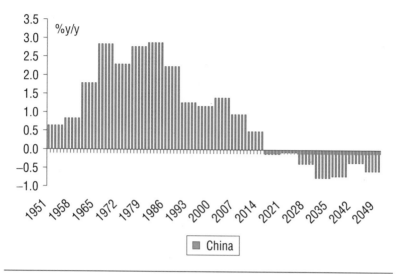

Figure 3.12   China's working-age population will drop soon

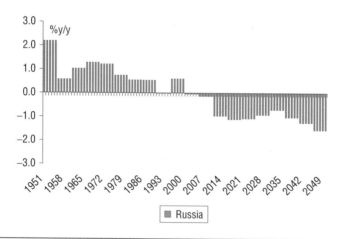

Figure 3.13   … along with Russia's

population) hasn't changed much over the last 300 years and is predicted to remain quite stable. If anything, it is now a little lower than the 40 percent recorded until the 1950s.

The dependency ratio of both young and old as a proportion of those aged 15–64, is predicted to rise only slightly from 55 percent today to 56 percent by 2050. On the face of it, this doesn't

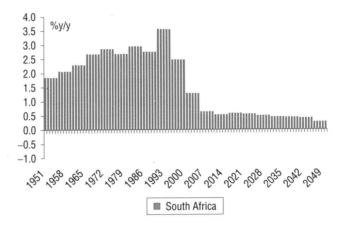

Figure 3.14   South Africa's is almost at a standstill

Source: United Nations/Haver Analytics.

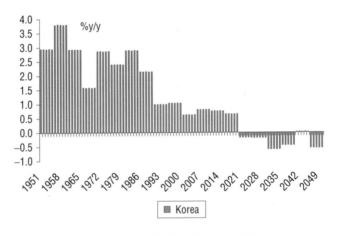

Figure 3.15   And South Korea's will fall after 2015

Source: United Nations/Haver Analytics.

suggest a massive change in our ability to look after and provide for the very young and for older people. To a degree, lower youth dependency might offset higher old-age dependency because fewer resources being allocated to education and childcare could make way for extra to be allocated to residential care for the aged, medical bills, and so on. Unfortunately, this observation is deceptively simple for at least two reasons.

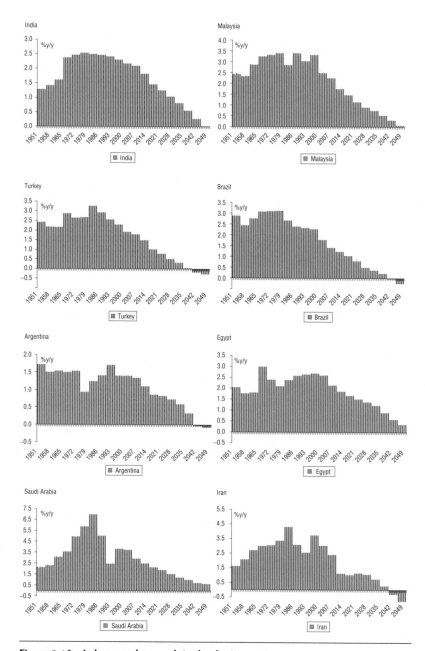

Figure 3.16 Labor supply growth in developing nations
Source: United Nations/Haver Analytics.

First, it presumes that childcare and old-age care are comparable and substitutes, when in reality, they are not. People in the public domain could make a case for spending less money on childcare, with the justification of fewer children, and fewer secondary school and university places, but to call for cuts in education and skill development budgets would be a much tougher argument. Is there, in fact, ever enough education? Can we really save money or cut funds allocated toward education in an increasingly competitive and globalized world where "human capital" is seen as one of the most crucial inputs to growth and prosperity?

Moreover, although both the very young and the very old have substantial care demands, the financial costs to society of caring for the elderly are calculated to be significantly higher than for the young. The elderly draw pensions, the size of which dwarfs payments made to children or to their parents on their behalf. They also require prescription drugs and medical care, the prices of which consistently rise faster than goods and services in general. The social costs of looking after the elderly, especially widows and widowers, are in a different league from those of supporting the young, not least because, for the most part, parents tend to their young privately and/or out of the family budget.

Second, the simple contrast between child and old-age dependency doesn't take into account the true significance of the change in dependency toward older age groups. In richer societies, the share of 15- to 64-year-olds in the population has risen steadily since the Second World War but is now peaking at just below 68 percent. By 2050, the share of this age group will have fallen by about 10 percent. Matching the 10 percent fall in the share of people of working age will be a 2 percent fall in those aged under 14 and a 12 percent rise in those aged over 65. By 2050, the very youngest will represent only 15 percent of the population, and the oldest will be about 26 percent of the population.

Taking into account a relative decline in the youngest age groups, a larger decline in the 15- to 64-year-olds, and a contrasting large rise in the over-65s, a few conclusions can be

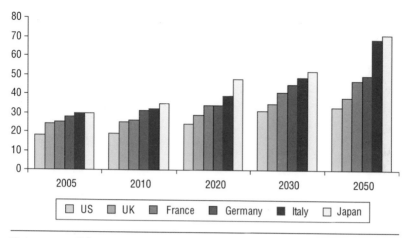

Figure 3.17 Old-age dependency rising rapidly in developed countries
Source: United Nations Population Division.

drawn about dependency. The child dependency ratio in the West is set to remain roughly stable at about 25 percent (of the working-age population), but the old-age dependency ratio is forecast to rise from 23 percent to 45 percent. This increase accounts for the entire rise of the total dependency ratio, which will stand at 71 percent by 2050. Actually, since the so-called Anglosphere (United States, United Kingdom, Australia, Canada, and New Zealand) has stronger demographic (that is, slower aging) characteristics than continental Europe and Japan, the aging and dependency numbers for the last two regions are even scarier.

The contrast is brought out in Figure 3.17 showing old-age dependency. In Japan and Italy, for example, the over-65s were roughly 30 percent of the working-age population in 2005 but they will represent about 70 percent by 2050. At the other end of the scale, America's over-65s were less than 20 percent of the working-age population in 2005 but will represent not much more than 30 percent by 2050.

In less developed countries (see Figure 3.18), the total dependency ratio is expected to fall from 57 percent to 54 percent by 2050, largely under the influence of a sharp fall in child dependency, from 49 percent to 32 percent. This offsets a rise in old-age dependency from 9 percent to 23 percent. India, Turkey, and

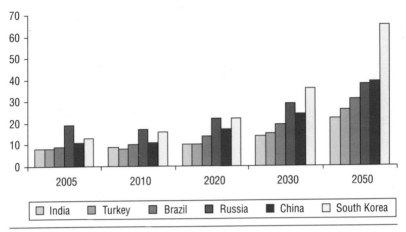

Figure 3.18   ... and in a few developing countries

Source: United Nations Population Division.

Brazil, for example, will still have low old-age dependency ratios in 2030. By 2050 they will be barely higher than those in the West today.

But again, there is no uniformity in the group. Russia, China, and South Korea will have rapidly aging societies from about 2020 onwards with the over-65s growing to become a larger share of the working-age population, than in the United States or the United Kingdom, by 2050.

The demographic dividend for poorer countries

In general though, developing countries should be able to reap the fruits of a demographic dividend. Their child dependency ratios will fall from roughly twice that of rich countries today to about the same, and their old-age dependency will rise but still only be half the level of rich countries by 2050. So this aggregate decline in dependency is one of the great hopes for growth and prosperity in the less developed and most populous parts of the world. As child dependency falls, pulling the total dependency ratio down, poorer countries have the opportunity to realize the economic and social gains that once accrued to richer countries. A decline in child dependency and stronger growth in the working-age population can be powerful growth drivers. The big difference of course is that the gains in rich countries can be documented as fact. The prospective gains in poorer countries depend on the assumption that child dependency will fall sharply, which is in turn a reflection of the assumption of lower fertility rates. This is also contingent on the occurrence of family planning, healthcare, and economic improvements. Moreover, and crucially, these demographic developments—the growth in the labor force especially—will turn on the ability of governments to provide adequately for both education and employment. Without these, sad to say, too many parts of the world could suffer the consequences of rising unemployment and social and political strife.

Conclusions

This chapter laid out three basic and important aspects of population developments to be expected over the next 40–50 years. World population growth is slowing down, but the extra three billion people who will inhabit the world by 2050 will almost all be counted in the developing countries, in particular in sub-Saharan Africa and the Middle East and North Africa. The largest declines in population are expected to occur in Japan, which has already started down this route, eastern European countries and Russia, Germany, and Italy.

The age structure changes that are expected, however, are similar within and between groups of countries, even if not identical. Some countries will age more slowly than others, but, one by one, we are all moving into the third stage of aging. In this phase, there will no longer be the rejuvenating effects of declining child mortality. Instead rising longevity and low or declining fertility combine to make our societies older. Youth depopulation will occur in several countries while in others, younger age groups will increase only very slowly. This aside, the focus will be on the stagnating or declining numbers of working-age people, while the older and elderly population groups expand strongly.

In richer countries, this is going to produce significant changes in dependency, that is, rising dependency of older people on a stable or declining population of working-age people, even as child dependency falls or stabilizes.

All countries are experiencing the same aging society characteristics, including emerging and developing countries. The demographic dividend—essentially a short-form for economic benefits that are brought by a fall in child dependency and a rise in the share of working-age people in the population, regardless of the elderly population size—has been pretty much exhausted in Western countries. In a few emerging and developing countries, this point is also quite close, but for most it lies some 20–30 years in the future, and for Africa, it is even further away.

Those countries that have lost, or that are losing, the demographic dividend will have to confront a series of economic, social, and political challenges to how they manage societies with rapidly rising age structures. But even for those countries that can still reap the dividend, demographics alone don't assure economic and social success. In the next chapter, I look at the type of developments that might be encouraged or promoted to defer or lessen the costs and disadvantages associated with aging societies.

Endnotes

1 J.R. Hicks, *Value and Capital* (New York: Oxford University Press, 1939).
2 China's population is actually going to carry on growing to about 1.44 billion by 2025–30, but then start to decline.
3 Ronald Lee, "The Demographic Transition: Three Centuries of Fundamental Change," *Journal of Economic Perspectives*, 17(4) (2003): 167–90.

Chapter 4

The economics of aging—
what is to be done?

> And in the end it's not the years in your life that count. It's the life in your years.
>
> —Attributed to Abraham Lincoln.[1]

Even if economics is not your specialist subject, or is only a distant relation to your favorite or expert area, you will find this chapter, on the economics of aging, conceptually simple. This is partly because its consequences are already affecting most of us—from families and governments to companies and employees (the themes explored here will be revisited with particular reference to conditions in the United States, Japan, and western Europe[2] in the next chapter). This is happening through two important areas in particular: labor markets and personal savings. The main concern about labor markets is the prospect of a stagnant or shrinking supply of people of working age. Ways of dealing with that include offsetting potential labor and skill shortages by increasing the retirement age, trying to get older people and females to remain active for longer in the workforce, increasing immigration, and raising productivity growth.

The question of savings is less obvious. Societies must save to be able to allocate funds for investment for the future, in factories and offices, transportation and energy, schools, and hospitals. This will involve sacrificing consumption today for projects designed to produce the means to consume goods and services tomorrow. If older people don't save, or they run down their savings, while a smaller working-age population does not save enough, via both private means and public pension schemes, to compensate for the shortfall, then a shortage of savings could seriously affect our future quality of life and have a significant negative impact on overall economic performance. These macroeconomic effects will be discussed in Chapter 6. Being prepared for the financial demands of aging societies is a topic no one can ignore.

How the rich world is aging

The characteristics of, and prospects for, emerging and developing countries are important but not as urgent as they are in advanced economies. In Chapter 7, I will look in detail at many of the overlooked demographic and economic phenomena in the poorer world, but in this and the next two chapters, the focus is on the United States, Japan, and western Europe. For these regions, the urgency reflects the two important economic effects of the three demographic megatrends of falling fertility, rising longevity, and rapidly rising age structure. The first is the hiatus, or decline, in the numbers of working-age people, that is aged 15–64. The second is the rise in old-age dependency as the numbers of those aged over 65 surge in relation to the 15- to 64-year-old age group. Table 4.1 shows how the population size and structure of different age groups is predicted to change in the United States, Japan, and western Europe over the next several decades.

The US population will carry on growing, with very small annual increases in the young and working-age populations but large increases in the elderly population. In fact, America's

Table 4.1   Key aging numbers for EU15, the United States and Japan 2005–50

| | | | | Population in millions | | | | | |
| | Percentage change | | | EU15 | | US | | Japan | |
	EU15	US	Japan	2005	2050	2005	2050	2005	2050
Population	−1	34	−20	457	450	300	402	128	102
0–14	−18	11	−35	75	61	62	69	17	11
15–64	−16	24	−38	307	259	201	248	85	52
Over 65	77	130	53	75	133	37	84	25	39
Over 80	174	119	156	18	50	10	31	6	16

Source: United Nations Population Division.

percentage gain in over-65s is the highest in the developed world. The pre-2004 European Union 15 (EU15)[3] population won't change much, but the structure will change more sharply, with the old and very old expanding significantly and all other age groups in decline. Japan's population is predicted to fall by 20 percent, with a structure more similar to the EU15 than the United States but with much more substantial youth and working-age depopulation.

In Japan today, there are 3.4 people of working age to support each person aged over 65 years, but by 2050, there will only be 1.3 people to do so. In the countries of western Europe, there are almost four people of working age for each person aged over 65 but again, by 2050, the number will have halved to about two. The United States is in a better position, marginally. Today, there are more than 5.5 people of working age to support every person aged over 65, but a halving to 2.9 is forecast by 2050.

By way of comparison though, an even more dramatic shift in age structure is expected to occur in China. Today, there are 9.2 people of working age to support every person over 65 years. By 2050, China will have little more than 2.5 people supporting each such person. As the numbers of working-age people shrink relative to those aged over 65, economic growth, living standards, and public and private finances will all be affected.

Will labor shortages crimp growth?

Gross domestic product (GDP—the value of goods and services produced in an economy) is not necessarily the best measure of economic welfare or living standards, but for most of us it will do just fine. The higher the level of GDP and the faster it grows, the more satisfied we are—or have been—that our societies are progressing, and our citizens are becoming more affluent. Economists look at many factors when trying to understand and predict economic growth. Some of them are cyclical, that is, the spending decisions of consumers, companies, and governments over short time periods of up to 18 months. But over a longer period, say from two to 10 years, or even longer, these factors and methods of predicting them are of little, if any, value. We cannot possibly know what the cyclical circumstances might be in 2010 or 2020 against which societies will make spending decisions, and there are few concrete ideas as to what sort of governments will be in office or what their priorities will be.

So over the longer term, we tend to look not so much at "demand" drivers of growth but "supply" drivers. In other words, we tend to look at the economy's capacity to expand, based on three essential drivers of GDP growth. Over the longer term, according to standard economic theory, these are: (a) the growth rate of the labor force, (b) technical progress that raises output per employee or output per hour worked, and (c) the amount of capital per worker.

Think, for example, of small family farms, where the number of people who work on the land is limited, where farming equipment and methods are quite dated and inefficient, and where there aren't even that many agricultural tools to spread around the family. A family might produce enough to eat and maybe even grow enough to sell in the local village or market town. But it isn't going to get rich without making some big changes. Somehow, it needs to get its hands on more labor and more (modern) tools and equipment to raise its productivity.

The "somehow" is the crux of the family's dilemma—and this analogy helps to convey the economic problem. The role of the growth rate of the labor force is clear. The faster the supply of labor increases, the stronger the impact on GDP. The technical progress (from better equipment) that raises workers' output is just a more complicated way of saying "productivity." The faster productivity increases, the more positive the impact on GDP and on living standards. And our third factor—capital per worker—is about how well endowed workers and employees are with capital equipment. This is perhaps the most difficult of the three drivers to predict, and in fact economists normally assume that the amount of capital grows at a fairly steady rate in line with the growth of the economy generally.

So the two drivers we focus on are labor force growth and productivity—and I have already demonstrated in the previous chapter what is likely to happen to the growth of the working-age population. This isn't identical to the labor force because some people who could work may choose not to, may be unable to find work, or may be discouraged from working for a variety of reasons. But as a proxy for the labor force, the working-age population is perfectly adequate. From here then, the math is as simple as it could be. If the labor force is growing by 1 percent per year, the contribution to long-run economic growth is 1 percent. Similarly, if the labor force isn't growing at all or shrinking by 1 percent a year, the contribution to growth is either zero or −1 percent a year.

Is it possible to boost the supply of workers?

If the labor force is stagnating or falling, the obvious solution would be to encourage people to have more children so they can grow up to become workers and employees in 20–30 years' time. Short of making procreation mandatory or imposing a 9:00 p.m. curfew on people aged under 40, this is of course easier said than done. Some countries are trying though, for example by offering tax incentives or one-off payments to women, but the overall effects have been modest.

So how to boost the supply of labor? There are two proposals, both of which would help to raise the supply of workers. One is to increase what is called labor force participation; the other is to raise immigration. Higher labor force participation means getting people who might otherwise not work for some reason into the labor force.[4] For example, the proportion of women and older people who could work but don't is generally speaking much lower than it is for men aged 20–64. Higher immigration, of course, simply means importing economically active workers.

Before looking a little more closely at these two measures, we should note the sheer scale of the task that confronts us over the next few decades. The International Monetary Fund (IMF) has considered the quantitative implications of trying to ensure that the number of working-age people as a share of the total population remains constant until 2050.[5] In advanced economies, for example, the overall participation rate would have to increase by a little over 10 percent, but this compares with a rise of just over 6 percent between 1960 and 2000, when, arguably, economic and social conditions were as favorable as they could be. The countries with the biggest challenges are Spain, South

Korea, and Italy, where participation rates might have to rise by 18–20 percent—an impossible task. In Japan, even if absolutely everyone aged 15–64 who could work did so, the size of the labor force would still decline between now and 2050.

One way to boost the participation rate of the workforce widely pursued in Western countries, is to raise the retirement age—a politically and socially contentious policy that governments are embracing, although with some trepidation. Again, to keep the proportion of workers in the total population constant over the next three or four decades, the retirement age in advanced economies would have to go up by seven years on average. This spans manageable increases of three years in the United States and the United Kingdom, 6–10 years in France, Germany, Spain and Italy but 10–12 years in South Korea and Japan. And older workers in Japan already have the highest participation rate of any major country. On average, Japanese workers tend to leave work at 64, which is five years past the current official retirement age and two years past the age at which full retirement pensions can be claimed. Japan has passed legislation recently to increase the official retirement age to 65 by 2025.

When we think about immigration as a way of keeping the relative size of the workforce constant, the challenge is both enormous, and its efficacy highly questionable. On average, in advanced economies in the four decades to 2000, total immigration as a share of total population was about 6 percent (of population in 2000). By 2050, immigration would have to grow so that it would account for about 30 percent of the population to keep the relative size of the workforce constant. Spain, which received very few immigrants in relation to its population size between 1960 and 2000, would have to increase its immigration to 40 percent of the population by 2050. Italy, Japan, Germany, and South Korea would have to increase the total number of immigrants so that they represented 30–40 percent of the population forecast by 2050, while France, the United Kingdom, and the United States would have to raise immigration to about 20–25 percent of the population in 2050, compared with levels of 2–10 percent between 1960 and 2000.

It is unrealistic, therefore, to imagine that any of these options alone will come close to being the solution. In reality, we will have to try and do a little bit of everything. We will have to continue to fight gender discrimination at work and create the conditions under which more women—if they wish to do so—can go to work and be mothers at the same time. We will have to combat agism in the workplace and encourage older workers to stay on in keeping with their health and abilities. We shall also have to devise socially acceptable and economically relevant immigration policies. Consistent with one of the main themes of this book, it is hard to envisage our societies evolving toward these goals without a strong or stronger lead role for government.

Raising participation and immigration

In advanced economies, more than 70 percent of men of working age tend to work. In Japan, which has the highest proportion of men aged 15–64 at work, the figure is more than 80 percent. However, participation rates are relatively low when it comes to women generally or older workers aged 55–64. Some people moreover believe that young workers in their twenties are showing signs of a lower commitment to stable and permanent employment. This is not a major problem to the extent that younger people spend longer in higher education or go to work and then return to school or college to acquire more skills or retrain. But it is, or will be, a problem if twenty-somethings delay work or career development or simply avoid long-term commitments to work. Several factors suggest why this might be happening, for example, adverse financial circumstances that tend to cause young people to spend additional years at home, inadequate skills and training in the information economy, exaggerated expectations about employment possibilities, and the temptation and ease of global travel.

In America, male participation in the first quarter of 2008 was about 73 percent, compared with over 75 percent in 2000. Female participation was 59 percent, also down from a peak of just over 60 percent in 2000, and the participation rate of older workers of both sexes, aged over 55, was just around 63 percent, compared with 57.7 percent in 2000. For 16- to 19-year-olds, where the participation rate is bound to be much smaller because of school and university attendance, the participation rate was 43 percent, compared with 52 percent in 2000. Although participation rates for some groups of people rose a bit in 2006–07, in line with the expansion of the economy, the levels in the first half of 2007 remained well off the peak rates registered several years ago. Participation rates are bound to decline far as long as the economic downturn continues.

It is curious that participation rates in the United States have fallen in recent years. As 50- and 60-somethings age and move toward retirement, participation rates of an aging labor force are going to decline. But in the United States, the 55- to 64-year-old participation rate has actually risen a little. On the other hand, the decline in female participation is something of a mystery, as is the very sharp fall in the participation rate of the very youngest workers. If these trends can't be reversed in the next several years, the overall outlook for the United States economy in the long term might not be as relatively bright as is often portrayed—that is, after the current economic and banking problems have ended.

Almost everywhere in western Europe, participation rates are lower than in America, but the most recent trend is the mirror image. Participation rates for many groups of workers in 2005–07 have actually risen. Overall, lower participation rates in the EU15 than those that occur in the United States are attributed to rules and regulations involving minimum wages, taxes, benefits, and pension packages and "hire and fire" laws that either discourage people from looking for work or restrict the ability or incentives for firms to hire.

EU15 male participation rose to 73 percent in 2006, not very different from what it was in 2000. But female participation rose over this period from 53.6 percent to 58 percent and for older workers from 36.6 percent to 45 percent. These last two increases are actually rather encouraging, given that the levels still remain rather low. The last several years have unquestionably seen some improvement in the growth rate and performance of western European economies. In a way, it would have been shocking if these increases hadn't happened. Western

European countries have slowly been amending their labor laws and trying to promote greater hiring of women and older citizens. The European Union's Lisbon Agenda, adopted in 2000, had many worthy economic and social goals that were supposed to, but won't, be realized by 2010. One of them was to raise overall participation to 70 percent with the lead role taken by women. So the scorecard might read that some progress has been made, but there is still a long way to go.

Women in Europe tend to have comparatively low participation rates, other than in Nordic countries where about 70 percent of women who could work do so. Most European countries have female participation rates around 50–60 percent but several countries have female participation rates of much less. Italy, Greece, Poland, and Croatia, for example, have female rates of 46–48 percent.

One of the main challenges for aging societies then is to encourage more people who could work to do so—assuming of course they want to. Because the groups with the lowest participation rates tend to be women and older workers, special efforts will have to be made to make it more attractive for more women to work and for older workers to stay on at work or to find economically useful and personally challenging work once they approach or pass the age of retirement.

Women to work

In many countries, it is still a man's world. That won't shock many women of course—even in more enlightened countries for female employment such as the United States, United Kingdom, and those in Scandinavia. But imagine the greater difficulties that many of today's developing, not to mention poorest, countries might confront in the next 20–25 years when they, too, start to experience the same aging pressures as the developed world and China are grappling with today.

China has a very high female participation rate, estimated at 70 percent. But most Asian economies have female participation rates of between 50 and 60 percent and India has the lowest at under 40 percent. A recent United Nations Survey[6] drew particular attention to sex discrimination and estimated its cost to Asia at between US$42 billion and US$47 billion each year. That is the equivalent or more of the entire GDP of many poor countries. Eliminating gender inequality at work could raise growth rates on average by about 0.3–0.4 percent a year and of course, for some countries, the gains could be materially higher. The costs don't end with sex discrimination as regards job opportunities. Inferior education for females in Asia is estimated to cost between US$16 billion and US$30 billion a year, to which have to be added the tougher-to-estimate economic costs of widespread violence to, and suppression of, women.

The Organization for Economic Cooperation and Development (OECD) has estimated that if all developed countries were to raise their female participation rates to the same levels as exist in Scandinavia, then economic growth rates would, for a while, increase by between 0.3 and 0.7 percent a year. There remain, of course, many obstacles and prejudices to raising female participation, not least the poor provision of adequate childcare and higher tax rates on second breadwinners in some countries. But it may be a potentially fruitful avenue for governments to look down because there seems to be a reasonably tight association between higher female participation and higher fertility rates. It could even be a win-win option for governments if they can bring this about.

You might think that the more women in work, the fewer children they would be inclined to bear. But the truth is a little different. Japan, eastern Europe and Russia, Italy, and Germany, and the European Union, in general, have the lowest female participation rates in the world, but they also have the lowest fertility rates. Sweden, Iceland, Norway, Denmark, the United States, and Ireland have higher fertility rates and higher proportions of women working. How so? Presumably if childcare is expensive or poor and the tax system penalizes women going to work, most women will have to make a decision between being a mum or a worker. The expense and quality of childcare might well be the more compelling factor that ultimately keeps women at home. On the other hand, if women can get affordable and readily available childcare and the tax system treats them in line with or better than men, the choice may become redundant since many women would like to be mothers and be able to pursue satisfying and productive work.

This shouldn't be beyond us to sort out. Governments and companies can do much more to provide adequate childcare facilities and flexible, family-friendly working arrangements to allow women to work at home, or in a factory, or office while bringing up their children. Governments can change housing and mortgage financing arrangements and incentives, which might allow younger people to start families earlier and, in particular, away from parental homes.

Can we strengthen brain as well as brawn?

Getting older workers into or back into the workforce represents a different sort of challenge and involves battling with different prejudices, which I examine in more detail in the next chapter. Some countries have achieved fairly high rates of older worker participation. Scandinavian countries and the United Kingdom, for example, record older person participation rates at 50–60 percent. In Sweden, it is almost 70 percent. But in Europe generally, on average, about 40 percent of Europe's 55- to 64-year-olds work. France, Italy, Austria, and Belgium have very low rates of older worker participation at 38 percent. Elsewhere, it is lower still. In eastern Europe, the rate is around 30–35 percent and in the case of Poland, it is as low as 27.2 percent. This is surely a waste of human capital in an economic sense and a waste of peoples' lives on a personal level.

The challenge will be to get people in their middle- to late-50s, who may be looking forward to changes in lifestyle and to a lighter, more enjoyable and personally satisfying workload, to soldier on regardless at work until the age of 65 or 67. Many would-be retirees may simply not want to carry on working that long, even if they knew they would live in reasonable health for another 15–20 years on average. The prejudices, predictably, are about agism in the workplace. Sometimes this derives from a simple work-specific preference for younger people. Other times, it is simply a reflection of the belief that as workers mature in age, they become less productive, less able to learn new skills quickly and less inclined to be innovative.

This may change in the future as older generations retire after a lifetime of work in the information society and with much stronger technology skills than current retirees possess. On the other hand, however much we can extend life expectancy and the period of good health in retirement—call it brawn for short—isn't there something reasonably basic about the deterioration of the brain as we age?

Some time around the age of 40 a gradual decline begins—barely perceptible at first—that for many people ends up with degrees of dementia. Medical science and the pharmaceutical industry are already experimenting with a variety of drugs to help augment memory and increase sharpness. Magazines and health professionals keep exhorting us to change our diets on the basis that certain types of food can improve our cognitive skills. Some psychologists think that listening to Mozart improves our mathematical and spatial reasoning. Best not buy your grandparents an iPod though because it is probably too late. These types of reasoning seem to depend on music lessons as children, rather than listening to a cracking aria or violin movement in an armchair. And then there's a cocktail of learning techniques, good sleep quality, physical exercise, and the avoidance of smoking and excessive alcohol intake that are hailed as meaningful ways of extending alertness and mental capacities into old age. Neurofeedback is a system that teaches people, either in a controlled medical environment or with the aid of a laptop, how to recognize, in real time, uncontrollable aspects of their physiology (like heart rate or brain wave) that occur in response to certain emotional stimuli. The idea is that by understanding one's emotions and natural body functions better, performance, concentration, and creativity can be improved.

Or become a nun. A study of 75- to 107-year-old inhabitants in the convent of the School Sisters of Notre Dame on Good Counsel Hill in Mankato, Minnesota (The "Nun Study"), has followed 678 Catholic sisters recruited in 1991. The group had remarkable longevity and an impeccable lifestyle. Some suffered from Alzheimer's disease, but many avoided dementia and senility altogether. The research put the sisters' mental and physical health down to a combination of adequate vitamin folate, verbal ability, positive emotions early in life, keeping the brain active, and maintaining good health and spirituality.[7]

All of the brain-enhancing methods discussed here represent perfectly sound pieces of lifestyle advice, designed to prepare better for an active old age. For many people in their fifties and sixties, though, however disciplined they may be in pursuit of these goals, it is still hard to imagine they're going to make an employer choose freely to take on a 64- or 67-year-old, let alone a still older candidate when a much younger one is available. Call it prejudice, common sense, self-interest, or whatever you like, but the world of work today simply doesn't function any other way for most positions, and is unlikely to do so in the foreseeable future.

Perhaps employer- or government-sponsored work environment programs will extend and sustain training and education for older workers, channel them into special types of work as they approach retirement, or even bring them together in special ways to give them access to appropriate employment opportunities. But such outcomes may be a long time away, and in the meantime older workers will find it hard to stay in work, despite a somewhat improved trend in recent years.

To a degree, there is no reason these exceptionally low rates of participation should persist. The experience of older workers and the nature of work that is becoming less physical and strenuous, more information-oriented, and easy to do at home should help to raise participation rates of 55- to 64–year-olds. The task should certainly be simpler than it might have been 25 years ago or than it might be, say, in many developing countries, where there tends to be far greater emphasis on agricultural, construction, and manufacturing labor.

Working longer to retirement

One fact that many people will experience is the rise in the official age of retirement or in the age at which people become eligible for full pension benefits. By extending retirement and or pensionable age, it's doubtful that governments have given

much thought specifically to providing for fuller, more enriching working lives for older people. Rather, the decision seems to
be mainly motivated by the desire to lower the pension payment
burden on the state in the future. Assuming, for example, that
our mortality tables are broadly correct and that men and
women retire at 65, then government pension obligations would
fall by 3 percent in money terms for each year that people work
beyond the age of 65 without drawing their pensions.[8]

In 1920, the normal retirement age in more advanced societies
was 70–74 at a time when male life expectancy was about 55–
60 years. So pension rights, such as they were almost a century
ago, were most unlikely to be drawn at all. Since then, life
expectancy has risen while the formal retirement age has fallen.
In 1960, the average retirement age in OECD countries was 65.
By 1995, it had fallen to 60–62. Pension providers, whether they
are the government or private companies, now have to pay pensions for the best part of 18 years for men on average and for
23 years for women. These payment periods compare with just
11 years and 18 years respectively, in 1970. If life expectancy
rises as many expect, then by 2030 or 2050, providers will be
paying pensions for even longer, unless the retirement age is
raised in line with life expectancy.

It is therefore clear that most people will be asked or forced to
work a little longer in the future. Since the 1990s, over a third of
OECD countries have passed legislation raising the pensionable
age for men and about two-thirds have done so for women. The
majority of countries now stipulate that by 2035 or earlier,
the pensionable age will have risen to 65 years or more, in some
countries equalized for both men and women. However, that's
the easy bit in a way. The hard part is to persuade employers
and employees to change their behavior and expectations,
respectively, and with a modicum of enthusiasm rather than res-
ignation and under duress.

Youth trends sap economic strength

It is not only the creation of jobs and suitable working conditions for women and older workers that will require our

attention. Youth needs to be considered too. Changes in the lifestyles and circumstances facing younger people have resulted in some weakness or decline in younger worker participation rates. Young people are, for example, spending longer in full-time education, taking extended career breaks, or retraining for a new career. None of these are particularly worrying, and it is possible to encourage students to complete their studies over a smaller number of years. But the more troublesome developments arise from young people who, for one reason or another, want to be single and stay that way, or become hard to employ or immobile for lifestyle and financial reasons.

For example, young adults have begun to stay single and to remain with their parents at home for longer. This has created another acronym social group, called "Kippers"—otherwise known as Kids in Parents' Pockets Eroding Retirement Savings. Maybe you know one—maybe you have one. The United Kingdom's Office of National Statistics, for example, reported in 2007[9] that the number of young people in their twenties staying with their parents had risen by 20 percent for males and 30 percent for females since 1992. The study suggested that 60 percent of men aged 20–24 and 40 percent of women were still living at home.

Inevitably there is—maybe always was—much social or street chat about today's youth being lazy, expecting too much from work, not being prepared to work hard, and so on. But the main reasons that many young people stay at home and/or remain single for longer are educational and financial. Many surveys find that the basic academic and literacy skills of school leavers in western Europe and America have been declining and that employers have to spend time and money training their youngest recruits in basic skills. In 2006, for example, *The Times* newspaper in the United Kingdom reported that the Confederation of British Industry had found that a third of employers had to send younger staff for remedial training in mathematics and English.[10]

In a globalized world, increasingly competitive and dominated by information technology, the search for steady and rewarding employment depends on young people having ever higher standards of literacy, numerical ability, and communications ability.

If they lack these skills, their ability to find and remain in suitable work will be compromised. They may have no option but to stay at home for longer since many may be not only unemployed but unemployable.

Single young females, as a social group, are nowadays much celebrated in magazines and the media—and do a lot of celebrating themselves. But, from a demographic angle, they too may be compromising their future. One of the reasons for youth depopulation is said to be the tendency on the part of women to stay single. A Japanese newspaper reported, for example, that 23.5 percent of Japanese women born in 1990 will never get married, up from 16.8 percent of women born in 1985, and that the average age of first marriage for women is now about 28.2 years, up from 23 years in 1950.[11] And this is not unique to Japan.

The average age of first marriage is about 28 years or higher on average in the United States and most European countries, and is creeping higher. The inclination to have fewer children later, or none at all, shows few signs of changing. Some governments have introduced fiscal measures to try to reverse the trend of declining births and birth rates. France offers tax and subsidy incentives to induce women to have more children, and the Spanish prime minister, Jose Luis Rodriguez Zapatero, announced in his 2007 re-election campaign that he would give families €2,500 for every child born in Spain. But to date, this type of monetary incentive has had only minor effects on the birth rate. A so-called longitudinal study (one that tracks the behavior and responses of a group as they grow older) undertaken in the United Kingdom was reported in a British newspaper to have shown that a third of British women who attend university would never have children.[12] According to the report, 40 percent of graduate women were childless at age 35 and a decade later, at the end of childbearing years, a third still had no children.

Lifestyle choices are clearly one explanation but the explosion of one-parent families or temporary two-parent families, reflecting the high incidence of divorce, is another. Divorce rates have been rising steadily, as is well known, and at the last count there were roughly 1.9 divorces per 1,000 people in the EU15, 2.3 in Japan, and four in the United States. As a share of marriages, these numbers work out at between 36 percent in Japan and 40 percent in the EU15 (though, as you might expect substantially lower in Italy, Spain, Greece, and Ireland), and 50 percent in the United States. So, whether out of choice or because one- and temporary two-parent families are less well equipped to bear and raise larger numbers of children, the odds are stacked heavily against any meaningful turnaround in youth depopulation trends. Fewer children and young adults, as should be clear by now, mean fewer workers in the future, and fewer workers and larger numbers of retirees and pensioners are precisely what aging societies are about.

Financial problems represent another key reason for the existence of Kippers. Growing numbers of young people can't afford to buy a house or even rent property, especially if mortgage finance systems make it difficult or expensive to borrow or if they discourage people from transferring their mortgages (or pension rights) when they move locations or jobs. While some people may scoff and recall how they had to leave the family home in their youth and become independent, young people face different circumstances today, at least in one important respect. Property prices, adjusted for inflation, in most countries in the OECD area, were at post-1945 highs in 2006–07. For first-time purchasers, buying property had become either unaffordable or only possible by getting a mortgage at imprudent multiples of income. The major benefit of the slide in house prices that began in several industrial countries in 2007 is the easing of the burden on first-time purchasers, the young and middle income workers, whose ability to live near work or move jobs has been impaired because of the cost of housing provided that adequate mortgage finance is available at a resonable cost.

How much immigration?

Immigration is perhaps an obvious way of offsetting the effects of shortages of labor in general or of specific types of skilled labor in particular. Countries such as the United States, Australia, and Canada became successful economies partly on the basis of immigration from what were the older economies of Europe. Could this have lessons for us in the twenty-first century? Will immigration be the key to resolving the problems of aging societies?

Immigration may provide the route to more labor supply and higher fertility—for a while at least. Naturally, not all the economics of immigration is positive. Higher immigration into already crowded cities in the West today adds to congestion, fuels demand for jobs and housing, and may displace existing employees. At the same time, the poorer countries from which immigrants depart are clearly at risk of an exodus of skilled workers they can ill afford to lose. But in the main, these are management issues to which we have to find workable solutions that are acceptable to most people. They are not, and cannot be seen as, reasons to oppose immigration in principle. Opening our economies to more migrants could have positive effects on economic growth and on the demographic challenges, but, as I argue later, the economic arguments are nowhere as convincing as is often assumed.

The main problem is that, to compensate for the stagnation or decline in the working-age population that will happen over the next 20–30 years, the scale of immigration will have to be way above current levels to have a material impact. Some countries, including the United States, Canada, Australia, and Ireland, will probably find that their demographics can be compensated to a degree by simply sustaining current levels of immigration. America takes roughly one million immigrants a year (net, that is, after allowing for emigrants) but actually needs only 110,000–120,000 a year until 2050 to keep its population stable. Australia took in a net 162,600 migrants—nearly eight migrants per 1,000 of population—in the year to March 2007. That contributed about 54 percent to the fastest annual growth in overall population recorded since records began in 1789. It could probably keep its labor force stable with a lower immigration rate for a while, but eventually, migrant numbers might have to increase regardless.

Other countries, including the United Kingdom and Denmark, however, may have to double their immigration rates to offset the impact of demographic change. But for most countries in western Europe, and in Japan, the idea of raising the immigration rate by between five and 12 times to offset the expected decline in the working-age population is a political nonstarter.

The first 15 member countries of the European Union had net immigration, until recently, of about 700,000 a year, but will actually need 2.5 million a year until 2050 to keep the population stable and 4.3 million a year to keep the working-age population stable. Japan has barely any net immigration but would need 300,000 a year and 600,000 a year, respectively to meet the same objectives. The realpolitik outlook for Western economies, of admitting significantly larger numbers of migrants in the foreseeable future, is poor—even in America, historically the most liberal and welcoming nation as regards immigration.

In Europe, for example, the "Polish plumber" has become a celebrated (though largely fictional) character in the wake of Poland's accession to the European Union in 2004. In the European referenda on the European Constitution in 2005, opponents to immigration used this character as a symbol of the threat of cheap east European labor to jobs and incomes of citizens inside the existing (i.e., west European) union. Of course, the citizens of so-called accession countries all have rights to live and work within the union in accordance with the European Commission's directives on labor and services.

The case of the Polish plumber demonstrates the ambivalence of Europeans. On the one hand, immigrants fill jobs and work for pay rates that many citizens of the host country would find unacceptable, and they contribute to the quality of life and to cities in enriching ways. On the other, especially in very recent years, many in western Europe, and the United States to some extent, have grown to view migrants with suspicion or worse. To a degree, of course, this has become intertwined with popular angst about security and terrorism, but for the most part, skepticism derives from economic and financial fears and insecurities that have grown in the last few years. These have been perceived, rightly or wrongly, as having been brought about by the combination of globalization, cheap labor, and concerns about the adequacy of affordable housing and meaningful jobs.

There is no question that in theory, a rise in immigration would swell the ranks of those of working age. Consequently, the first-round effects should include higher economic growth, bigger tax revenues, low inflation (as a result of downward pressure on wages and salaries), and possibly higher birth rates because migrant women coming from countries with higher fertility rates will tend often to have more children than native-born women.

However, there are at least three major problems with the theory. First, as noted, the scale of immigration required to offset native demographic trends and the loss to economic growth is extraordinarily large and unrealistic—certainly as things stand today politically. Second, these positive effects of immigration may be much more short-lived than they are made out to be, so that immigration doesn't really offer a stable, long-term solution. Third, sooner or later, high immigration may also involve costs to the host society too, including those of dependency, welfare, social disharmony, and pressure on infrastructure and social facilities.

None of this is to argue, of course, that immigration has no economic role to play, for it clearly has. Immigration should also be welcomed for a host of other social, cultural, and political reasons. The policies adopted with respect to immigration cross many disciplinary backgrounds, of which economics is but one and perhaps not the most important one. That said, from a contemporary and practical standpoint, higher immigration might not make a material and enduring contribution to the economic consequences of aging societies.

Productivity is the holy economic grail

If the potential to boost labor supply and offset a rising age structure in society via the participation and immigration routes is limited and temporary, the main alternative lies in the form of higher productivity growth, in other words, higher levels of output per person per hour worked. Productivity growth is often cited as a positive factor for aging societies—but this is probably more out of hope than confidence. Rising productivity would add to the contribution made by any increase in labor force participation, and the faster productivity grows, the more it will cushion the impact of any labor force slowdown or even shortages. More sophisticated developing countries typically have high rates of productivity growth. Limited opportunities to consume and poor social care arrangements normally mean citizens save a high proportion of their income. These savings tend to end up being collected by financial firms and are used to finance investment, which supports higher productivity growth rates. As people move from labor-intensive, low productivity farming into higher productivity, more capital-intensive manufacturing or services jobs in cities, the economic benefits start to accrue quickly.

Most advanced economies have had relatively slow rates of productivity growth in the last decade or two, and, to some degree, demographic constraints over economic performance have come to be more fully recognized. But this doesn't mean rich economies cannot increase productivity growth. Until the 1990s, our economies were based on a mixture of plentiful supply of labor, large-scale production, consumerism, traditional goods and services with a long shelf life, and stable employment and career patterns. Today's information economy, however, has entirely different modes of production and organization. It demands flexibility, innovation, and continuous improvement in skill levels and education standards; it rewards merit and achievement as opposed to seniority; it prizes individual creativity rather than machines—and it may be a tougher world into which to integrate millions of extra retired and old people.

But for the moment, the United States at least is still basking in the afterglow of its own productivity spurt, the productivity growth rate having doubled during the 1990s and until about 2005. Previously, America's productivity growth rate was a rather unimpressive 1.4 percent per year on average, but between 1990 and 2005 the underlying rate of productivity growth rose to about 2.7 percent per year, largely under the influence of powerful technological advances in the information and communications technology (ICT) industries. Although ICT hardware firms and industries were the first to benefit from the Internet, microchips and so on, other industries and employees followed as ICT hardware and software were incorporated into such diverse activities as retailing, transportation, wholesaling, manufacturing, financial and business services, health and education, and leisure. If American productivity were to carry on growing at 2.7 percent a year and the growth in the labor force, as I showed in the previous chapter, slowed to just +0.5 percent per year, then the country's trend growth rate would be 3.2 percent a year. This is so much faster than the growth of America's population over the next few decades (0.8 percent per year for the next 25 years) that the economic outlook would be bright indeed.

Of course, America's productivity may not grow this fast in decades to come, and some economists have pointed out that slower productivity growth since 2006 offers some evidence that the 1990s surge has more or less burned itself out. But even if US productivity is more like 2 percent per year, this would still leave America with absolute and relative advantages.

The EU15's prospects might look bleak by comparison. western Europe has not enjoyed such good productivity performance, at least until 2006–07, when economists started to detect the first hopeful signs of a revival. Before then, productivity growth in the pre-2004 European Union 15 member countries had been little more than 1 percent per year. And it is not as though the European continent is populated by technological philistines and antiquated manufacturing.

The reasons for Europe's relatively low productivity performance have been the subject of much discussion and collective soul-searching. Let us assume, though, 1 percent per year growth in productivity for the next 30–40 years. Europe's working age population is expected to be stable until 2010 and then to drop by 0.3 percent per year between 2011 and 2030 and by 0.6 percent per year from 2031 to 2050. Unless Europeans can make some big changes in the nature of labor force participation, a simple addition shows a deteriorating growth outlook from 1 percent a year in the next five years to 0.7 percent a year in the next 20 years and then 0.4 percent a year in the following two decades. Western Europe's population is going to remain pretty much unchanged until 2025–30 and then start to fall by about 0.2 percent per year, so at least there will be no population pressures on the sharing out of income and wealth. But GDP growth of 0.4 percent a year, even if the population is falling by 0.2 percent a year is a damning and unattractive outlook.

So, then, productivity is going to be a big issue in aging societies, determining to a significant extent how to extract rising living standards when economic growth rates might otherwise decline with changes in the labor force. If only there were an elixir for higher productivity growth. As our societies age, the search may get harder. Older societies will probably invest less in capital equipment (which boosts productivity), and much of the capital equipment older societies use may get modernized less often. Moreover, it is a widely-held view that the productivity of people, once they reach the age of 50–55 years, starts to ebb and that their drive to innovate and explore the new frontiers of technology weakens.

Cell phones, with a multitude of functions apart from the boring one of making a phone call, appeal to the young, not the old. The same goes for MP3 players on which you can watch DVDs, blog, and do instant messaging. More importantly maybe, broadband penetration and use of the Internet for purposes other than e-mail and information searches are almost certainly going to become more widespread over the next 10–15 years—and these are almost certainly central to enhanced productivity in the information age. Of course, as today's more tech-savvy young people grow into middle age and then retirement, their familiarity with technology will set them apart from today's retirees. Nevertheless, aging societies may need new innovations to boost and sustain access to, and use of, the Internet and the technologies that have yet to happen.

The BBC reported in 2006 on a telecommunications regulator research study that said only 28 percent of people aged over 65 in the United Kingdom have home Internet access, compared with 57 percent for the United Kingdom as a whole.[13] This isn't an unusual observation, and researchers from the United States, western Europe and Australia have found diminishing use of the Internet, including e-mail, going up the age scale, especially among those over 65. The reasons are not surprising, revolving around the failure, or weakening of, perceptual (audio and visual), cognitive (attention and memory), and motor (haptic or sense of touch) capabilities.[14]

Aging populations will also require us to spend more money on, and work more in, the health and old-age care sectors. The provision of goods and services in these sectors is not subject to global competition as are, for example, cars and electronics and they also tend to be quite labor-intensive. These characteristics tend to be associated with lower rates of technical progress and of productivity growth. So the responsibility to raise productivity that will fall on the next generations of working-age people will be all the bigger.

The point is that raising productivity won't come easily or quickly. It will require investment and innovation, which in turn require that there should be enough savings around to finance them. And it will require a favorable legal and regulatory environment to allow tomorrow's productivity to materialize. It is argued, for example, that one of the reasons that productivity growth in western Europe and Japan has failed to match performance in the United States is because of red tape, overly regulated labor markets, and barriers to the creation of new businesses, innovations, and patents.

In any event, the most valuable investment that we can make for the long term is probably investment in education. And it seems increasingly likely that provision of higher standards of education for most people through their (longer) working lives will have to be an expanding function of government and of employers. Human capital investment, in other words, is going to be a relentless requirement that will challenge the possible presumption that education budgets can be cut as youth dependency ratios decline.

Will we be able to finance retirement?

Societies and individuals have to save to provide for the future. Our savings, collected by pension funds, insurance companies, banks, and other financial institutions, finance the physical and human capital investment that increases the efficiency and productivity of workers—and in turn, creates future growth. If we don't save enough or find that the growing population of over-65s starts to cash in its savings, we shall be compromising our future, at least economically and financially.

When it comes to paying the bills for retirement and elderly care, pensions, and healthcare, we all hope that our personal savings pots and government finances will be large and strong enough to write the checks. But the only judgment we can make today in the West is that they won't. If we don't save enough, or run down our savings in the future, or if governments accumulate debt more rapidly (what economists call "dis-saving") there will be significant implications for the living standards of both young and old.

Individually, many of us spend much of our lives trying to squirrel away some of what we earn, plus money we borrow, into assets. For most people, the most important investments are property, pension assets, life insurance policies and other savings products, and bank deposits. Baby boomers have been privileged, having accumulated over a few decades unprecedented quantities of such assets, whose prices have been on a strong rising trend—with some interruptions of course.

There are many reasons to save. We may save to buy property or pay for that holiday to the Galapagos Islands. We may also save for a variety of "just in case" reasons. The main motive to save more is to help maintain our worldly pleasures and enjoyment of life when we stop working and retire. We may even want to pass some of our savings pot on to our children. With rising life expectancy, people now have additional reasons to save, namely to pay for what is becoming increasingly expensive old-age care, especially when mobility and ability in the home begin to decline.

Individuals are thought to go through different saving and consumption phases during their lives, known in the jargon as the "life cycle hypothesis." According to this, people try to smooth their consumption over time, resulting in large changes in their savings habits. The young don't save and, as they grow up into young working age, tend to borrow to support or improve their lifestyles. As they advance into their forties and fifties, they are probably at or close to the peak of their capacity to earn, spend and save. This may still be true for people in their early- or even mid-sixties nowadays. But by the time work stops or winds down and retirement begins in earnest, the theory says that savings normally stop, too. In fact, the elderly normally have to live off or sell their assets, especially the riskier varieties, in order to finance their consumption and eventually old-age care.

In the real world, it's not always obvious how true this hypothesis is. We have some evidence today to show that in Japan, personal savings have fallen from about 15 percent to 3 percent of disposable income since 1990. Aging probably has a lot to do with this, if not everything. But in America, which is aging a lot more slowly than Japan, the household savings rate has also fallen from about 8 percent of disposable income (long-term average until about the early 1990s) to around zero. This basically means that individuals have reduced their savings or increased their borrowing. Debate about the measured collapse in personal savings continues, after over a decade or more, but it is fair to point out that on any measure, the US personal sector in the aggregate has been dis-saving for several years.

If individual savings tend to stall or decline with advancing years, the key question for the future is the extent to which the sharp rise in the elderly population will spend their savings to finance the longer retirement years of consumption. And remember, while they do, the stagnant or declining numbers of working-age people as a group are likely to save less in total in the absence of any changes in savings behavior. People of working age today, and in the future, should save more in preparation for retirement because they won't be able to rely on company and government pension schemes as the boomers have done.

Saving less with age, saving less anyway

We can see in Table 4.2 the savings rates of the heads of households in six major industrial countries according to their age group. The patterns are not wholly convincing, but bear in mind this is a snapshot taken by researchers in work published mostly in or around 2000. It doesn't tell us anything about the context

Table 4.2   How Savings Change with Age (%)

Age	UK	Canada	Japan	Germany	Italy	US
25–34	6.22	1.5	11	11	13.26	8.72
35–44	9.42	4	20.15	14	15.57	14.21
45–54	12.24	6.5	17.6	16	17.65	14.75
55–64	7.62	10	19.7	10	17.94	10.81
65–74	11.36	6	20.2	7.5	16.52	−4.88
Over 75	19.82	8	26.45	10	15.7	−6.54

Note: Ages are for head of household and the savings rates (as a % of income) in each age group are for all households in the group.

Source: Stephen A. Nyce and Sylvester J. Schreiber, *The Economic Implications of Aging Societies: The Costs of living Happily Ever After*, (New York: Cambridge University Press, 2006); p. 26.

of the time the snapshot was taken, the trend leading up to it, or what has happened since. Nevertheless, the comparison is sufficiently revealing.

All younger households save less than older ones in all the countries shown. Mostly, households headed by 35–54 year olds have the highest savings rates, though this wasn't true in the case of the United Kingdom or Canada. Households headed by over-65-year-olds generally had lower savings rates than younger and middle-aged households, except in the United Kingdom and Japan. The United States actually provides us with the clearest picture of a decline in savings in older age groups.

In recent years, savings rates for all age groups combined have fallen significantly in the United States, Japan, and the United Kingdom. They remained steadier in most of the EU15. One reason for this may be that it is only since 2005 that economic performance and confidence have improved in the EU15. Another might be that most EU15 citizens tend to worry more about the adequacy of retirement pension systems than do their peers in the United States, United Kingdom, Australia, and Canada, for example, where private pension provision and funded public pension schemes are more common. And ultimately, it's also possible that the good times of the last 10–20 years have fostered a culture of credit (more borrowing) and consumption (less saving), which might well reverse, at least for a while, in the wake of the slowdown in growth in advanced countries that commenced in 2007.

But the culture of saving for a rainy day isn't being helped by poor financial education relevant to the contemporary world and by the rude awakening of enormous changes to our pension systems. Across the OECD, surveys show very low levels of financial literacy in general and of understanding the need for retirement savings. An OECD online Question and Answer session unearthed some of these problems: in the United States, for example, four out of 10 workers are not putting money aside for retirement whilst in New Zealand many people are unwilling or unable to save for retirement, with 30 percent of households spending more than they earn. In Japan, one survey stated that 71 percent of respondents had no knowledge about investment in the stock and bond markets, while in Canada one survey's respondents believed choosing the right investments for retirement was more stressful than going to the dentist.[15]

Changing pension schemes

For many years, companies, especially in the United States and the United Kingdom, provided employees with pension schemes, known as defined benefit schemes where the pension is based on an employee's salary, either just before retirement or averaged over a longer period of time. But these schemes are rapidly being altered or terminated because of the inexorable rise in life expectancy. In a nutshell, the longer pensioners and their partners or spouses live, the greater the increase in the company's future pension obligations. Making adequate employee pension provision has become increasingly expensive for companies, not just in terms of funds to be set aside to pay benefits but also because companies are often asked by pension fund trustees to make good the difference between the value of their assets (investments) and the estimated value of their liabilities (benefits). Financial tensions have been fuelled by weak stock market performance and low interest rates, and these have also contributed to the demise of defined benefit schemes. You can see why companies have gone off the idea. For example, UK private sector companies added about £30 billion to their pension liabilities in the two years to March 2007 just by recognizing the longer life expectancy of the members of their pension schemes.[16] For every additional year of life expectancy, companies might have to add about £15 billion to the UK private sector's pension liabilities, boosting the pension fund deficits for many, if not most, companies. For a while, of course, companies' defined benefit schemes will continue to pay pensions to existing members of the scheme, provided the company remains solvent and that the scheme isn't terminated for some reason. But it is rare nowadays for private sector employees to be able to join defined benefit schemes.

Instead, many employees in advanced economies nowadays—outside the public sector—are invited or required to join so-called defined contribution pension schemes whereby employees pay an amount of money regularly into their scheme. Some employers may help them to manage their funds by providing an additional contribution and online access to a range of funds from financial firms. At retirement, the pension will be based not on the employee's salary but on the value of what has been accumulated in the pension scheme. And this depends on what has happened to the prices of the assets that have been bought and put into the pot. In other words, the employee now bears the risk regarding the value of the pension (and how long it might last) whereas in the defined benefit scheme, the company bore the risk. Many employees, younger ones especially, do not understand the full implications of these changes, and consequently a generation may grow into retirement without adequate resources on which to retire.

Retirement and savings in the United States

A recent survey, conducted in America, makes for rather disturbing reading about the savings habits and retirement provisions of people today, let alone in 10 or 20 years. According to the survey, American workers are slow in recognizing how the US retirement system is changing, and even those who are aware of change are not adapting to it in ways that would secure a comfortable retirement.[17] Among the survey's findings, the most relevant include these points:

- Nearly half of workers feel less confident about employer pension scheme benefits, but most are not changing their savings behavior.
- Forty-one percent of workers said they were in a defined benefit plan, but 62 percent said they expected to receive a pension from such a plan. Similar observations were made about workers expecting free health insurance in retirement even though fewer companies are offering this benefit.
- Twenty-four percent of workers and more than 35 percent of retired people report they have long-term, old-age care insurance, but the latest data indicate that only 10 percent of retired people actually had such insurance they could rely on.
- Only 18 percent of people know about retirement age changes and the ages at which they might qualify for full pension eligibility.
- Most workers have negligible levels of savings, and most of those who haven't put any money aside for retirement have little savings altogether.

Allowing for the fact that this is a survey of American workers only and that pension and savings rules and regulations vary between countries, the last point about low or inadequate levels of savings raises one of the most important points. What is adequate for retirement? A complicated question that all but the very rich have a tough time answering. But we know what too little is. Table 4.3 shows the savings reported by participants in the US survey, according to their age:

Clearly, older workers reported higher levels of savings than younger workers, much as you might expect, and a third of retired people fall into the lowest category of less than US$10,000. But the table also shows that 77 percent of workers under the age of 35, 62 percent of workers aged 35–44 and 45 percent of 45- to 54-year-olds, had savings of less than US$50,000.

The source of these findings is the Washington, DC–based, Employee Benefit Research Institute, whose mission is stated as "promoting the understanding and furtherance of employee benefits national policy." Even if you might expect such an institute, dedicated to the advancement of sound employee-benefit

Table 4.3   Savings reported by different age groups in the United States

	All workers	25–34	35–44	45–54	Over 55	All retired people
Less than $10,000	35	50	36	24	26	32
$10,000–$49,999	23	27	26	21	14	23
$50,000–$99,999	13	10	14	15	11	12
$100,000–$249,999	15	8	16	19	20	20
More than $250,000	14	5	8	21	28	14

Note: Numbers are in %; savings exclude the value of main residence and of defined benefit plans

Source: Employee Benefit Research Institute and Matthew Greenwald and Associates Ind., 2007 Retirement Confidence Survey.

programs, to emphasize the inadequate level of savings among most age groups, it is by no means alone in its observations. A comprehensive study by economists at the US Federal Reserve Board also found some rather disturbing evidence.[18] Although its authors did note that most households (with a member aged over 51 in 2004) had wealth that was well above the level needed to finance what they call poverty line consumption, they admitted their definition of poverty was somewhat arbitrary and based on official criteria related only to the affordability of adequately nutritious food expenditures. They also found that about 12 percent of households didn't have enough savings, even after taking into account the value of Social Security (pension) and welfare (excluding medical) benefits. A further 9 percent of households were quite close to the poverty line.

The results of the Federal Reserve's study didn't point to any imminent threat to the comfortable retirement aspirations of the leading edge of the baby-boomer generation, although the 21 percent who *do* face such a threat constitute a significant percentage. But this observation does not extend to younger baby boomers and certainly not to those following the boomer generation. Only if these groups of individuals save more might they be able to fend better for themselves in retirement and lessen the pressure for future tax increases and public spending reductions.

Some of the longer-term consequences of the savings problem may not be evident yet. For a while we may find that the baby boomers still working up to or even past normal retirement age will continue to save. They may be all too keen to hang on to their assets in retirement, maybe even to add to them. They may want to transfer them to their children or keep them for as long as possible before having to sell them to finance residential care, for example. They may feel it appropriate to keep or build their savings simply because they have longer life expectancy and can't predict for how long they will need those savings.

In the end, though, there are some hard conclusions we can draw. The whole question of retirement and retirement lifestyle is subject to more uncertainty than since the end of the Second World War. This should make working-age people, especially younger ones, want to save more, not less, but there is little evidence so far that the message has hit home. In the future, we will probably be forced to rely less and less on adequate and comprehensive government pensions. If we don't put enough to one side, then financial hardship really will beckon for many. Governments have already lowered pension payments, putting pensioners' consumption at risk, and this could be exacerbated as pensioners face mounting costs in, and during, old age. Today's workers (tomorrow's pensioners) are also being forced or encouraged to undertake much greater self-provision as regards retirement income.

In short, more and more people may face having to save more for old age, receiving less from the government upon retirement (certainly in relation to their earnings while at work), and finding that their self-provided pension plans may fall in value or not keep pace with inflation. Managing and overcoming these circumstances successfully will require that financial education be taken much more seriously and that public policies try to achieve a better balance between the desire to consume and the necessity to save.

Endnotes

1 Quoted by US Senator Robert C. Byrd (West Virginia), Senate speech, June 28, 2007.
2 The term "Europe" refers throughout to the countries of western Europe, unless specifically defined to include the whole of Europe, including the countries of eastern Europe.

3 The term "EU15" refers to the 15 member countries of the European Union before the accession of 12 countries in eastern and south-eastern Europe in 2004. These are Austria, Belgium, Finland, Denmark, France, Germany, Greece, Ireland, Italy, Luxembourg, the Netherlands, Portugal, Spain, Sweden, and the United Kingdom.

4 Labor force participation basically measures the number of workers of different types and ages relative to the size of their groups in society.

5 International Monetary Fund, "How Will Demographic Change Affect The Global Economy?" *World Economic Outlook*, (IMF: Washington, DC, (September 2004).

6 *Economic and Social Survey of Asia and the Pacific*, UN Economic and Social Commission for Asia and the Pacific. (April 2007).

7 "Eleven steps to a better brain," *New Scientist*, No. 2501 (May 28, 2005): 28.

8 OECD "Pensions at a Glance." Public Policies across OECD Countries (Paris: 2005).

9 Office of National Statistics, *Social Trends* 37 (2007).

10 *The Times*, "School leavers lack even basic skills warns CBI." August 21, 2006.

11 *Daily Yomiuri Online*, December 21, 2006.

12 *Sunday Telegraph*, "I chose a career over children and have no regrets," April 22, 2007.

13 BBC News, "Older People 'missing out' online, http://news.bbc.co.uk/1/hi/technology/5146222.stm.

14 And, I suppose, most of them still know how to write a letter and actually think it's the "right" way to communicate.

15 See OECD, "Ask the economists: The pensions challenge—financing retirement," www.oecd.org/asktheeconomists, for this reference as well as other questions and answers on pension topics.

16 *Financial Times*, "Pension liabilities rise by £30bn," (citing a study by consultants KPMG.) April 24, 2007.

17 Employee Benefit Research Institute, "The Retirement System in Transition: The 2007 Retirement Confidence Survey," Issue Brief No. 304, Washington, DC (April 2007).

18 David A. Love, Paul A. Smith, and Lucy C. McNair, *Do Households Have Enough Wealth For Retirement?* Federal Reserve Board (Washington, DC, March 2, 2007).

Chapter 5

Coming of age: United States, Japan, and Europe

> *Population aging has economic consequences because our economic behavior and capabilities vary in systematic ways with age, and, in particular, abilities tend to decline later in life.*
> —Ronald D. Lee, Global Population Aging and its Economic Consequences.[1]

OK, so we're getting older. So what? In fact, some say, good for us. First, longevity is something to be welcomed and enjoyed. From the point of view of individuals, as opposed to societies or countries, few would argue with that. Second, the slow growth or decline in population means we do not need to chase economic growth anymore which, in any case, is bad for the environment and congestion. This view, however, is less widely embraced than the first. For one thing, it disregards basic instincts in human behavior. Moreover, economic growth is essential to living standards generally and to the creation of resources needed to finance economic and social goals. There is a limit to how much you can redistribute resources from a finite pot of wealth. (A little later, I show how sustainable growth in some Western economies will slow significantly over the next few years and why this needs to be addressed.)

Third, the demographics of aging are temporary and will vanish in the long run once the baby-boomer retirees have moved on to another world. This is true, but the much-quoted expression that "we are all dead in the long run" applies in force. Its author, John Maynard Keynes, meant that economists always talk about the long-run tendency of shocks to diminish and of economies to return to some sort of equilibrium.[2] As though that mattered to people today or economic and social conditions likely to prevail in the foreseeable future! Long before aging societies return, if indeed they do, to some sort of equilibrium, we and our children and their offspring will have to cope with and manage the consequences of aging.

A fourth dismissive argument goes like this: Other adverse demographic shocks, for example the two world wars of the twentieth century, had no lasting negative economic effects. So why should aging and extended retirement be different? I would like to spend a little time on answering this. While it is self-evident that there was no long-lasting economic decline after either world war, despite the slaughter of millions of young men, this is a strange and rather narrow lens through which to view the impact of demographic change. Apart from the appalling human cost, there was a significant economic cost of both wars, estimated to be more than 4 percent of world GDP (far bigger in belligerent countries, of course). About two-thirds of this was related to war deaths and the rest to the loss of world trade. And while there were indeed economic recoveries after each of the two conflicts, they were not akin to the kinds of adjustments we face now. At the time there was a multitude of political, social, and economic factors at work, many the result of war itself, in what was essentially a long-term trend of improving health, falling infant mortality, and higher fertility.

The First World War claimed the lives of about 10 million men, mostly under the age of 40, and, because of the plunge in fertility during the conflict years, there was much discussion after 1918 about "surplus women" and the risk of depopulation. Fertility rates rose again as normal family life resumed, and, because of the continuing sharp fall in death rates, overall population continued to rise in the interwar years. There were no constraints on economic expansion from labor shortages, and social change encouraged a more active participation by women in the labor force. Thus, the dire economic interwar period in the United States and Europe occurred in spite of favorable demographic trends.

The Second World War claimed over 50 million people, including large numbers of women and civilians. But fertility rates actually started to rise in several countries during the war, even prior to the birth of the boomers. Moreover, social and economic changes in the organization of public policy, work, and employment helped to facilitate the shift back to a peacetime economy and then sustain economic expansion. There were labor shortages, but only temporarily and until millions of combat personnel had returned to civilian jobs. The baby boomers, of course, were in the process of being born and growing up— and were ideally positioned to pick up the baton of economic growth as the first postwar rebuilding phase turned into the 1960s. No one had reason to worry about labor shortages, diminishing youth, or large changes in old-age dependency.

Aging in advanced economies

Japan is at the leading edge of rich country aging, and Europe is not far behind. In both we can already observe the characteristics of demographic change. But in many ways they are very different. Japan's culture has historically been associated with exceptionally low female employment but a strong seniority bias to employment and compensation. Many, but by no means all, European countries have relatively high female participation rates but very low rates for older workers, who are encouraged or given incentives to retire early. Japan is a rapidly aging economy in a younger and most dynamic economic part of the world. Europe has the Atlantic on one side, an even faster aging Russia on the other, and some of the poorest or most troubled countries of the world to the south. But both regions face the prospect of a pronounced worsening of their budgetary positions, which will force governments, sooner or later, voluntarily or otherwise, to alter their structures of taxation and public spending to accommodate social and economic change. Japan, Italy, and Belgium already have exceptionally high levels of public debt relative to the size of their economies while many other countries in western Europe are either close to leaving, or are already out of, the comfort zone, where public debt is roughly 60 percent of GDP. Both regions will have to give more serious thought and attention to legislative and regulatory changes designed to instigate or nurture reforms to childcare, work, retirement, and old-age care systems and financing.

America has to do many of these things too, and it will be interesting to see whether this bastion of market-related solutions will be able to find more effective ways of addressing aging society problems than the more state-oriented policy framework in Europe and Japan. In a way, America doesn't have to look to its geography and economic relations overseas because of its size and productive power, but in important ways its dependence on the rest of the world is becoming ever greater. The biggest example is the country's dependence on foreign capital inflows, mainly from China and other developing countries, to pay for the vastly greater amount it spends on goods, services, and income from abroad than it earns from its exports of those things. In 2007, this current account deficit, as it is called, amounted to US$730 billion or the equivalent of 5 percent of GDP. Although this represented some improvement over the $856 billion deficit recorded the previous year, it probably pushed America's foreign debt up to about 23 percent of GDP. The state of America's internal and external finances, then, is stressed. But this is nothing compared with the financial challenges awaiting the Administration that will be installed in January 2009, and its successors, because of the coming escalation in healthcare and, to a lesser degree, pension spending and the number of people who might look forward only to poverty or deprivation in old age. I look at this in more detail in Chapter 6.

But in contrast to Japan and western Europe, the United States is expected to have a stronger demographic structure, including a rising population and a slowly growing labor force. It has labor markets that function well from a strictly economic viewpoint. Employment rates for women and for older workers are relatively high, and the unemployment rate has been relatively low at between 4.5–5 percent since 2006, though it has been rising since 2007 and looks set to continue to do so. People tend to be more mobile from the point of view of both location and job. It has—or had—a highly sophisticated mortgage market to support home ownership and geographic mobility.[3] It

is renowned for its top universities, plethora of Nobel Prize win-
ners, volumes of patents and technological and innovative
prowess, and it continues to draw millions of "tired, ... poor, ...
huddled masses yearning to breathe free ....,"[4] albeit with some
recent but growing opposition.

Accounting for growth in Japan, western Europe, and America

The contrast between the economic prospects for the United
States and other advanced regions, from a demographic standpoint, can be seen more clearly below. I'll start with Japan
because it is interesting to reflect on the way in which it has
been catapulted into the forefront of aging. In 1945, Japan was
younger than the United States, western Europe, and China. Its
median age of 22.3 years was about 18 months younger than in
China, five years younger than in southern Europe, and about
seven to eight years younger than in western Europe, and the
United States. Today, Japan's median age of 43 years is three
years older than in Europe, seven years older than in the United
States, and 10 years older than in China. Its population of 127
million is expected to drop to below 90 million by 2050 and
might have fallen back to its 1930 level of 65 million by 2100.

But between 1950 and 1995, Japan's pool of workers grew by
almost 2 percent per year, as shown Table 5.1, and this contributed about a third of the country's impressive 6 percent
annual growth rate in GDP until the early 1990s. Labor force
growth, of course, wasn't the only factor that powered Japan's
economy in the decades following the Second World War, but
it was a key ingredient and contributor. After 1990, as is well
documented, Japan succumbed to a bust, following the vigorous expansion of the economy and the surge in asset prices
over the previous decade. From then until 2005 the economy
grew at little more than 1 percent per year, but this includes the
recovery period that started in 2004–05. During the 1990s, the
economy stagnated, falling into recession on three occasions.

More troublesome than this was the country's helpless drift
into deflation, first as asset prices such as land and equities
fell sharply, and subsequently as consumer price inflation

Table 5.1   Japan's shrinking workforce

	Population		Average	Average	Real GDP
	15–64 years (millions)	Change (millions)	annual change (thousands)	annual change (%)	%
1950	49.85				
1995	87.19	37.34	830	1.7	6.0
2005	84.88	−2.3	−230	−0.3	1.0
2025	72.33	−12.6	−628	−0.7	1.3
2050	52.33	−20	−800	−1.1	0.6

Source: United Nations Population Division, *World Population Prospects*: The 2006 Revision; and author's estimates.

disappeared and then became negative. Many factors that lie beyond the scope of this book contributed to Japan's economic decline in the 1990s, elements of which pervade the Japanese economy to this day. The actual fall in the workforce was hardly large enough to have been a significant factor on its own, but it is almost certainly not accidental that the turn in Japan's economic fortunes coincided with a turn in its population and labor force trends.

Even if labor force factors were of relatively minor significance, their role in the future promises to be of more consequence. Japan's pool of potential workers is going to fall by 0.7 percent per year until about 2025 and then by a little more than 1 percent per year. Strictly speaking, this means that the country's economy is going to decline at that pace, more or less, before allowing for other factors such as productivity growth and improvements in the stocks of both physical and human capital. But the latter could well be compromised by the negative consequences of aging for both private savings and public finances. For what it's worth, in 2006–07, productivity was growing at about 1.5 percent per year—far better than in the previous decade but still not fast. If this stayed unchanged or even rose a little, as suggested in Table 5.1, Japan's economy would still stagnate.

Note that there are about 1.5 times as many 65-year-olds as children under 14 years today, but that by 2050, there will be 3.3 times as many. Renowned for longevity, the Japanese people may not disappoint. The population of 80-year-olds will become about 40 percent bigger than those aged under 14. The over-90s may number about five million and some 500,000 people are expected to be living on three digits, so to speak.

Western Europe's experience of aging may be little different to that of Japan and is also related to the fall in the size of the labor force, as shown in reports by the European Commission (Table 5.2). In fact the European Central Bank undertook to examine some alternative scenarios but could not conclude that western European growth prospects were materially different from those proposed by the Commission. The steady deterioration and then decline in the number of workers accompanied by cautiously optimistic estimates for productivity growth and labor utilization (or hours worked per worker) continue to point toward steadily lower growth rates in the future.

America's situation is a little different. The bad period in American economic history since 1945 straddles the 1970s and 1980s when productivity growth fell back sharply, at times to a mere 1 percent a year on average. But steady labor force expansion and, in the 1990s, a surge in productivity growth—partly related to the introduction and diffusion of new technologies and a significant rise in female participation in the labor market—helped sustain high growth rates. Since 2000, though, there has been a marked fall in labor utilization, which seems to be continuing. In other words, the total number of hours worked has been falling. A lot of people may not recognize this as being remotely related to their own experience. But because the participation rate in the labor force overall has been declining, this is the result for the whole economy. I have assumed this will stabilize and then turn around in the future. I have also assumed that after a cyclical decline in productivity growth now and in the next few years, it will pick up again. Neither of these may happen, of course, or they may turn out much better than expected. But the extrapolations I've used here suggest that the US economy will grow quite slowly in the next few years but then chalk up about 2.5 percent per year growth further out.

Part of this derives, of course, from the fact that America's working-age population is going to keep growing, unlike that of

Table 5.2 European growth drag will be larger than the United States

	Euro Area				US			
	Working-age population	Productivity	Labor utilization	Real GDP	Working-age population	Productivity	Labor utilization	Real GDP
1960–80	0.7	4.8	–1.2	4.3	1.6	2.1	–0.1	3.6
1981–00	0.5	2.1	–0.3	2.3	1.1	1.5	0.6	3.2
2001–05	0.4	0.8	0.1	1.3	1.1	2.5	–1.1	2.5
2006–10	0.2	1.1	0.8	2.1	0.7	1.5	–0.5	1.7
2011–30	–0.3	1.8	0.2	1.7	0.3	2.2	0	2.5
2031–50	–0.6	1.7	0.1	1.2	0.2	2.2	0.2	2.6

Notes: All figures are % change per year over the periods; working-age population is the population aged 15–64; productivity is output per hour; labor utilization is the total hours worked per worker; real GDP growth is the result of adding the prior three columns.

Source: "Macroeconomic Implications of Demographic Developments in the Euro Area," Occasional Paper No. 51 (August 2006) European Central Bank; and author's estimates.

western Europe or Japan. The same applies to the United Kingdom, Australia, and Canada—all of which will add two–three million to their working-age populations in the next 45 years or so. The reality is that these correspond, over 40 years, to gains that range from 21 percent in Australia, 12 percent in Canada, and 3 percent in the United Kingdom. So while the good news is that these countries can at least look forward to some growth in their working-age populations, the virtual stagnation of employment means that growth is going to slow down regardless. In the United Kingdom, for example, the Treasury's long-term economic projections hold out the prospect of economic growth running at about 2 percent per year, almost 1 percent lower than in recent years, and then only if immigration continues to expand by about 150,000 people per year.

Two major conclusions can be drawn from this simple accounting exercise. First, while the United States and western Europe seem to be converging in terms of underlying growth rates, the gap will open again after 2010, when the European labor pool starts to contract. In neither case does the assumed pick-up in productivity growth offer enough to bring growth back to the levels experienced in the past decades, nor does labor utilization rise sufficiently to compensate for the slower growth in the working-age population overall. Slower growth over time will slow or stall the improvement in living standards and will impose pressures on government budgets as it lowers the growth of tax revenues. Second, the weakness of growth ingredients highlights precisely where efforts have to be made to redress the changes in overall age structure being brought about by aging.

Removing the sex and age barriers to work

These efforts will have to go far beyond the so-far limited attempts many countries have made to reform pension systems and payments. They will have to home in on retirement and labor market reforms, most urgently perhaps in western Europe. Moreover, in this context it is important to recognize and understand just how the basis of our societies is changing. Chikako Usui, at the

University of Missouri, argues that in the modern economy people will eventually have a wider mix of skills, more career changes, more options to work full- or part-time, and an extended phase of work into full retirement. Women will find more and more male jobs opening up for them. She maintains that Japan, for example, has been an economy built around stable and career-oriented jobs and incomes and a "bullet" retirement exit from work, but that the information economy is changing the structure of work and learning. Its characteristics are intermittent employment, continuous education and training, and gradual retirement.[5]

In a similar vein, optimists believe Western economies are on course to reveal just how much more productive tomorrow's smaller or more limited labor force will be, and they tend to play down the problem of old-age dependency. They say the new economy will allow older, healthier workers to pay their way and that technology and productivity will empower tomorrow's workers and enrich our societies. This Panglossian outcome is possible, but before grasping this as a realistic prognosis, it will not hurt to remind ourselves of how far we still have to go.

Barriers to female employment

Existing barriers to labor force participation among women have to be lowered or eliminated. The participation rate of women has been rising in recent years, in particular in Japan and the EU15. In Japan, for example, over 10 years ago there were about 8.7 million people in part-time jobs, representing about 16.5 percent of the workforce. In 2006, there were 11.25 million, representing nearly 21 percent of the workforce. If you add on temporary and contract workers, the total of nonregular workers amounts nowadays to about a third of all workers. Roughly 80 percent of part-time jobs are held by women, and about two-thirds of women part-timers work to support their families. Spain, Italy, and Germany have also created about 20 million part-time jobs in the last 10 years as full-time employment stagnated or fell—and, similarly, women are heavily represented in these positions.

The fact remains that fewer than 50 percent of women are in paid employment in Italy, Greece, Spain, and Poland, and barely more than 50 percent in France and Japan, compared with more than 70 percent in Switzerland and Scandinavia. And it is of small comfort that the number of women at work has been growing a little faster than that of men if this is purely due to the expansion of part-time jobs that reflect government job schemes and attempts by firms to keep costs down. Part-time work, for example, pays about 50–60 percent of the hourly rate of full-time work and women frequently earn 20-30 percent less than men. Employers often don't offer much in the way of training and education and don't, or don't have to, pay benefits, including housing allowances and family time off, which are given to full-time staff. As they're cheaper to employ, it is small wonder that during the Japanese and western European economic recovery since 2004, most of the job creation has been in part-time occupations and positions. The preference for part-time positions represents a way that employers can essentially lock in low paid (mainly female) labor in the secondary job market. This simply drives a thickening wedge between the part-time and full-time job markets, with higher skills and pay on the one side and lower on the other, and a hurdle between that's too high to clear.

There is another reason for concern about any imminent breakthrough in the quality of female job creation. Women should be ideal recruits into the information economy, but the story so far is only mildly encouraging. Women have low and even falling shares of information technology-specialist employment (for example, software and IT specialists), but in information technology-using employment, they have very high shares in office and secretarial occupations and low shares in scientific and professional jobs.[6] This difference in gender-work concentration tends to be associated strongly with low female pursuit of computer science and engineering qualifications in higher education.

Gender-work differences in the information economy can't possibly be viewed through the same glasses as in, for example, the steel and automobile industries. Whether from a fairness or from an efficiency standpoint, it cannot make any sense at all for these differences to be allowed to persist when every demographic perspective and many governments insist that raising the participation of women is a key goal. It's one thing to say it, of course, another thing to make it happen. That will require strengthening the law to support equal treatment of men and women in employment, education, and training, and more specific funding of education and training schemes designed to entice and encourage women in the information technology disciplines currently dominated by men. Other initiatives will have to follow to encourage flexible hours and teleworking, equal pay, and the removal of social and access barriers that prevent or restrain women from using information technologies to the full.

Stories appear from time to time, of course, that do suggest that employment practices, law, and attitudes are in flux as companies and governments attempt to move with the times. Japan, again, provides some interesting illustrations. Enter Hiroko Matsukata. She is an educated, chain-smoking, sometimes rather outspoken comic book character who has assumed cult status for millions of Japanese women aspiring to recognition in the male-dominated workplace, where all but 10 percent of managers are male. This make-believe character is the antithesis of the much decried lazy, comfortable lifestyle of modern times and has a powerful weapon to help her get on at work, a "Man Switch," which transforms her career drive and success rate. It is of some significance, perhaps, that such a character should command widespread public attention, though this alone will solve little.

Then again, in 2007, it was reported that the Japanese electronics giant, Matsushita (with brand names such as Panasonic and Technics) had struck an agreement with its labor unions to put the bulk of pay increases into special allowances to encourage workers to have children.[7] The same report said Nippon Telegraph & Telephone, Japan's main telecommunications company, was allowing fathers and mothers of children under nine to work shorter hours, and Canon had started a program to pay for fertility treatment for workers and their spouses.

And Japanese labor laws recently changed to allow workers who head one-parent families to take up to a year off work after the birth of a child and to receive up to two-thirds of their pay.

During 2007, a fierce debate began in Germany, which has one of the lowest birth rates in the world at 1.3, about the need for expanded childcare. The family affairs secretary, Ursula von der Leyen, proposed a tripling of nursery or childcare places for the under-threes and other encouragements for women to have more children. Currently only about 5 percent of under-threes have access to a nursery place, and the government's goal is to raise this tenfold. Now, you could criticize the German proposal because you can't play gesture politics with this. You cannot simply propose the goal of vastly expanded toddler-care without also indicating how the program is to be financed and how it will be supported by the provision of more buildings, facilities, staff, and training. That said, the debate, not to mention any legislation, is only in its infancy at the time of writing. But the ferocity of the reaction was more noteworthy than any policy omissions. Some said the government's proposal was a throwback to life in the former communist German Democratic Republic—though, truth be told, between 80 and 90 percent of infants attended state crèches or kindergartens in 1989 (the year the Wall came down), and even today in the territory of the former GDR, 20 percent of under-threes have access to a nursery place. Others complained that the proposal amounted to a de facto state subsidy to families to turn women into "baby-machines" and that family values would be degraded. This is simply to demonstrate both the need for comprehensive reform and not just piecemeal measures, and that opposition and resistance lurk.

It is clear that our societies have a long way to go. Concerted attempts to reform and change in the areas of education and labor markets plus the implementation of more family friendly policies are liable to persuade more women to go to work while at the same time being able to rear children and eventually help these women work for longer as well. Such initiatives would include flexible work patterns, tax incentives, adequate paid parental leave, and high quality and affordable childcare. The fact is that France and Denmark, which have among the higher birth rates in western Europe, have a higher proportion of women at work and much more comprehensive childcare arrangements. In France, for example, 40 percent of under-twos and almost all three-year-olds attend free nursery. And another thing: women would probably find their work and lifestyles a lot more practical if their menfolk would share more childcare. While this is for couples to sort out themselves, it also means changes in employer practices as regards men, too; for example, concerning time off, flexible hours, and paternity leave.

Barriers to older workers in employment

Breaking down the barriers to the employment of older people is also essential, but the prospects today are bleak. In the rich world, about half of people aged 55 to 64 were in paid employment in 2005, but this was skewed heavily in favor of men. About 61 percent of men of that age group were in employment (more than 70 percent in Japan, Switzerland, and Norway, about 67 percent in the United States and the United Kingdom, 53 percent in Germany and 43 percent in France) compared with 42 percent of women (62 percent in Norway, 55 percent in the United States and Switzerland, 48 percent in the United Kingdom and Japan, 37 percent in France and Germany, and 21 percent in Italy). If we don't do something to change work and retirement patterns, the proportion of older inactive citizens per worker in countries in the Organization for Economic Cooperation and Development will rise from 38 percent today to 70 percent in 2050 and, in Europe, to 100 percent. The scale of the task ahead for different countries can be seen from Table 5.3 which slots the OECD nations into boxes, depending on how high the current rate of employment is for older workers and how significant the change in old-age dependency is expected to be by 2050.

In the top left of the table, most Scandinavian countries, Switzerland, and the United States have relatively smaller burdens to shoulder than, say, southern European countries and some eastern European countries in the bottom right. But Japan, the Czech Republic, and Portugal also have much to do.

Table 5.3   Raising the involvement of older workers

Participation rate of 55–64s	Change in old-age dependency		
	Moderate	Large	Very large
High	Scandinavia Switzerland US	Canada New Zealand	Japan
Average	N'lands, UK	Australia, Finland, Germany, Ireland	Czech Rep., Portugal
Low	Belgium, Turkey	Austria, Hungary	Greece, Italy, Poland Spain, Slovakia

Source: Live Longer, Work Longer, OECD (2006).

The involvement or participation of older workers could potentially rise over the next decades for two reasons, though neither of these should be taken at face value. The first is that many people seem to want to work longer after they retire. The second is the lifting of the retirement age.

It seems that many people who might once have taken the option for early retirement have chosen to stay on at work or to look for alternative employment after they formally retire. Participation rates for the over-50s and over-60s, in other words, have been inching up here and there. One comprehensive survey of more than 21,000 adults in 20 countries and territories across all five continents, comprising nearly three-fifths of the global population, was published in 2007, revealing some interesting attitudes toward aging and retirement.[8] The main findings of the survey indicated that people would rather be forced to save for retirement by mandatory schemes than pay higher taxes or be obliged to take lower pensions, that government could not be relied upon to provide for them in old age and that, given health, they would want to remain active. In fact, they asserted that they would remain productive for far longer than might have been expected in the past.

The media often like to focus on older personalities to show work-life after retirement. Take, for example, the retirement of former Federal Reserve chairman Alan Greenspan. At the age of 78 he became president of his consulting firm Greenspan Associates LLC, embarked on a demanding series of lectures and speeches, published a successful book, and became a consultant to many high profile companies. But be careful about taking these "data points" as indicative of a real change. Many older people want to work longer, or feel they could, but businesses have been slow to choose them over younger workers for reasons they say are to do with innovation, renewal, and cost. And in any case, how many of us at 60 or 65, let alone 78, can claim to be on a par with Alan Greenspan? Those few of us with very good contacts, deep and long insights into government and official decision-making, well-rounded management and entrepreneurial skills, and experience may well find that we will be in demand as non-executive board members, consultants, and so on. That is about it though, at this point.

Governments in many countries have begun to raise the retirement and/or pensionable age and to equalize them for men and women (though many of these measures will only become effective in the next 10 to 20 years). Critics say such moves are aimed only at trying to curb the costs of people retiring formally at aged 60 or 62, bearing in mind growing life expectancy after retirement. However, there's no question that raising the retirement or pensionable age is an important step in the attempt to keep people at work for longer and thereby to sustain the overall supply of labor (and taxpayers) in the economy.

Later retirement is more than just a matter of law

On its own, however, raising the retirement or pensionable age will almost certainly fail to achieve the hoped for results. To make it effective, you have to implement a wide array of labor market policies, such as giving incentives to employers to recruit older workers—or punishing them according to the law. Without this larger context, all that will happen is that a pension-financing problem will be replaced by an unemployment-financing one. So, if you have to work until 65 or 67 to be able to retire or draw your full pension, it will only benefit you and society if you have a real job to do until you reach that age.

Changing employment practices and retirement finances must go hand in hand. The first problem is a cultural one, namely that of age discrimination. People over the age of 50 tend to be first fired, last hired. Their skills tend to atrophy as they are often passed over when it comes to training. Poor or inappropriate working conditions drive many into early retirement. A survey on age discrimination in the United Kingdom in 2006[9] revealed that more people (29 percent) reported suffering age discrimination than any other form of discrimination, especially after 55, when the incidence of prejudice rose significantly. The survey suggested that almost a third of people believed there is more age prejudice than five years ago, and most thought it would get worse. And a third of people thought that the demographic shift toward aging societies would make life worse in terms of standards of living, security, health, jobs, and education. In an attempt to address some of these issues the United Kingdom government introduced new rules for the workplace in October 2006. It is now illegal to make employment decisions or advertise positions based on someone's age, and there is no longer an upper age limit regarding unfair dismissal and redundancy rights, which means older workers' rights are now aligned with those of younger workers. Moreover, employers have a "duty to consider" any request by employees to stay on beyond compulsory retirement, and employers must give people at least six months' notice of their retirement date.

It is a start, but combating age discrimination goes far beyond the law. The work environment, the nature of work, and the education and skills required for work have to be considered from the standpoint of both employers and older employees. Older workers may have special needs to do with mobility, transportation, sight, hearing, time off, a different sort of work-life balance, and so on. So, to succeed in getting more 55–64s or even 55–70s to continue to work, the struggle against age discrimination must remain a priority.

Companies, governments, and public employers will have to spend money on, or provide for, education and training throughout people's working lives. They will have to restructure compensation arrangements so that older people are paid according to what they do, not to their status or seniority. And all the social partners—government, companies, and labor unions— have to challenge the culture in which work, success, and management constantly emphasize, or are made to appeal to, youth and in which older workers are encouraged to scramble for retirement and disability benefits.

Governments have also connived in the low job participation rates, especially of older workers, in many western European countries by encouraging early retirement schemes. Introduced over the years in European Union countries such as Austria, Belgium, Finland, France, Germany, the Netherlands, and Spain, as well as in Australia, such schemes comprise large-scale, state-subsidized spending programs designed to combat rising unemployment especially among young people. The programs were partly successful in that they led to significant falls in employment among older workers. But the irony is that employment rates for younger workers did not rise as a result. Getting older people to retire early with appropriate incentives was the easy bit. Getting younger people into work proved to be hard or impossible without other reforms to the labor market. To make matters worse, early retirement schemes, once seen as a way of helping the young unemployed, subsequently became a quasi-entitlement that, once entrenched, have proven very hard to reverse.

Thus, we can see that increasing the retirement age alone is not the solution. The agenda for getting more older citizens to stay on at work and—what is more difficult, to find alternative work after formal retirement—is long and complex. First, we have to tackle the financial incentives in pension systems and early retirement schemes that force or encourage people to stop work early. Second, we have to dismantle barriers to employment from age discrimination, costs, and inappropriate or unsuitable job protection rules. Third, we have to improve the attraction of hiring or retaining older workers in the information economy through training courses and refreshers while providing assistance for better occupational health and safety in the workplace.

A Singaporean model for all?

In 2007 the Singaporean government announced that it would propose a law, to become effective in 2012, requiring companies to rehire older workers after the age of 62 because it wants to raise the participation of workers aged 55–64 from 53.7 percent to 65 percent. The proposal noted that Singapore would be home to half a million people aged over 65 by 2020, many with inadequate savings, and that the new law would need to be accompanied by both significant changes in the mindset and employment practices of corporations and more funds allocated to firms to underpin the new system. Clearly, the authorities recognized the need for consultation, and the legislation has yet to be framed. However, it is interesting that government officials focused attention on several other areas that would need attention for the new rules to work. These included greater efforts to bring women into work and encourage part-time and flexible working; the speeding up of wage reforms away from seniority-based to job-worth and performance-based compensation; the recruitment of more professionals, executives, and managers to tackle the problem of future skill shortages; and attention to fair employment practices, for example improved working conditions for older people. On the face of it, this approach to raising older worker—and female—participation looks just right. In fact, there is no provision to increase the mandatory retirement age, per se, and a fairly comprehensive agenda to increase employability. And in Singapore—a model of what can be called "managed democracy"—it is probably going to work.

Who's for change?

Over time, western Europe, Japan, and the United States will probably move, more or less slowly, to improve the prospects for, and functioning of, older societies. There are many questions though, such as how, at whose instigation, and at whose cost? Reform and improvement of childcare, education, work, healthcare, and retirement arrangements will have to remain a priority for years to come. This is going to involve many, sometimes very hard, social and financial choices and it is inconceivable that these can be made without having government or public authorities take on a stronger and more proactive role.

In several Western societies, this sentiment is already evident as many voters tire of ineffective governments or political parties that have become almost indistinguishable. The middle ground in politics moved to the right in and after the 1980s with a strong emphasis on individualism as the baby boomers became employees and entrepreneurs. It shifted back to the left, under the influence of the so-called Third Way advocated by former President Bill Clinton and former British Prime Minister Tony Blair, who sought new ways of combining the economics of individualism with a greater social role for the state. A sort of middle way for middle-aged boomers, if you want. Nowadays, despite the continuing popularity of some parties of the right and center-right, the consensus seems to be changing again, with more emphasis placed on social (and environmental) goals as the boomers move beyond middle age. Interestingly, "the contented," as J.K. Galbraith might have called them, have few qualms about articulating demands for stronger government protection of their (middle class) communities, benefits, and privileges.

Pretty soon, most voters are going to be aged over 50, and the effects of aging can be seen in voting patterns—though sometimes in unexpected ways. In national elections in Australia in 2007, baby-boomer votes were decisive in the return of the Labor Party to government for the first time in 11 years with the 40- to 54-year-old age group voting strongly for the winning party. But in the French presidential election in the same year, the center-right victory was attributable to a combination of the "gray vote" and very young voters. Nicolas Sarkozy received 68 percent of the votes of the over-70s and 61 percent of the votes of those aged 60–69, as well as more than half the votes of those aged 25–34.[10]

In the 2008 United States presidential election campaign, the Democratic candidate, Barack Obama seemed to be scoring well not only among the young but also among the younger and middle-aged boomers, who have leaned toward the

Republican Party in recent elections. Many factors influence voter swings, including nothing more complicated than a time for change mood, but it may be no coincidence that by 2008, the political mood was shifting to the left in the younger economies of Australia and the United States but going in the other direction in France and Germany and also the United Kingdom, Denmark, and Switzerland. About one thing though, voters seem quite clear. They are looking for change in an environment where they have grown to feel insecure and uncertain. Demographic change may not be the most widely publicized factor in voters' priorities, but it is both a cause and effect of the changing political agenda.

For western Europe and Japan, the principal aging burden is expected to derive from pensions expenditure, with healthcare playing a supporting role. For America the issue is the opposite, namely how to afford the vigorous increases expected to occur in healthcare financing, with pensions an important but subordinate problem. These are part of even more important macroeconomic changes that lie ahead. It is to these topics that I now turn with a view to establishing if the evolution of aging societies brings with it serious threats to our savings and, fundamentally, our wealth.

Endnotes

1 Ronald D. Lee, "Global Population Aging and Its Economic Consequences," (American Enterprise Institute Press: Washington, DC 2007).
2 Keynes, John Maynard, A *Tract on Monetary Reforms* (London: Macmillan, 1924), ch. 3.
3 The US mortgage market will continue to go through significant change in the wake of the so-called subprime fiasco in 2007, named to reflect the financing of mortgages for borrowers who either had poor or no credit histories. Rising delinquencies and foreclosures, a sharp fall in construction activity, and falling house prices in 2007-08 became worrisome developments in what will probably be the the worst banking crisis and credit crunch since the 1930s. The Federal Reserve was forced to provide emergency financial assistance to the banking system. The US Congress, which had already been considering measures to address financial practices and innovations deemed responsible for the subprime fiasco, also began to embark on regulatory and legislative measures to try and stabilize the financial crisis.

4 Emma Lazarus, "The New Colossus," inscribed on the Statue of Liberty.

5 Chikako Usui, "The Demographic Dilemma: Japan's Aging Society." Asia Program Special Report, No. 107, Woodrow Wilson International Center for Scholars (January 2003).

6 OECD, "ICTs And Gender," (Paris: March 29, 2007).

7 *Financial Times* "Japan pay deals offer workers baby bonus," March 22, 2007.

8 HSBC, "The Future of Retirement: What The World Wants" (2006).

9 "How Ageist is Britain?", *Age Concern* (2006).

10 Cited in Wolfgang Munchau, "Europe sways to the center-right swansong," *Financial Times*, May 21, 2007.

Chapter 6

Will aging damage
your wealth?

> *Money is a singular thing… over all history it has oppressed
> nearly all people in one or two ways: either it has been
> abundant and very unreliable or reliable and very scarce.*
> —J. K. Galbraith, *The Age of Uncertainty.*[1]

In a very important respect, money is at the heart of the aging
debate. Both citizens and governments will have to pay attention to the financial resources needed to ensure that some form
of crisis does not shock them. There will be pressure on the
personal savings needed for retirement and on government
budgets. Government spending on the retired and elderly will
soar in coming years—and much faster than the underlying
rate of economic growth can finance. So decisions will have to
be made about spending priorities and about the level and
rates of taxation needed to maintain orderly government
finances. Failure to address these issues now can only lead to
more wrenching changes in the future.

In advanced societies many people fear that population
aging is a serious challenge that they may not be up to and
could even prove to be an economic and social disaster. We
fear a significant increase in pensioner poverty and in the tax
burden on younger people. We don't really want to recognize
that governments will face tough choices about how and how
far to raise taxation and how to restructure social programs to
make way for age-related public spending. And it is not only

aging that's going to demand adequate funding: Climate change, education, and social infrastructure will also exert additional strains on the public purse in the next 10 to 15 years, let alone subsequent decades. Without the will to adapt and come up with new solutions in good time, the outcome may involve varying degrees of economic degradation and financial turbulence. And that's bound to damage your wealth.

Will there be enough in the personal savings pot?

It is, of course, impossible to predict how the value that human beings place on saving as opposed to consuming will change. There is a reasonably robust theory—the life cycle theory already considered in Chapter 4—that suggests people accumulate wealth between the ages of 30 and 60 for retirement, after which they tend to save less or "dis-save." It is possible that as individuals become more accustomed to longer and healthier periods of retirement, they will tend to hang on to their savings, or save more, to finance their longevity. But the overall tendency toward lower savings expected for the population as a whole in old age seems about right.

Currently, the stock of accumulated savings in most rich countries remains substantial, and with the new savings coming from developing countries, especially China, there is more than enough to finance private and public investment around the world. Consequently, the average level of world interest rates is relatively low. This is not good for pensioners living off their savings or for pension plans that have to make their investments work harder to remain solvent. But it has certainly been beneficial in other respects for asset prices. However, too many people do not save or save enough, and if aging societies were to be characterized by a chronic shortage of savings, interest rates on average would probably be higher.

Accumulating resources for retirement during their working lives isn't the only reason people save, but it's one of the most important and involves a variety of assets that typically include public and private pensions, bank deposits, equities and bonds owned directly or through mutual funds, and property. In different countries, people choose to save in different ways, often reflecting different cultures, financial infrastructure and products, and regulations affecting financial services companies.

For many countries, property is by far the most important asset that households own. Until 2007, the sustained and vigorous rise in house prices stimulated at least two major financial changes. First, the rise in housing wealth went hand in hand with a significant growth in mortgage debt, encouraged by low interest rates and the expectation of ever-rising house prices. Second, households, especially in the United States, used housing wealth as a substitute for saving in other ways. Similar developments have occurred in the United Kingdom, Australia, Spain, and Italy where home ownership rates are high. If it transpires that the last 10 to 15 years of housing feast (as far as prices are concerned) turn into some years of housing famine, people may end up saving more in traditional ways. Even so, the longer-term trend for savings does not appear robust.

Savings patterns and trends in Japan

Japan's reputation for having exceptionally frugal citizens has already been undermined. For decades after the Second World War, Japan's household savings rate was around 15 percent of disposable income. It soared to 20 percent in the mid-1970s as Japan, along with most other economies, responded to the economic instability and rising inflation of that period. But this was the high-water mark. Since that time, the savings rate has fallen steadily, reaching a mere 3 percent of disposable income in 2005–06.[2]

In the past, high savings rates in Japan have been attributed to a variety of factors, not least the prevalence of an extended family system, bequests to children, and savings for retirement. But the sustained decline has been associated strongly with both the income and jobs slump in the 1990s and the impact of aging. The savings rates of people aged over 60 in particular, but also of people in their fifties, have been dropping. The main reason seems to be a combination of lower public pension benefits[3] and higher rates of consumption—much as one would expect.

The pace and extent of aging is liable to keep savings rates relatively low for the foreseeable future for three reasons. First, the number of households of retired people in Japan is going to grow rapidly, so that by 2025 there will be more of them than there will be households comprising members aged 30–50, the prime years of saving. Second, the savings rate for thirty-somethings today is roughly 5-7 percent of disposable income, compared with the 25–28 percent saved by today's retirees when they were in their thirties. While this can be explained by several factors, including productivity growth, financial innovation, and improved financial security, the trend toward lower savings appears to be strongly age-related. Third, the returns on savings in Japan are still remarkably low. Short-term interest rates in the middle of 2008 were still only 0.5 percent, and yields on Japanese government bonds remained in a range of 1.7–2 percent.

This throws up some interesting ironies. The first is why Japanese households don't own more risky assets such as equities; the second is that pensioners would probably welcome some inflation if it caused interest rates to rise. For the record, Japanese households owned about ¥1500 trillion of assets (roughly US$12.5 trillion) in 2006, according to Bank of Japan data, of which 51 percent was in cash and deposits, and equities a mere 13 percent. This excludes (small) holdings in investment trusts and equities held in insurance and pension assets. Compare this for example with households in the United States whose direct ownership of equities and indirect ownership via mutual funds is around 30 percent of their total assets. And this excludes equities owned in pension and life insurance assets.

Regardless of how the Japanese prefer to hold their assets, it is clear they are growing them far more slowly, and it is even possible that, before long, Japan's overall household savings rate will become negative. In other words, older households will start to run down their savings as the surge in the elderly retired population begins to use them and accumulated wealth for consumption. The new savings of younger households may not compensate for this.

Savings in the United States

In the United States, a long-running debate has focused on the collapse of the household savings rate. For decades after the Second World War, the savings rate averaged about 8 percent of disposable income, but this began to decline in the 1980s and has at times been negative since the spring of 2005. In this context, negative simply means that households consume more than their income by running down savings or running up debt. We also know from national income and balance of payments accounting that America's huge external deficits reflect levels of national and personal savings that are too low in relation to investment. Simply put, US households have been undersaving, or overconsuming if you prefer.

The patterns of savings in the United States are quite revealing. The Federal Reserve Board publishes a Survey of Consumer Finances, every three years, which goes into great detail about family finances according to age groups, income levels, ethnic origin, employment status, and educational attainment among other things. This is the most robust evidence available to support observations about saving behavior, but different economic, social, and financial conditions in other countries might well yield a different picture.

In general, the 2004 Survey[4] noted three major changes occurring over the previous years. First, strong house price appreciation was the most significant factor in boosting households' assets. Second, households had been reducing their ownership of equities. Third, the amount of debt relative to assets had grown sharply, mostly as a result of a strong rise in mortgage debt, and this was a big contributor to the rising share of interest payments that families had to pay out of their incomes. The bulk of personal assets were held in the form of equities, mutual fund shares, and pension and life insurance policies. The survey reported that the heads of households aged 55–64 were the biggest holders of equities, an observation that applied to almost all other forms of financial assets. This corroborates the view that savings and wealth accumulation tend to rise with age until the late fifties and early sixties, after which they tend to decline.[5]

Low savings in recent years, or even running down of savings, doesn't mean—yet, at least—that the personal sector is struggling. At the end of 2008, it owned US$40.6 trillion of financial assets of all types, and it had liabilities or debts of US$19.6 trillion, of which about US$11.4 trillion was mortgage debt. So the difference or net worth was still clearly a very large number and the equivalent of about five times total personal income.

But away from these top-down numbers, the net worth of different types of families reveals a rather more interesting picture. It is with the rich middle-aged that most of this financial wealth is concentrated. In 2004, the median net worth of families where the head was aged below 54 (64 percent of all families) was less than US$145,000. In the family group, where the head was 55–64 (15 percent of all families), median net worth was US$249,000, and in those headed by over-65s (21 percent of families), it was less than US$200,000. More dramatic is the dominance of high income earners: the top 10 percent had a median net worth of US$924,000, the next 10 percent had US$311,000, the next 20 percent had US$160,000. And for the rest, it was less than US$72,000, including a tenth of that for the bottom 20 percent. Most families, then, have precious few resources on which to retire as things stand now.

Savings in Europe

It is no accident that the United Kingdom and Spain have the lowest personal savings rates. To a degree, this has been the result of the vigorous property price boom after 2000. In the United Kingdom, the household savings rate of 2.5 percent in the first quarter of 2008 wasn't quite as low as it had been in the 1950s but by more recent yardsticks, it was a record low. In bigger continental European countries such as France, Germany, and Italy, savings rates tend to be much higher, in the region of 8–11 percent of disposable income and, while they move about a bit from year to year, they don't exhibit the same strong downtrends that have been noted for Japan, the United States, the United Kingdom, the Netherlands, and Spain.

There are many reasons for higher personal savings rates in western Europe, and they involve differences in culture, greater

financial insecurity with regard to pensions and unemployment and the depth and breadth of the financial services
industry. This is also reflected in the ways people tend to hold
assets, and you can see this as you travel northwards from the
Mediterranean. The further north you go, the more likely it is
that you find not only higher levels of financial wealth but also
higher household participation in equity markets and higher
contributions to plans offered by institutional asset managers.
According to a report from the European Central Bank, in 2003
only around 25 percent of households in France, Germany,
Switzerland, and the Netherlands owned equities directly and
via financial companies, compared with more than a third in
the United Kingdom (and almost a half in the United States).
More Italian, German, and Belgian households owned bonds,
and fewer of them owned equities directly or indirectly than
in France, the Netherlands, Sweden, and the United
Kingdom.[6] In Spain, only 3 percent of households owned equities compared, say, with 38 percent in Sweden and 31 percent
in Denmark, while in the United Kingdom, three-fifths of the
entire assets (£3.846 trillion at the end of 2006) owned by
households comprised equities and life insurance and pension
fund reserves. Like the United States, though, country statistics show a heavily skewed distribution of wealth. In the
United Kingdom, Office of National Statistics data reveal that
in 2003, the richest 1 percent owned 21 percent of personal
wealth, the top 10 percent owned 53 percent, and the top 25
percent owned 72 percent.

So, in response to the question about whether there is
enough in the personal savings pot, the position can be summarized as follows:

- Savings rates have been falling in Japan, the United States,
  the United Kingdom, and Spain, among others, in some
  cases to historic lows.
- Household assets and net worth are generally speaking at
  high levels, but declines in asset prices and particularly in
  house prices could undermine this. Meanwhile, households in only a handful of countries hold enough risky

assets, such as equities, which it is hoped will appreciate in value over time, though it should be acknowledged that there has been a strong tendency to own riskier assets indirectly via pension funds and other asset managers.

- Those in their fifties and early sixties, immediately prior to retirement, are responsible for the bulk of personal savings in advanced economies, while the savings of those at the very top of the income and wealth ladders eclipse those of all others.
- Most middle-income and low-income earners have low or negligible savings pots. These and younger workers in general may find they are dangerously savings-"lite" not only as they approach retirement but also if house prices stagnate or fall.

Less generous pensions

The key issue, especially for people who look to the government for pension income support, is that governments are already reducing pensions perhaps to the lower limits of what is politically acceptable. The good news may be that there is precious little scope to cut them further. Figures for pensioner poverty (defined as the proportion of 66- to 75-year-olds with income that is below half the median population income) emphasize this point: it is highest in Ireland at 30 percent, next highest in the United States, Australia, and Japan at about 20 percent, and then still fairly high, at 10–15 percent, in Italy, the United Kingdom, France, and Germany. It is negligible only in New Zealand, Canada, and the Netherlands.

In Luxembourg or Greece an average earner with a full career can still get close to 100 percent of income in retirement benefit, but elsewhere it goes sharply downhill. You will get more than 75 percent if you retire in Austria, Hungary, Italy, Spain, the Netherlands, Portugal and Finland, 50–75 percent in Germany, Poland, France, Sweden, Belgium, Japan, Australia, and the United States, and less than 50 percent in the United Kingdom, Ireland, and New Zealand. Germany once had one of the more generous pension systems in the European Union, accounting for about 12 percent of GDP. But pension reforms adopted in 2001 aim gradually to lower the pension-for-earnings replacement rate from 70 percent to 62 percent by 2040. The quid pro quo for this, of course, was attempts to encourage greater use of private pensions, which of course entails a shift toward higher personal savings.

A report published by the OECD in 2007[7] found that the United Kingdom state pension system is the meanest of the developed countries belonging to the organization, and confirmed that Greece has the most generous.

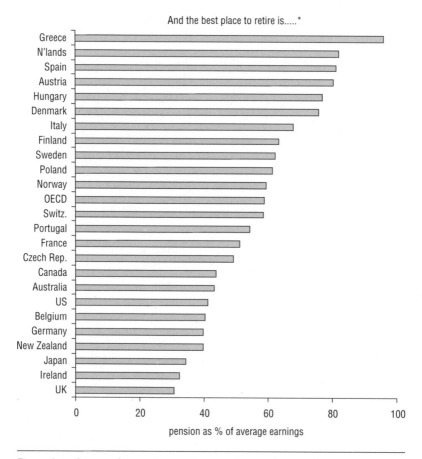

Figure 6.1 **Gross replacement rates: how pensions replace earnings**
* Gross pension entitlement as percentage of individual preretirement average earnings.
Source: "Pensions At a Glance," OECD, Paris, 2007.

For someone on average earnings who retires in 2050, the state mandatory pension in the United Kingdom would be equivalent to 31 percent of their earnings before retirement. This compares with about 40 percent in the United States, Australia, and Germany, about 50 percent in France, 59 percent across the whole of the OECD countries, 60 percent in Sweden, and 68 percent in Italy. The UK government has already tabled legislation to address this by raising the age of pension entitlement to 65 by the 2020s and then to 68 by the 2040s. It will also re-establish the link between pensions and earnings (as opposed to prices) in 2012 on the basis that earnings tend to rise faster (than prices).

Nearly all the 30 member countries in the OECD have made changes to their pension systems since 1990, and about half have introduced major reforms that alter future retirement benefits to a significant degree. These vary from the simple raising of the age at which full pension payments can be claimed to more complex changes in the way in which earnings are measured when calculating pension benefits. They all have one thing in common, though, to reduce the pension promise made to today's and future retirees compared with their predecessors.

If you consider, for example, the accumulated pension benefits that retirees who had been on average earnings can expect to receive, the average in 16 OECD countries has been cut by 22 percent for men, from 10.7 times annual earnings to 8.4 times. And for women, the cut has been a little larger at 25 percent, from 13 times annual earnings to 9.7 times. Major reforms have been undertaken in Austria, France, Germany, Italy, Sweden, and Finland—all of which were among the highest spenders on pensions. But some, with lower pension spending commitments, such as Japan, South Korea, Mexico, and Turkey also introduced significant reforms. In the case of the last three countries, the motivation seems to have been less to do with the immediacy of aging than with the recognition that exceptionally generous pension systems would not be sustainable. In Japan's case, the incentive was rather different and related to both the urgency of aging and the associated sharp rise in pension spending as a share of GDP. In some countries, as noted, the pension entitlements of employees who have average earnings will be significantly lower in the future. For those who have less than average earnings, the reductions will be even more painful. As things stand, unless employees are able to put away some of their income into savings, schemes of one description or another, poverty in old age will loom as a serious risk.

More self-reliance for retirement savings

The main messages to emerge from this discussion, therefore, are the need for greater self-provision and for governments to act sooner rather than later to put pension and healthcare funding onto a sounder footing. About 30 countries have opted for some form of privatized pension scheme or for compulsory saving schemes. Most of these are smaller countries in Latin America and eastern Europe, but Chile, Mexico, the United Kingdom, New Zealand, and Sweden have all introduced schemes (or will) that require employees to contribute a specific percentage of earnings to an individual account managed by a public or private asset manager. Other schemes require employers to provide private retirement arrangements, financed by the employer and or employee and some, such as Australia, have a compulsory private savings scheme to supplement the basic pension scheme. The problem for employees, of course, is that all such schemes involve administrative costs and, what is more important, expose their savings to the vagaries of the market and to the risk that their retirement savings at retirement may be worth less than they had planned or expected. For these schemes to succeed in building adequate savings for retirement, moreover, it is assumed—indeed required— that workers start making contributions early in their working lives and continue to do so for the 45 or so years that they will be working. The later people start to save or contribute, the more they have to save out of their wages and salaries to match the OECD pension average of 59 percent of earnings at retirement.

Is this the right way to go? Does it mean that government economic and social policy from now on will have to take into account stock market valuations to make sure employees will be properly protected in retirement? And this goes just as much for developing countries, from Chile to China, which have adopted, or propose to introduce, private pension arrangements. Of course, it would be impossible over any length of time—and undesirable—for governments to influence stock market valuations. But not to do so means that employees' savings, through defined contribution pension plans, or private plans, could potentially fail to grow adequately or even to decline. And that means that people will have little choice but to become much more financially literate and build and manage their savings throughout their working lives and indeed, after retirement.

Government spending and more public debt

In the absence of major changes in public policy, population aging will cause government financial surpluses to fall or deficits to get bigger. Governments in Western economies already face enormous financial obligations over the next 20 to 40 years. From a demographic standpoint, public finances have realized pretty much all the gains from the fall in youth dependency that has occurred in recent years but have not yet encountered the drag arising from old-age dependency. It is sometimes said that lower youth dependency will pay for higher old-age dependency. In other words, less spending on midwives, neo- and pre-natal care, kindergartens, schoolteachers, and youth facilities, and more on healthcare and pensions, residential care, care providers, mobile care services, and geriatric departments. But it would be a delusion to think that the youth savings will pay for the old-age spending.

It has been estimated that transfers payable to a person over 64 are about 27 percent bigger than to a younger person and 76 percent bigger than to a child.[8] Though the data were published some time ago, it is unlikely that the relative costs have fallen. More recently, Ronald Lee stated that in California, taking into account federal, state, and local expenditures to both the elderly and the young, the elderly receive about three times as much per head as do children.[9] Population aging, therefore, is going to cost money. The radical change in age structure that is coming inevitably means more spending on older people than governments could possibly save by spending less on fewer young people. Since 40–60 percent of public spending is sensitive to the age structure of the population, and we know a few things about age structure, it is clear that the burden of public spending is going one way only. It's only a question of how far and how fast.

We'll see below some estimates that have been made that try to account for perhaps lower spending on education and unemployment benefits, and the extent to which this might offset the rise in age-related spending. Remember that age-related spending, of course, goes beyond pensions to include healthcare, long-term care and disability, and long-term incapacity and unemployment expenditure. But take as a starting point estimates made by both the International Monetary Fund and the OECD[10] that such spending would rise by about 7 percent of GDP in the OECD, on average, by 2050. This is on top of the roughly 3.5 percent of GDP that the OECD thinks its members will have to spend on social and energy infrastructure over the next 20 years.[11] Age-related spending currently represents about 19–20 percent of GDP in OECD economies, and so clearly the jump from this to about 27 percent of GDP will be of great significance. Think of it this way. If your income is 100 today and grows by 5.5 percent each year for 45 years, it will increase eleven times at a compound rate. If you spent 20 percent of your income today on, say, housing, but 27 percent in 45 years, your housing payments will have grown 15 times at a compound rate. To stop being worse off, you will need either a lot more income or to reduce your spending on other things. For governments, the choice is the same.

Age-related spending: pensions

Pensions are the largest component of age-related spending. Some countries have funded private pension systems where employees save a part of their incomes, invest them privately or in employer- or government-provided schemes, and then draw an income from the accumulated pension pot when they retire. But most countries have so-called Pay-As-You-Go (PAYG) systems, which are basically ways of transferring money, not saving it. Retirement pensions paid to contemporary retirees are financed by the tax or social security payments made by contemporary contributors, that is, today's employees. Some countries have elements of both systems.

PAYG pension systems are a liability of the state. They work according to the principle that the government receives pension contributions (a percentage of wages and salaries multiplied by the number of contributors) and pays pensions (a percentage of earnings times the number of recipients). Their significance derives from the fact that governments do not have to collect peoples' savings or invest people's money and they can use contributions to redistribute wealth, for example, by paying rather more generous pensions to lower paid employees and smaller ones to the better paid. A flat-rate pension does this in effect but means-tested and other rules for paying pensions are used as well. Because of the prospective decline or stagnation in the numbers of working-age people and rising life expectancy, public pensions are now growing as a share of governments' total financial liabilities. In a nutshell, as the dependency ratio rises, the value of all future pension (and healthcare) liabilities will rise too.

Governments only record in their financial statements the actual amounts they pay in a calendar or financial year, not the estimated value today of the entire pension promises they have made to current and future retirees. If you know roughly the demographic characteristics of the population, have a reasonable estimate for life expectancy after retirement, and take account of the flow of retirees in future years, then it is possible to calculate the government's total fiscal liabilities as they appear today. We shall see below why governments do not publish or base policies on this information: the numbers look frightening.

Whether the main pension system is PAYG or funded by individuals, the problem for aging societies is the same. How do you transfer resources to growing numbers of pensioners, who are mainly consumers, from a relatively or absolutely dwindling number of workers who produce more than they consume, that is, save? If people save more for retirement, interest rates and returns on financial assets could be lower than they might be otherwise. If savings decline as the age structure increases, asset prices might suffer as they are sold to finance longer retirement.

Longer lives, lower fertility, and rising dependency ratios are having profound implications on PAYG systems. The core PAYG problem, though, is not so much longer lives (which could be addressed simply by increasing the retirement age), but falling fertility and excessively low birth rates. After all, PAYG systems are little more than Ponzi schemes.[12] They depend, for their financial integrity on there always being enough workers to pay ever-greater amounts to the (growing) retired population. It is self-evident that as the working-age population stagnates or falls, that there will be insufficient savings to pay the retirement bills. The faltering math of PAYG systems has brought to the forefront of public debate the urgency of policy adjustments and focused attention on the need to pursue some combination of higher levels of tax to finance state pensions, lower pension benefit entitlements relative to earnings, and a rise in the retirement or pensionable age. Some countries such as Spain and the Netherlands have pension systems that are strongly related to earnings. Others such as the United Kingdom and New Zealand, have more or less flat rate pension systems, while Australia and the United States, for example, have a blend that, in Australia's case, provides for compulsory private savings. Clearly, the more the pension system is characterized by flat rate payments, the greater the risk and likelihood of growing pensioner poverty.

Age-related spending: healthcare

Healthcare costs are already rising relatively quickly for non-demographic reasons. These include relatively low productivity in the healthcare sector, which employs labor much more intensively than other "industries," wider and more expensive healthcare insurance premiums, the introduction of new and costly prescription drugs, and more expensive diagnostic and treatment techniques. The emphasis that continues to be placed on good diets and tackling obesity, exercise, and antismoking campaigns is vital in allowing us to lead longer and healthier lives. But this also calls for an ever-rising quantity and quality of medical care and pharmaceuticals for the prevention, diagnosis, and treatment of a variety of diseases. There is no evidence yet that healthcare benefit growth is slowing down much, if at all, and it does not seem likely that there will be much relief from these cost pressures in the future. The growing number of elderly people will continue to demand ever-greater amounts of medical care to maintain mobility and for inpatient treatment and long-term chronic disease management, especially in later years.

Age-related spending in OECD countries

The size of age-related spending in relation to GDP varies a lot from country to country. In France, Germany, Italy, and Sweden, for example, it is about 17–19 percent. In the United Kingdom, Switzerland, the Netherlands, Japan, and Canada age-related spending is lower, at 12–14 percent of GDP. America's share, for the time being, is a relatively lowly 8 percent.

Recent research from the OECD about how much additional age-related spending is in prospect in its member countries is summarized in Table 6.1.

Clearly, the estimated average increase for all OECD countries of 7 percent of GDP by 2050 masks many differences between countries. The average for the Euro Area is about 9 percent, but France, Germany, and Italy are a little below this level, while Spain is well above. It isn't the worst affected though. Portugal, Ireland, and Greece (not shown on this table) will have to find amounts from 14 to 17 percent of GDP to pay for their aging populations. The United States, the United Kingdom, and Japan are about average on this standardized comparison, Australia and Canada a bit higher, and Sweden a bit lower. But New Zealand's challenge is clear.

Table 6.1   Additional public spending on pensions, healthcare, and long-term care

| | Change from 2005 levels, in percent of GDP | | | | | | | |
	Pensions		Healthcare		Long-term care		Total	
	2025	2050	2025	2050	2025	2050	2025	2050
Euro Area	1.1	3	0.9	2.2	1.5	3.7	3.5	8.9
France	1.2	2.1	0.4	1.7	1.5	3.5	3.1	7.3
Germany	0.2	2.2	1.5	3.6	0.8	1.9	2.2	7.5
Italy	0.2	0.4	1.6	3.8	1.3	2.9	3.1	7
Spain	1.8	7	1.6	4.1	1.1	2.4	4.5	13.5
US	0.9	1.8	1.5	3.4	0.4	1.7	2.9	7
Japan	0.3	0.6	1.9	4.3	1.1	2.2	3.4	7.1
UK	0.7	1.7	1.4	3.6	0.6	1.9	2.8	7.2
Australia	1	1.7	1.8	4.2	0.5	2	3.3	7.9
Canada	0.8	1.7	1.9	4.1	0.6	2.1	3.3	7.9
New Zealand	3.2	5.9	1.8	4.2	0.6	2	5.7	12
Sweden	0.1	0.8	1.4	3.2	0.3	1.1	1.8	5.1

Source: Boris Cournede "The Political Economy of Delaying Fiscal Consolidation," Economics Working Paper No. 548 Paris: OECD, March 9, 2007.

The European Central Bank, using some rather more optimistic estimates made by the European Commission and more favorable assumptions about labor market participation, reckons that in the European Union, pensions, healthcare, and long-term care spending will rise by 4.3 percent of GDP by 2050. Savings in education and unemployment benefits could bring the total increase down to 3.4 percent of GDP. The 20 years after 2010 in particular will see the need for about two-thirds of this extra spending. The largest age-related spending increases are expected to occur in Spain, Ireland, Belgium, Portugal, and Greece (6–9 percent of GDP) and the lowest in Austria, Sweden, the United Kingdom, Germany, France, and Italy (4 percent of GDP or less).

Without higher taxes, other spending cuts, or both, the chances of being able to achieve those higher spending estimates are finely balanced in all these countries. In recent years, the average annual increase in GDP, measured in nominal or money terms, has been about 5 percent in the United States, a little lower in western Europe and about 0–1 percent in Japan. Assuming economic growth alone has to finance the estimated increases in age-related spending, all industrial economies would have to maintain an equivalent growth rate at the very least. But several would have to increase their growth rates by about 1–2 percent per year, foremost among them the United States, Germany, Japan, and Spain. Since the underlying trend in real economic growth—about 3–3.25 percent per year in the United States and 2 percent in the European Union—is declining with aging, we don't have to dwell any further on economic growth as a possible solution. Higher inflation might help—but that's another matter to which I will return.

America's healthcare and public spending explosion

In the United States, it's not so much pensions that are going to strain the federal budget as healthcare. Overall, spending on healthcare is about two times as much per person as in the whole of the OECD on average. Despite this, Americans actually have slightly lower life expectancy. Social Security, which pays out pensions, and Medicare and Medicaid, which are the two main federal healthcare programs, together account for roughly 8 percent of GDP. And the Office of Management and Budget predicts this will rise to 13 percent of GDP by 2030, though this is probably a rather optimistic projection.

Social Security accounts for 21 percent of federal spending and about 36 percent of mandatory spending, which is defined as programs funded according to rules regarding eligibility or other payment criteria and which pays cash benefits to the elderly and disabled. The main component is Old Age and Survivors Insurance that pays benefits of nearly US$450 billion to 40 million people. In 1935, when President Franklin D Roosevelt introduced the scheme, it paid US$35 million to 200,000 retirees. The Congressional Budget Office estimates that by 2016 the scheme will be paying roughly US$800 billion to 50 million people. Medicare provides subsidized medical insurance for the elderly and certain disabled categories, and accounts for 23 percent of federal spending. Medicaid is a joint federal-state program that funds care for the poorest citizens and accounts for 13 percent of federal spending.

The Congressional Budget Office reported at the end of 2005 that the combination of Social Security and healthcare spending would rise from 8.4 percent of GDP to 19 percent of GDP by 2050. But depending on whether or not policies are undertaken to address the surge in expected spending, the range of the increase might be between 7 percent and 22 percent of GDP. Even the central assumption of a rise of 11 percent of GDP is significantly greater than the average 4 percent of GDP or so that most European countries and Japan are going to have to find. Former Federal Reserve Chairman Alan Greenspan told the House of Representatives Budget Committee in 2005: "I fear we may have already committed more physical resources to the baby-boom generation in its retirement years than our economy has the capacity to deliver."[13] He went on, needless to say, to urge the Congress to speed up fiscal changes to prepare for this eventuality—which, predictably, it has not.

It is worth reminding ourselves of the magnitude of America's age-related spending issues in the years ahead. Remember the over-65s are expected to double as a share of the population (to nearly 20 percent by 2025) while the 20- to 64-year-olds drop from about 60 percent to 55 percent and the 0- to 19-year-olds from 30 percent to 25 percent. Projections of healthcare spending in particular are especially alarming in view of America's relatively favorable aging profile compared with, say, Japan.

One research paper noted that if healthcare spending were to grow over the next 40 years as it has done over the last 40, then eventually it alone could account for 18 percent of GDP, compared with 12 percent of GDP for Japan.[14] It said that the United States may well be in the worst long-term fiscal shape of any OECD country, despite its slower aging. Along with that of Norway and Spain, healthcare spending in the United States has grown the most rapidly since 1970 at around 5 percent per year in real terms. The lowest growth rates at just over 2 percent per year occurred in Canada and Sweden.

Another paper drew attention to the scale of healthcare spending and vulnerability of the economy ahead of the demographic changes to come. It revealed that the more than US$11,000 per head, that people over the age of 65 spend on personal healthcare, was about four times as large as younger people spend. The older group spent about 2.5 times as much for doctors' services, three times for prescription drugs, four for hospital services, 10 for home healthcare, and 30 for nursing care.[15]

Growth rates in healthcare spending have considerably outpaced the growth of GDP in all countries, but the Kotlikoff and Hagist research paper emphasized that three-quarters of the growth has not been accounted for by aging, per se, but by the expansion and increase in benefit levels, again especially in the United States. Much of the growth here has been the result of the introduction of costly diagnostic treatment such as CT[16] scanners. Given what is known about aging composition, the authors calculated that if benefit growth stabilized, the biggest financing problems would be in Canada and Germany, but if past growth was projected forward, the United States would be by far the country most at risk from adverse fiscal consequences. They argue that, unlike other countries, the United States lacks the institutional mechanism and the political will to control spending and that America's elderly are politically well organized to secure growing transfers for their members in each generation. For example, the recently legislated Medicare prescription drug benefit, which came into effect in 2006, is expected over the next decades to cost more than US$12 trillion in today's money, of which today's elderly will not pay a cent.

Remarkably, the Trustees of the Social Security and Medicare trust funds issued a message to the public in their annual report for 2007.[17] They said the long-run growth rates in spending are not sustainable as things stand and that, for the first time, they were issuing a "Medicare funding warning"— a technical provision that would soon require the president, by law, to propose, and Congress to enact, corrective legislation. In the report, they drew attention, as always, to the projected rise in Social Security spending from 4.2 percent of GDP in 2006 to 6.2 percent by 2030, but they noted that under current arrangements, this increase would start to tail off. In fact by 2081, they thought the share of GDP would still be 6.3 percent of GDP. But on healthcare, they emphasized that the 3.1 percent share of Medicare in GDP would grow to 11.3 percent of GDP.

To put into perspective the estimated total increase in Social Security and healthcare spending of about 10 percent of GDP, I would remind you that total federal revenues in 2006 amounted to 18.5 percent of GDP. The only time the tax share of GDP was higher was during war (the Second World War and Vietnam), in a recession (1981–82) and in the capital gains tax-driven revenue surge arising from the stock market bubble of 1998–2001.

The Trustees also noted that the actuarial balance (a measure of long-term solvency) in Social Security could be achieved over the long term by various measures including an immediate increase of 16 percent in payroll tax revenues (levied equally on employers and employees) or an immediate reduction in benefits of 13 percent or a combination of the two. The same calculation for the Hospital Insurance trust fund indicated that actuarial balance could be achieved via an immediate 122 percent increase in payroll taxes or an immediate 51 percent cut in spending programs or some combination.[18]

The signature of the trustees at the end of the report, including that of one Thomas R. Saving, follows a chilling warning that if the growth in healthcare spending did not abate very soon, "then the bleak fiscal future portrayed in these reports will be bleaker still." The only question America and other advanced economies have to answer, if the fiscal consequences are not to be overwhelming, is when, not if, healthcare spending growth will be made to slow down or be restructured.

Another alarming report appeared in 2007 showing how the United States government's methods of budgetary accounting, especially as regards health and pensions, grossly understates the degree of financial stress and indiscipline. Corporations in the private sector are simply not allowed to get away with the sort of accounting that neglects to value pension and benefit liabilities properly. The authors reckon that, accounting fully for explicit and promised obligations, the US national debt would be US$63.7 trillion, equivalent to seven times the official estimate made in October 2007 and to nearly five times GDP. They estimated the annual budget deficit in 2006 would have been US$2.4 trillion or 20 percent of GDP.[19] The data are based on estimates of the difference between the present value of the government's spending commitments, especially including Social Security and healthcare spending programs, and its projected tax revenues and other income. The number US$63.7 trillion is impossible to grasp, but it is enough to note that it is larger than the entire capital stock of the United States, which is to say, land, buildings, roads, cars and other consumer durables, homes, factories, and financial assets. This does not include the very substantial value of human capital in the form of education, skills, and training, but the implication is that unless the government acts soon to remedy this extraordinary fiscal imbalance, tomorrow's workers may face an extraordinary tax burden.

The main problem of course is that until now Congress has been unwilling or unable to legislate meaningful fiscal changes to address the problem. If anything, policy has been leaning the other way: George W. Bush's administrations pushed for significant reductions in taxation, and Congress approved these as well as the new and expensive program for prescription drugs. In years gone by, the emergence of a "peace dividend" was a welcome bonus with which to finance growing mandatory spending (see Figure 6.2). For example, from the late 1960s to the mid-2000s, defense spending fell from about 9 percent to about 3 percent of GDP. During this period, mandatory spending rose from 3 percent to 8 percent of GDP. But now that the inexorable growth in mandatory spending is about to begin, and bearing in mind that defense spending is again rising as a share of GDP (4 percent at the latest count), there is no sight of any possible peace dividend in the foreseeable future.

The starting position for aging as far as the United States is concerned is one where personal and national savings are at historic lows and where the country can expect a very significant expansion in federal spending—especially on aging. While there was a more meaningful debate about these matters during the 2008 presidential and congressional elections, the prospects for action much before 2010 look poor.

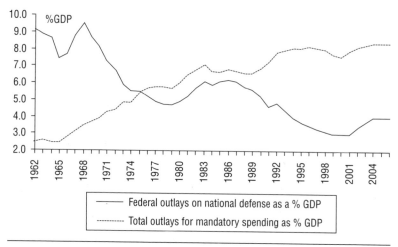

Figure 6.2   Who will pay as the peace dividend fades?
Source: Haver Analytics.

Paying for aging

As we have seen, raising the retirement pension age by two to three years and watering down or withdrawing pension and health benefits in the future probably form the opening salvo of responses to aging societies. From 1990 to date, 16 OECD countries have implemented major pension reforms, the over-all effect of which has been to lower the amount of benefit for the newest workers by about 25 percent compared with what they would have received without those reforms.[20] While it is possible that governments will try to cut their pension outlays further in the next five to 10 years, the limits may already have been reached in some countries, as we have already seen. So the next stage is going to see governments having to tackle the tough issues of tax and non–age-related spending as well. In other words, public policy will focus more and more on deci-sions about how to raise taxes and from whom and about how, if possible, to economize on public expenditure so as to make way for additional age-related spending.

The main focus will almost certainly fall on the tax system and on the question of who will pay. No one could doubt that baby boomers have benefited hugely from rising consumption, based on the strength of their numbers, their incomes, and their wealth accumulation. Their children and grandchildren will probably find tougher financial conditions since their numbers will be in decline or increasing much more slowly. The coming generations of workers, then, will have to pay more, one way or another, not only for their own retirement but also for existing retirees. They may even end up paying more while at work than they themselves might expect to receive when they retire.

Tax decisions will have to be tackled with great caution. If you raise taxes to punitive levels on inheritance, wealth, and other forms of capital, the effect is to discourage savings when saving is exactly what you want people to do. If people do not save enough, there might not be enough investment, and this could put upward pressure on interest rates. If you raise income or social security taxes to an excessive level, it will discourage companies from hiring and people from working, when more labor effort is precisely what you want. The major alternative is a shift in the tax system from these kinds of taxes to higher or new consumption taxes, such as a value-added tax or a sales tax. But these are regressive—since everyone pays the same tax, they're unfair to less well-off people.

There has already been a shift to consumption taxes in many regions, including the European Union, Australia, Canada, Japan, and Switzerland, and this shift may go further, not least because these taxes are thought to encourage savings and do not penalize labor. But for societies to accept such a shift, it is probable that fairness or equity will involve higher rates of tax for better-off individuals, high-income earners, and companies. The status quo, in short, cannot and will not last. In fact, it seems absurd to think that for the last few years most countries have been on a mission to cut taxes for individuals and companies when this can only mean that the burden on future generations to pay for aging will be larger.[21] Unfortunately, because governments in democratic societies are normally fixated on what will work for them at the ballot box next time around, there is only a weak—or no—incentive to tackle the problem of "who's going to pay for grandma and grandpa?" over the longer term.

In any event, it will simply not be possible, beyond a certain point, for governments to raise taxes or reduce benefits for the younger members of the population to accommodate aging. It is unclear when exactly that point will be reached, but it probably lies within the next 10–15 years. It is the equivalent point at which an individual might file for bankruptcy or a company would be wound up or acquired by another. What happens when it is governments in this kind of trouble? Well, of course, governments do not go bust, do they? Actually, they do, technically, and often when the budgetary and debt positions have become so unstable and unsustainable that creditors and investors stop lending. The result, historically, has included a variety of forms of financial crisis, including higher interest rates, currency devaluation, and sometimes, political unrest and change of government.

Fiscal versus fallen angels

The least controversial way for governments to proceed, if political reforms to spending are hard to achieve, would simply be to allow government borrowing and debt to rise. In the best circumstances, high and sustained rates of economic growth might take care of the servicing of that debt and its eventual repayment. But faster economic growth is what aging societies may find difficult to achieve. So public authorities would issue bonds or savings products to the public, much as they do now, but in ever-larger volumes. As a policy, this can be justified to the extent that such rises are temporary or will be used to finance investment to generate new revenues or productivity growth in the future. But if governments simply allow borrowing and debt to increase over the long term, because they are unwilling or unable to finance consumption and social transfers in other ways, they are sowing the seeds of trouble.

Currently, Japan has the highest level of public debt to GDP in the OECD (in 2006) at about 180 percent. Italy and Greece have public debt levels that are about 120 percent of GDP. The countries with the lowest debt as a share of GDP are Australia, New Zealand, Ireland, Denmark, Spain, the United Kingdom, and Finland. In these countries, the share is between 15 and 45 percent. The middle ground is occupied by Sweden, the Netherlands, the United States, Canada, Germany, Portugal, and France where the share is between roughly 60 and 80 percent of GDP.

We don't really know what the right number should be, the one that separates fiscal angels from fallen angels. But most economists think that 50–60 percent of GDP is high enough, assuming that the outlook is for broad stability. The European Union, for example, has set a level of 60 percent as one of the entry criteria for admission to the Euro Area (countries with the single euro currency) and encourages countries to aim for this level over time. On this basis, Greece and Italy clearly have excessive levels of public debt even today. The same could be said of Japan, even though more than half the government's debt is actually held by agencies of the government itself.

It has been some years since the global economy was focused on a budgetary crisis in any of the more advanced or larger economies. For the most part, budgetary positions have been broadly stable. Steady and high rates of economic growth have kept tax revenues buoyant, and low inflation has allowed low interest rates to contain government interest payments on the national debt. Neither of these beneficial factors can be relied upon forever, and if economic conditions deteriorate, then rising levels of public debt could indeed again become a threat to stability. Before long, the age-related spending burden will grow, and the longer-term budgetary consequences will be more evident.

It is important therefore that governments use the opportunity of favorable economic times to strengthen their financial positions. Historically, the failure to correct structurally weak fiscal positions has sometimes led credit-rating agencies to downgrade government debt. This has the effect of making borrowing more expensive and might even act to discourage investors and lenders who might want their money back. The reason we want to know how aging societies will pay for demographic change is because countries that do resort to sustained and large increases in public debt may well end up first having their credit downgraded and then confronting some sort of fiscal crisis with rising inflation and interest rates, and then, probably recession.

There is a long list of examples of countries that have gone bust, so to speak. They reached the point where they had to default on their obligations to investors, amid financial chaos and economic ruin. To take a relatively recent and major example, in 2001 Argentina defaulted on its foreign debt in the midst of an economic crisis. Images around that time of Argentine citizens in Buenos Aires queuing up to withdraw money from banks or send their pesos abroad were shocking enough. They got worse after the government froze all bank accounts for a year, allowing people to withdraw only small amounts of money. Widespread street protests and violence to property followed. Eventually, the then president declared a state of emergency, which prompted still more violent protest, including several deaths and the fall of the government. The president fled his palace by helicopter.

The thought seems preposterous today that similar developments might occur in the United States, a European country, or Japan. But it is not. The possibility of a financial crisis, in some ways similar to that experienced by Argentina, is real. Just because the idea seems far-fetched and that financial markets brush it off as a tail risk (that is, at the extreme end of a bell-shaped probability curve) does not mean it is unlikely. Rich countries may not have defaulted in as dramatic a fashion as Argentina in the past, but they have certainly defaulted. The way they have done it, in the last 50 years at least, is via inflation—or some mix of inflation and currency devaluation. Some European countries experienced such developments in the 1970s and until the 1990s, prior to the birth of the European single currency, the euro. In the 1960s, US President Lyndon Johnson's Administration was fighting against the communists in Vietnam and for social progress at home. This guns and butter program kicked off a sequence of higher government borrowing and money creation that was carried to new levels in the Administration of President Richard Nixon. Rising levels of inflation and interest rates were already well established before the oil producers hiked the price of crude in and after 1973. The United States was certainly not alone in experiencing higher inflation in the 1970s but if there was good news, it was for governments. Inflation erodes the real value of government debt and debt obligations. If you own a mortgage, you would welcome some inflation. Your debt is fixed, your mortgage rate might be, and as inflation rises and pushes up your income and the value of your house, your financial burdens diminish. The same goes for governments because inflation erodes debt and debt interest payments in real terms while it strengthens tax receipts.

Several countries today are not in the best of financial health. As already noted, Italy, Belgium, and Japan have extraordinarily high levels of public debt in relation to GDP. Most other rich countries have lower levels but not so low that they are immune from the continuous deterioration that would happen if trying to finance the costs of aging societies without a carefully planned series of fiscal and financial reforms. Today, with central banks focused strongly on the maintenance of low inflation, it seems unlikely that inflation will rise significantly and over an extended time. But who is to say that over the next five to 10 years the world won't succumb, for one reason or another, to higher inflation again? As already suggested, aging societies could be inflationary if public deficits and debt were to keep growing. Bad fiscal policies often create pressures for bad monetary policies, in which central banks eventually end up monetizing debt, or, in effect, printing the money to finance the debt. Strange as that may seem today, with central banks in many economies, east and west, retaining an aura of inflation-fighting credibility, it is not at all strange to imagine that this resolve might diminish in the light of growing fiscal stress with all its political repercussions. And that could end up, in some cases, in higher inflation and eventually, even capital flight and financial crisis.

Will aging societies inflate or deflate?

Throughout most of recorded economic history, inflation has been the exception to the rule of roughly stable prices. So has deflation. For most of the nineteenth century, inflation was subdued or prices actually fell, except when spurred by wars and the gold discoveries in the Americas and South Africa. The peacetime parts of the twentieth century were marked by the savage deflation of the 1930s and the sharp rise in inflation in the 1970s, but at most other times and in the first years of the twenty-first century, inflation has been low or falling. The most dramatic instance of falling prices in advanced economies, since 1945, occurred in Japan in the later 1990s. However, during 2002 and 2003, the United States and some European countries were also alarmed by the prospect of slipping into deflation. The threat passed, and by 2007–08, the dominant concern had again become rising inflation, mainly as a result of soaring food and energy prices. The housing and financial crises that began in the second half of 2007 will probably cause overall inflation to decline again in the near future, but many economic commentators and analysts believe that much of the recent rise in inflation is a harbinger of higher inflation in the future, whatever the outcome in the next one to two years.

So is our recent history of low and stable inflation also at risk from aging? To answer this, I need to underline that inflation is sometimes not what you think it is. If petrol or gas prices rise, is that inflation? If workers demand and get higher wages, is that inflation? Strictly speaking, the answers are no. First, inflation is a sustained rise in the overall level of prices, not just a few items, however important they might be. Second, as the economist Milton Friedman was renowned for having said, inflation is always and everywhere a monetary phenomenon. In other words, you cannot really have inflation in the absence of relatively loose monetary and credit conditions. Accordingly, whether aging societies will be inherently inflationary or deflationary and whether, therefore, interest rates are likely to be higher or lower is hard to say because no one can know what money and credit policies might look like in 10 or 20 years. But we know enough to say a few things about where cost and price pressures in society might arise.

According to conventional thinking, low inflation is a sort of handmaiden of aging societies. It could even be worse than low inflation. Maybe deflation. Many people associate older societies with low inflation or stable prices because the pattern of consumption is likely to change toward lower priced goods and services. Labor unions may become even less relevant to wage setting, and older people tend not to vote for inflationary economic policies because they depend on the stability of fixed retirement incomes. In the extreme, the temptation is to conjure up images of decrepit and stagnant societies, living off past wealth and characterized by deflation. However, history reveals that low inflation, rather than deflation, is the rule and that periods of low inflation occur more frequently, and for longer, than periods of high inflation.

But high or higher inflation can and does occur for a while when the circumstances are propitious. There will be significant labor market developments that might cause inflation to rise. The working-age population will stagnate or contract. If this cannot be offset, then there might be growing shortages of labor in general or of certain types of skilled labor in particular. In fact, this isn't even theoretical anymore, because in Europe and Japan, for example, labor shortages are already quite widespread, ranging from agricultural laborers to engineers and medical staff.

It would be serious enough if such shortages arose naturally for demographic reasons as described. But governments should take heed. Some people with high skill levels are not waiting for the consequences of aging societies to become more apparent. Hostile to the social consequences of immigration or anxious about high levels of taxation, they are already looking for pastures new. In Germany, for example, the Federal Statistics Office announced in 2007 that 155,290 people emigrated in 2006, in line with the numbers leaving in the chaos after the conclusion of the Second World War. More to the point, these emigrants included well-educated managers, consultants, doctors, dentists, scientists, and lawyers. Skilled people are the last that advanced societies can afford to lose (even if they end up emigrating to other advanced economies), especially if the overall skill levels of immigrants are materially lower.

In the United Kingdom, the official number of people emigrating rose from 249,000 in 1995 to more than 350,000 10 years later. The *Daily Express* newspaper reported in 2007 that applications at one consultancy from people looking to emigrate had risen 80 percent since the start of the year.[22] People with skills and with English as a mother tongue are in particular demand in Australia, Canada, and South Africa and, according to the newspaper report, local community burdens and tensions as well as a host of social issues including crime, the dearth of good schools, and rising tax rates were given as the main reasons. But the reasons for the emigration of skilled workers (not to mention associated reports in the right-of-center media) matter less, from an economic point of view, than do the skill shortages they leave behind.

Capitalism has a very simple way of addressing shortages and surpluses of key resources. Prices rise or fall, respectively, to address the imbalance. In this case, shortages of labor should raise the reward to labor—or wages and salaries—relative to the reward to capital or profits. This need not but could also occur with wages rising not only relative to profits but in absolute terms as well. Rising wages could then result in rising prices and so trigger rising inflation if central banks didn't intervene to break the momentum. Moreover, if governments tried to achieve steady economic growth rates when our potential to sustain those growth rates had been lowered by falls in the working-age population, this may also be a source of inflationary pressure from time to time.

Thus, the answers to aging and inflation or deflation may not be known for many years yet, during which time a host of other factors could have a significant bearing on the outcome. But over the long term, the demographic position in advanced economies should certainly be associated with a change in income distribution away from profits and toward wages and salaries, a stronger wage and compensation structure for workers with advanced skills and education, and the possibility of a shortage of savings and rising government debt. Such an environment could easily be consistent with a world where price inflation may well be higher than it has been in the last 10 to 15 years.

There is of course one type of inflation we love. We like sustained and significant increases in both house and equity prices. If you're a more sophisticated investor, you might also derive comfort from rising prices for commodities, art, wine, and so on. Over the last 20 to 30 years, property, stock markets, and commodities, for example, have delivered stunning returns to investors. In 2007, as I have noted, the unfolding crisis in housing markets and in the banking and credit industry set off declines in several asset prices in ways that were quite unfamiliar and unexpected. Maybe, this was a foretaste of how financial markets could react in the face of the economics of aging societies.

Will aging damage your wealth?

It is often said that the main demographic factor during these last decades in which equity and property prices have risen so strongly was the baby-boomer generation itself. In other words, the strong long-term upswing in equity and property prices in the 1980s and subsequently can be attributed to the boomers moving into their forties and fifties—the prime earning and saving years. The other side of this argument is potentially worrying and has prompted some to predict that aging societies will face a meltdown in asset prices.

As the boomers move toward, and into, retirement, they may well be inclined to sell off their assets and run down their savings in order to finance old-age consumption and care. If the boomers sell their equities and their houses—or even trade their bigger houses for smaller ones—to whom will they sell? After all, their hapless and possibly indebted children and grandchildren are going to belong to a working-age population that is smaller and may be less well equipped to buy assets.

The result could be an overhang of property, in which house prices decline. Similarly, if older people need or want to sell equities and the demand from potential younger buyers is not robust, then stock prices would decline too.

You can find these kinds of meltdown scare stories being written in populist and tabloid media nowadays, and for the most part, they are just that—scare stories. To begin with, the boomer generation's bulge after the Second World War, and its experience with asset prices, is really only one observation. It is impossible to infer anything about behavior without many more observations about surges in the 40- to 50-year-old age group and asset prices. For one thing, global life expectancy was still only 47 years in 1950 and closer to 65 in rich countries. Furthermore, lots of things affect the prices of assets. Demographic factors may be important but so are innovation, productivity, global savings trends, inflation, and interest rates. With hindsight, three powerful trends in the last two decades turbo-charged the rise in asset prices—baby boomers apart. First, the sharp decline in interest rates as inflation fell and economic stability became more entrenched. Second, the rapid expansion of savings in emerging and developing countries looking for a home—mostly in the financial markets of the richer OECD countries. Third, and probably the main factor, a long and vigorous global credit expansion, which started to go into reverse in the second half of 2007.

The idea that asset prices may not behave in the future as they have in the past is a very serious point. It is a warning of risk to investors but also to us all as aging societies move into uncharted waters. Just for a moment, go back to the life-cycle hypothesis that suggests savings rise into middle age or just after and then drop off or reverse in old age. Now think about this happening for an entire population. Total savings, then, rise as baby boomers reach their fifties and sixties, and then fall. The implication is that asset prices might rise while savings rise and labor is plentiful and then stagnate or fall as savings decline and labor becomes scarce. Similarly, as labor becomes scarce relative to capital, the return on capital should fall or increase more slowly relative to the return on labor. These changes could be reflected in relatively low or lower interest rates, in lower dividend flows from companies and in slower stock price appreciation.

The empirical evidence, such as it is, is not convincing. There was a bulge in the 40- to 60-year-old population in the 1920s and 1930s, but there was certainly no lasting boom in equity or property prices then. Far from it. After the Second World War and until the 1970s, this age group fell as a share of the total population—and yet share prices rose steadily. Since the early 1980s and until very recently, share prices did rise strongly, but not all baby boomers have been siphoning off their savings into an array of financial assets. American and Japanese, as well as other Anglo-Saxon boomers, have not been diligent or prolific savers at all. Savings rates in these economies have actually been falling, especially in the United States.

This does not really sit comfortably with the theory, which says that the boomers "should" still be raising their savings. In practice, the assessment is complicated because housing wealth has, for many people, become a substitute for savings and there is little question that fast house price appreciation, and acquisition of second homes (for enjoyment or renting out) have all been viewed as alternative ways of saving for retirement. With house prices starting to fall in several countries, it is unlikely that housing alone will be seen as a way of saving.

Less buoyant returns but new opportunities

Why might returns on our investments not be as high in the future as they have been in the past? Historically, the real return on equities, that is, after adjusting for inflation, has been about 6.5–7 percent per year. In the 1980s and 1990s, of course, the returns were rather higher, but previously they were lower, and the concern here is only about longer-term trends. The real return on bonds has been roughly about 2 percent per year. Of course, investors have to pay fees and charges in the course of buying, selling, and owning financial assets, so that the in-the-pocket returns would of course be a little lower than those mentioned. But leaving this aside, these historical numbers serve as a benchmark for the future. Taking into account the historical returns on equities and bonds, the average weighted real return has been about 4–4.5 percent. Some experts believe that real returns may drop by about 0.4–0.5 percent per year over the next decades. This may not seem a lot, but it is a 10 percent fall in returns regardless. Moreover, these long-run trends in real returns may be of little relevance if, for example, some years from now, retirees were to experience rising inflation at a time when they were shifting more of their assets into fixed-income savings products.

The empirical work on this subject, it should be said, is ambivalent. Much of the work suggests there is a relationship between rising average age and lower asset returns, for example, as older people have less appetite for and tolerance of risk. But the links are thought to be tenuous, at least as far as the last decades are concerned. One prominent analyst, James Poterba, argues none of the empirical findings provides strong and convincing evidence of the amount that asset prices will change as a result of population aging.[23] Another, Robin Brooks, didn't find a strong historical link between demographic factors and financial markets, drawing attention to the finding that in the United States at least, older people do continue to add to their savings for a while after retirement and then don't run them down much.[24] If that were true and also true over the next 30 to 40 years, then there should be less reason to fear negative interest rate and asset price repercussions.

As noted, all the empirical work is, by definition, based on the limited aging experienced so far. There are some reasons to be relaxed. First, the broader the mixture of financial services and systems, the more opportunity people have to save appropriately for retirement, and the more likely it is that this will act as a stabilizing force on asset prices and returns. And second, globalization could help. I shall discuss the relevance and implications of globalization in more detail in Chapter 8.

Open borders and open financial markets mean that you or your pension and life insurance providers have the opportunity to invest in a variety of foreign countries and markets. Many people may already own properties overseas or the shares of foreign companies. Institutional asset management firms certainly do, and their allocations to foreign assets have risen steadily over the last 10 to 20 years, in line with accelerating globalization. In the future, developing countries and emerging markets should be the dynamic, high growth, high return economies for the very opposite reasons to Western economies. They will be the ones with the still rapid expansion of working-age populations, even though many of them are aging very quickly, as I explore in the next chapter. But for the time being and probably until about 2030, these countries are likely to attract more and more of our savings, the returns to which should be appreciably higher than they might be in Western economies. Globalization, as I later explain, is certainly no panacea for aging societies any more than it is a godsend for all developing countries. But in the main, the world is a better-off place with it than without it, and as Western countries age, it will be to their benefit to allow globalization to evolve. If it does not, then the loss of overseas investment opportunities would, of course, be the least of our problems.

Maybe the only conclusion is that financial markets will not collapse as the boomers retire in droves, but that they may be at some risk from lower real or inflation-adjusted returns than have occurred in the past. This would of course vindicate the warning that "past returns may not be a good guide to the future." If there is a time to panic, it is not yet.

Safe as houses?

House prices, on the other hand, could and do behave quite differently from equities and other asset classes. Because of the significance of housing to people as the biggest purchase they ever make, and the most valuable asset they own, what happens to house prices is no small matter, financially, economically, or politically. It is also worth noting that housing is a totally different type of asset from anything else. It is illiquid in the sense you cannot turn it into cash easily or quickly. There are no common valuation methods that allow us to be aware of how much property is worth. Housing markets are highly fragmented, and are often distorted by property taxes, planning regulations, and social phenomena like divorce and single-parent families.

As a result of these traits, house price cycles tend to last for long periods, certainly in real terms. Consequently, the interest in housing takes on an additional twist, if for no other reason than the possibility of a most unfortunate coincidence: It is quite possible that a downward movement in the housing market, due to "normal" cyclical factors could coincide with a phase when the change in age structure begins to have a more marked impact on the supply of and demand for houses. Fewer people at the young end of the age spectrum would mean less demand for houses. The surge in retirees would imply an overhang in the supply of houses for sale. The price effects coming from a more structural source would then reinforce the consequent price effects from the cycle.

In 1989, two American authors argued that housing demand in the United States would grow more slowly in the 1990s and in the twenty-first century than at any time since 1945 and that house price performance would be the mirror image of the house price appreciation in the 1970s, when real house prices rose by about 20–30 percent.[25] They said that the reason for the latter was the bulge in the leading edge of the boomers, namely people who reached the age of 20–40 and typically the prime age for house purchase. They then suggested that as the prime age group grew older, housing demand would start to stabilize and then decline. Their prediction was that real house prices would drop by more than 40 percent between 1987 and 2007, or roughly 3 percent per year.

This pessimistic view did not materialize as the authors expected, though the demographic foundation was sound. In fact, in the United States, house prices in real terms rose by about 5 percent per year to reach their highest levels ever in 2006–07. And America was not the only country that enjoyed a housing boom or even bubble in the 1990s and in the early years of this century. Even though house prices slumped in several countries in the early 1990s, they surged almost everywhere in the following years, especially in countries such as the United Kingdom, Australia, Ireland, Spain, and even France and Italy. By 2006, the value of residential property in OECD economies, in inflation-adjusted terms, stood at its highest level since 1945, except in Germany, Japan, and Switzerland—and even in these three countries, prices were rose in the first half of 2007.

The end of this house price boom, however, became apparent in 2007 and is already leaving a nasty legacy for homeowners, especially those with mortgages. But from a demographic standpoint, the legacy will be still worse if people are obliged to carry larger mortgage debt into their retirement years and/or be forced to work for longer so as to service those mortgages. The house price boom meant that purchasers either had to borrow far more to get on to or higher up the property ladder; or they had to wait until much later in life to do so, by which time they may already have started a family and needed a bigger and more expensive home—and mortgage.

Prime-age house buyers in decline: who will buy?

Although these earlier expectations of a demographically induced weakness in house prices did not materialize, the conclusions were correct in principle. The expected stagnation—and in many countries fall—in the 20- to 44-year-old group remains as robust today as it was 20 years ago—and even more so and more imminently. This prime home-buying age group will stagnate or fall as a share of the total population or in absolute terms, encouraging us to ask just who will buy the houses that will be sold by the boomers and their children.

In Figure 6.3, the countries are ranked by the change between 2000 and 2050 in the share of the 20- to 44-year-olds in total population. The 14 countries shown together had about 1 billion 20- to 44-year-olds in 1980 and about 1.04 billion in 2000, a rise of 40 million. In the two decades to 2000, the share of 20- to 44-year-olds rose substantially in South Korea, Spain, Mexico, and Italy, and was broadly stable elsewhere, except in Japan where it dropped by 10 percent. But between 2000 and

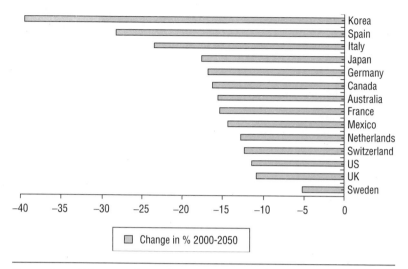

Figure 6.3   Prime-age house buyers (aged 20–44)

Source: OECD, "Aging Pyramid." (Paris) at http://www.oecd.org/dataoecd/52/31/38123085.xls.

2050, this age group will decline by about 240 million to just under 800 million, lower even than in 1980. By 2050, Sweden's share falls the least. Most countries, including Mexico, see a fall of between 10 and 17 percent, but the drop in Spain and Italy is considerably larger and the surprise tail-ender is South Korea with a near halving of its 20- to 44-year-old group.

Moreover, rates of owner-occupancy have generally been rising over the last 20 to 25 years to high levels. According to one report covering 16 countries,[26] owner-occupancy was recently over 70 percent in six countries and between 60 and 69 percent in five. The lowest rates were in Germany (42 percent) and Switzerland (35 percent). Aging does not mean specifically that owner-occupation cannot rise further, which would clearly be positive for housing markets in years to come, but for most countries the levels are already high or at all-time highs. Moreover, as the share of prime-age house purchasers falls, there is a looming likelihood of an emerging oversupply of housing. The bulge in the over-65s is hardly likely to be made up of people accumulating more property. Indeed this age group will increasingly be likely to move to smaller houses, flats, or sheltered housing or to sell outright if they move into residential care.

Last, there is also some limited evidence that house prices behave markedly less well when considering the age of homeowners. An American research report concluded that the prices of homes of those aged over 75 years had risen between 1 and 3 percent slower in real terms compared with the prices of homes of all owners.[27] The main reason cited was that older people tended to spend less time and money on refurbishment and maintenance leading to some deterioration in the quality of housing for sale. Again, this is quite under-standable. Older people have much less motivation and intent than younger people to make capital gains from the eventual sale of their houses or to trade up to larger, more expensive homes. And physical factors are certainly a strong reason why the do-it-yourself customer is typically aged 35–49 and not 65 or older.

If older people did spend more time and money on maintaining or refurbishing their houses, in theory, there might be several benefits. A higher-priced home obviously means on a personal level that, upon sale, there is more to pay for extended residential care. It also means there might be a bigger amount to pass on to children and grandchildren. There is a social benefit too because higher-valued homes yield higher property tax revenues to local authorities or to the government. So, maybe there is some mileage in having governments choose to encourage older people to make or keep their properties clean, green, and pristine.

Wealthy and healthy?

The next time you buy a house or something from a financial services company, read the small or large print that says that the past may not be a reliable guide to the future and that the prices of assets may go down as well as up. Then read it again. Financial services companies are referring to the risk you alone bear from buying something that is more risky than the cash you have in the bank, not to the consequences of aging. If they were, they might have to say that over the long term, the returns to your investments might be lower than you have experienced in the past. And further, that you might have problems selling them for gain in the future to fund retirement partly because of the more limited supply of younger-age buyers.

While there is little evidence to suggest that asset prices will go into meltdown as a result of population aging, it is nonetheless likely that the economics and politics of aging will contrive to lower the long-run return on assets. The "first principles" reason is the coming relative scarcity of labor, which should push up labor returns (wages and salaries) relative to capital returns (profits). Theoretically, this would involve a slower rise in asset prices, slower growth in dividend payments from companies, and lower overall returns. But there are scenarios in which interest rates might well end up higher on average because of inflation and because of the possible financing strains in both the personal and public sectors. And if and when these happen, asset prices would stagnate in real terms or fall.

There is no doubt that upper-income groups can fend for themselves, not having to rely on basic state pensions and publicly funded and provided healthcare. But for the bulk of families, certainly at the bottom of the income tree but also for middle-income groups too, the inadequacy of savings and or pension provision looms as a serious problem. And for most people and companies, it seems inescapable that the tax burden will rise in years to come.

If governments cannot or do not manage the age-related expenditure burden that lies ahead, the likelihood is that fiscal stress will intensify, and there is a point beyond which some countries would be vulnerable to a broad spectrum of unpleasant macroeconomic outcomes. But now, it is time to move on and consider the demography and the implications of the new powers in the global economy and of the countries in the world where most population growth is predicted to occur.

Endnotes

1   John Kenneth Galbraith, *The Age of Uncertainty*, (Boston: Houghton Mifflin, 1977).
2   For a full economic demonstration of how and why the personal savings rate has fallen and among which age groups, see Charles Yuji Horioka, "The Dissaving of the Aged Revisited: The Case of Japan," National Bureau of Economic Research, Working Paper 12351, Cambridge, Mass. (June 2006).

3 Benefits were reduced in several ways as a result of changes made in 2000, including a 5 percent cut in the earnings-related component of the pension for newly retired people, the temporary suspension of indexation of wages to pensions, a new means test for people aged 65 to 69 and the announcement of a gradual rise in the retirement age from 60 to 65 beginning in 2001. Further pension reforms were introduced in 2004.

4 The 2007 survey is expected to be published during 2008.

5 In general, 56 percent of families reported saving more than in the previous year. In families where the head was aged over 35, about 58 percent saved. Among families where the head of household was over 74, only 46 percent reported saving. The richest Americans save the most, unsurprisingly. Among the top 20 percent of income earners, 70 to 80 percent of families saved while in the bottom 40 percent, only 34 to 44 percent saved. The strongest reason for saving given by all families was retirement (34.7 percent), followed by "liquidity" (30 percent) or emergency, "rainy day" money.

6 European Central Bank, "Macroeconomic Implications of Demographic Developments in the Euro Area." Occasional Paper No. 51 (August 2006).

7 OECD, "Pensions At A Glance," Paris (June 2007).

8 David M. Cutler, James M. Poterba, Louise M. Sheiner, and Lawrence H. Summers, "An Aging Society: Opportunity or Challenge," Brookings Papers On Economic Activity (1990:1).

9 Ronald D. Lee, "Global Population Aging and Its Economic Consequences," (American Enterprise Institute Press: Washington, DC, 2007).

10 OECD, "Fiscal Implications of Aging: Projections of Age-Related Spending." *Economic Outlook* 69, Paris (September 2001).

11 The International Monetary Fund has published rather different estimates for the countries of the Group of Seven (G7), suggesting an average rise in age-related spending of about 4.2 percent of GDP to 2050. While this estimate applies to a much smaller sample of countries, there are also some differences in definitions and calculations compared with the OECD numbers used here. See, for example, International Monetary Fund, *World Economic Outlook* (April 2007), Chapter 1, pp 24–27.

12 A Ponzi scheme, known widely in financial and credit circles, takes its name from one Charles Ponzi, an Italian immigrant to the United States. In the 1920s, he devised a policy to profit from anomalies in the market for international postage stamps. He was able to offer big returns to one group of investors but only by borrowing more money from the next group and so on. This system of borrowing ever-greater amounts of money from new investors to pay off existing investors works so long as the underlying price of the asset continues to rise. Once it stops rising or falls, the scheme collapses as people want their money back.

13 Testimony before the Committee on the Budget, US House of Representatives, March 2, 2005.

14 Lawrence J. Kotlikoff and Christian Hagist, "Who's Going Broke? Comparing Healthcare Costs in ten OECD Countries," NBER Working Paper 118833 (December 2005).

15 Jennifer Jenson, "Health Care Spending and the Aging of the Population," Congressional Research Service Report for Congress, Order Code RS22619 (March 13, 2007).

16 CT stands for computerized tomography. This type of scanner is a special type of X-ray machine that emits beams rather than X-rays and delivers more detailed images for diagnostic purposes.

17 The 2007 Annual Report of the Board of Trustees of the Federal Old-Age and Survivors Insurance and Federal Disability Insurance Trust Funds, Washington, DC, 2007.

18 In a different analytical context, Ronald D. Lee (2007) has suggested that to maintain current federal programs on spending for the elderly, while balancing the overall federal budget, benefit levels would have to be cut by 30 percent at each age relative to the position in 2005, taxes would have to be raised by 38 percent, or there would have to be some combination of the two, given what we know about the change in age structure up to 2030. The further out in time you go, of course, the bigger the numbers get—and for European countries, where aging is more severe and publicly funded programs are more generous, the adjustments to spending and taxation might have to be larger still.

19 Jagadeesh Gokhale and Kent Smetters, "Do The Markets Care about the $2.4 Trillion US Deficit?" *Financial Analysts Journal* 63, No. 2 (March/April 2007).

20 www.oecd.org/asktheeconomists.

21 For a comprehensive discussion about how financial burdens related to aging societies are underestimated and effectively distributed between today's and tomorrow's taxpayers, see Laurence J. Kotlikoff and Scott Burns, *The Coming Generational Storm* (Cambridge, MA: MIT Press, 2004).

22 *Daily Express* "4,000 people a week trying to leave UK" (August 5, 2007).

23 National Bureau of Economic Research, "The Impact of Population Aging on Financial Markets," September 2004.

24 Robin Brooks, "Demographic Change and Asset Prices," prepared for G-20 Workshop on Demography and Financial Markets, Sydney (July 23–25, 2006).

25 Gregory N. Mankiw and David N. Weil, "The Baby Boom, The Baby Bust and The Housing Market," *Regional Science and Urban Economics* 19 (1989): 235–258.

26 Bank for International Settlements, "Housing finance in the global financial market." CGFS Papers No. 26 (January 2006).

27 David T. Rodda and Satyendra Patrabanush, "The Relationship Between Homeowner Age and House Price Appreciation." Abt Associates Inc., Cambridge, MA. (March 30, 2007).

Chapter 7

Waiting in the wings: aging in emerging and developing nations

> *Unlike plagues of the dark ages or contemporary diseases we do not understand, the modern plague of overpopulation is soluble by means we have discovered and with resources we posses. What is lacking is not sufficient knowledge of the solution but universal consciousness of the gravity of the problem and education of the billions who are its victim.*
> —Martin Luther King, Jr., award acceptance speech, May 1966.

The implications of population aging in emerging and developing countries are barely publicized and less well understood than those for advanced countries. This is largely because most of them have not yet reached the point at which demographic change threatens their development and economic prospects. But they are heading there, and for the same reasons—falling fertility and rising longevity. The most significant challenge facing the developing world is the even greater lack of preparedness for aging than is the case in industrial countries. This is understandable. For most developing countries, the dependency ratio of older people to the working-age population is still declining because the latter is still rising quickly enough. With some exceptions, notably China, it is not until the 2030s, and after, that the working-age population will start to decline, resulting in a sharp increase in dependency thereafter.

Not all developing countries and emerging markets will face growing populations. Russia, and most of the countries of eastern Europe and the Balkans will experience a fall of between 13 and 35 percent in population size in the next 40 years or so. The population of most of the Caribbean islands will decline too. As we have noted, China's population will start to fall between 2030 and 2035, as will Thailand's after about 2040. By and large, though, the populations of most developing countries will continue to expand, if at slower rates of growth, the bulk of it occurring in sub-Saharan Africa and the Middle East.

There will also be marked differences in the working-age population numbers among developing countries. In China and South Africa, for example, the working-age population is currently close to a turning point. South Africa's working-age population is barely rising now and is expected to contract slightly after 2015–20, before rising again modestly after 2030. This is almost exclusively because of HIV/AIDS, the incidence of which is assumed to get no worse now and gradually to lessen. Of course, this assumption may prove off the mark. But in China's case, other factors have contrived to bring the 15- to 64-year-old age group to the point of an early peak. From about 2010–12 onwards, China's working-age population is predicted to decline, slowly at first, and then quite rapidly after 2030. In other major developing countries, there is no such alarm. In India, Malaysia, and Turkey, the growth of the working-age population is set to continue for another 40 years or more, although at steadily slowing rates. By 2045–50, growth will have all but stopped. In Latin America, Chile will be one of the first countries to experience a fall in working-age population from about 2030, followed by Mexico from about 2035, and then Argentina and Brazil after about 2040.

In the meantime, the decline in dependency ratios will continue to pay the so-called demographic dividend in the form of higher rates of economic growth, income, and savings. Notwithstanding the serious credit crunch and economic slowdown in Western countries that began in 2007-08, the rich world will benefit over time from lucrative export markets and attractive returns in equity and other markets in developing countries. The high rates of savings will be reflected in relatively strong balance of payments positions, which, in turn, mean that developing countries will recycle financial capital back to industrialized countries. The developing world as a whole will continue to enjoy the benefits of an expanding labor supply for about another 20 to 25 years, but it is not too early at all to pay attention to the speed with which many countries are aging and what this implies.

Aging faster than rich countries

While the proportion of over-65s in industrialized countries took almost 50 years to double to its current rate of about 15 percent, this age group in most developing countries will double in just over 20 years. In 2005, the over-65s represented about 6 percent of the population in Asia and Latin America and just over 3 percent in Africa. By 2030, the Asian and Latin American proportions will have almost doubled before rising to 17.5–18.5 percent by 2050. The countries of the Middle East, defined to include Turkey and several central Asian republics, will show a similar pattern. For example, the over-65s who now account for 4.5 percent of the population will double their share by 2035 (9 percent) and then triple it by 2050 (13.4 percent). Africa is aging much more slowly, the over-65s doubling as a proportion only by 2050.

The main position can be seen in Table 7.1. It shows the expansion in the numbers of older citizens, defined a little more broadly to include those aged over 60. The global forecast for 2050 is nearly 2 billion, nearly three times as large as it was in 2006, but the bulk of this growth is expected to occur in the developing world. Its share of the world's over-60s will grow from 70 percent to just over 88 percent.

So, although the over-60s will represent a much larger proportion of the population in more developed countries, the developing world in 2050 will have an age structure much like the developed world today. Put another way, today's over-60s in the developing world are roughly twice the number of those in developed countries. By 2030, they will be three times and by 2050, four times as numerous. China has 144 million people aged over 60, roughly 11 percent of its population. By 2050, it is expected to have 438 million—more numerous than

Table 7.1 Here come the over-60s

	Over-60s (millions)			Percent of population			Change 2006–2030		Change 2006–2050	
	2006	2030	2050	2006	2030	2050	million	percent	million	percent
Developed economies	248	363	400	20	29	32	115	46	52	61
Less developed	440	1,014	1,568	8	14	20	574	230	1,128	256
Least developed	40	89	171	5	7	10	49	222	131	328
World	688	1,377	1,968	11	16	22	689	200	1,280	186

Source: United Nations Population Division, Population Aging 2006.

the entire population of the United States at that time and representing 31 percent of China's population, compared with America's 27 percent. India, by contrast, has 85 million over-60s, or roughly 7.5 percent of its population. By 2050, Indian over-60s will number about 335 million or 20 percent of the population.

The speed with which developing countries are aging will have material financial consequences. Industrialized countries have had a long time to accumulate wealth, and industrial and social infrastructure, build institutions, and realize high levels of income. It is against this backdrop that they are now on the verge of experiencing the challenges and consequences of aging. Developing countries, on the other hand, are going to encounter rising median age, rapidly growing numbers of elderly citizens, and eventually sharply rising dependency ratios at much lower levels of income and development.

Most have rather immature or limited social and pension insurance systems, and many have stressed or primitive healthcare systems. They can, of course, hope that fast economic growth over the next 30 years or so will pay for accelerated development in old-age and healthcare systems. As things stand today, however, "growing old before they get rich" seems the apt description. If low income, social stress, and poverty prevent them from adopting policies to address aging now, then aging itself will prove a severe drag on their development when it arrives.

It is probable that in many emerging markets, rising levels of prosperity and the evolution of a larger middle class will be associated with a shift in healthcare policies from communicable to chronic and noncommunicable illness and disability (assuming that the incidence of HIV/AIDS gets no worse). In many countries, though, especially the poorest, healthcare tends to be available mainly in cities, whereas it is in rural areas that older people live. Their access to healthcare is also limited by inferior literacy, poor infrastructure, and transport as well as poverty.

Demographic dividend and dependency

For the most part, though, developing countries can expect to continue to enjoy their "demographic dividend" for a good few years yet. Emerging market giants such as China, India, Brazil,

Turkey, Mexico, and Argentina can expect expanding labor supply and rising urban working populations to continue to support strong rates of economic growth and social development. Most people would include Russia as an emerging market giant too—but Russia's demographic profile is so poor, by comparison, that it doesn't seem appropriate, in this sense, to put it in the same category. Russia's extraordinary economic growth and development, especially since the crisis in 1998 when it defaulted on its external debt, has of course been a source of much satisfaction to both Russians and to external investors. It is important to bear in mind though that the success of these last several years has been based largely on Russia's immense energy and basic resource endowments and the sustained rise in commodity prices—not on demographic factors at all, which if anything, have been pulling Russia in the wrong direction. Quite how this balance of forces will swing in years to come remains to be seen, of course, and I will elaborate on this later.

The key element of the demographic dividend is, for the time being at least, falling fertility and the effect this is having on lowering the overall dependency burden of both younger and older members of society on the economically productive population. Closer to the middle of this century, falling fertility rates, if sustained, will change the demographic dividend into what we might call a demographic deficit, much as it is for industrialized societies today. The bulge in the 15- to 64-year-old group will shift up, and more people will reach retirement age or the limits of physical labor just as the flow of new workers starts to wane as a consequence of lower fertility rates. For the time being, though, lower overall dependency ratios should continue to yield beneficial economic results.

The overall picture can be seen clearly in Figure 7.1 that shows youth and old-age dependency ratios for Asia, Latin America and the Caribbean, and Africa, compared with industrialized countries. The overall height of the bars measures combined dependency, the two shades representing young and old-age dependency.

In Asia and Latin America, total dependency ratios are still declining and are expected to do so until the late 2020s. The

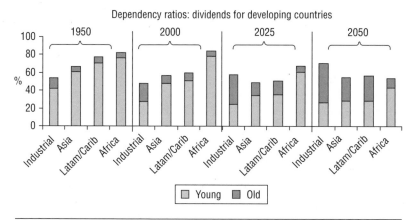

Figure 7.1   Dependency ratios

Source: United Nations Population Division.

patterns are identical to the earlier ones of industrialized countries with falling youth dependency the main driver. But Figure 7.1 indicates clearly that between 2025 and 2050, a meaningful change will be occurring as rising old-age dependency more than offsets the more restrained decline in youth dependency. African countries are predicted to experience a similar overall pattern but because it is anticipated that youth dependency will continue to decline until the middle of the century and beyond, total dependency will carry on falling. This could imply that the prospects for successful African development may brighten and more because of "made in Africa" factors than anything to do with aid initiatives, charities, or celebrities in rich countries.[1] Will the demographic dividend then tend to continue to favor developing countries in general and the poorest of them in particular?

This is a crucial question now and will become increasingly relevant to developing countries and emerging markets in the next 10 to 20 years. The answer, based on historical evidence, is that a fall in the total dependency ratios is a necessary but by no means a sufficient condition for sustainable and fast economic and social enrichment. From Figure 7.1, it is clear that Asia and Latin America have had and will continue to have, comparable overall dependency ratios, and the youth-old age mix also looks quite similar over time. To date, however, the economic, social, and educational achievement records have been firmly in favor of Asia.

Asian strengths and weaknesses

Asia's critical success factors to date, aside from the demographic dividend itself, have been identified in education, flexible labor markets, openness to trade and foreign investment, and well developed financial markets. Growing access to, and improvements in, the quality of education has been partly the result of investment in the sector, financed by the high savings ratios that are typical of "dividend" countries. More flexible labor markets have allowed the region's economies to absorb growing numbers of workers more easily and allowed workers to move across jobs and regions. Developed financial markets have allowed the region's economies to harness and mobilize the savings of the expanding working-age population successfully for productive investment. This is not, however, an unmitigated success story.

Despite the fact that they have experienced some of the most impressive growth rates in the world in the last 10 years, unemployment has still tended to rise, especially among younger workers. According to the Asian Development Bank, youths aged 15–24 in Asia make up 25 percent of the working-age population but 50 percent of the unemployed. In the next 10 to 20 years, as working-age populations expand and urbanization brings more and more rural workers to the cities, Asia, including (and maybe especially) China and India, is going to have to pay particular attention to job creation and to the circumstances of domestic, as opposed to export growth.

Managing urban growth will remain a major issue along with rural-urban income and wage inequalities, job creation, and the fuller provision of social and healthcare facilities for the urban population. Asia boasts some of the finest, most interesting, and modern cities in the world. The parts of these and other cities that tourists tend not to see are home to nearly 600 million slum-dwellers, or roughly half the world's total.

They are the victims of excessive growth in the labor supply in urban areas, have little in the way of social and income protection, and are the most exposed to poor social infrastructure, pollution, and congestion. Even nonslum urban residents splinter into the masses and a core of highly educated, healthier, richer citizens. Literacy rates lag badly behind in rural areas, where urban migrants of course originate. In poorer countries, such as Bangladesh, communicable diseases in urban areas are as common as they are in rural areas, because of poor sanitation and housing and health infrastructure as well as low levels of financial and technical support.

The thorny issue of adequate social insurance for aging populations is not yet seen as a major problem.[2] The effects of pension spending in the next 10 to 20 years are not considered especially onerous—in part because of limited coverage and low replacement rates. However, the impact is likely to be greatest in the cases of South Korea and Taiwan, followed by Singapore and Hong Kong, and then China. In the next one or two years, however, even that impact is rather modest.[3] It only starts to worsen between 2010 and 2025, intensifying from 2035. The impact on China's social insurance system is estimated at about 2 percent of GDP between 2010 and 2025, growing to 5 percent of GDP in the following 10 years. So there's a pretty big window—roughly 10 to 20 years—through which Asian countries can try to remedy or prepare their social insurance systems for the next 40 to 50 years; but no one should imagine this to be either inevitable or successful, and we will doubtless learn in years to come of more alarming statistics pointing to the failures of public policy with regard to pension and healthcare provision for Asia's elderly.

Gender discrimination

Last, Asian countries have a particular demographic problem in the form of the economic and social costs of gender discrimination.[4] The United Nations says that discrimination against women in Asia has obstructed their participation in the labor force, lowered their productivity, and wasted valuable resources. It noted that there was a gap of between 30 and 40 percent between the workforce participation rates of men and women and that female participation rates of less than 40 percent were common in India, while they were about 50–55 percent in Malaysia, Indonesia, the Philippines, and Singapore. At the other extreme, China had a female participation rate of 70 percent. The costs to Asian economies (based on a study of seven countries between 2000 and 2004, accounting for two-thirds of Asia's output and three-quarters of its population) of gender discrimination were estimated at between US$42 billion and US$47 billion per year (excluding Japan, which alone would have recorded costs of US$37 billion a year). The biggest costs were incurred in India, Malaysia, and Indonesia.

In addition to this, the United Nations estimated that the costs of discrimination against women in the education system accounted for up to US$30 billion a year. The exclusion from education of so many females for largely cultural reasons was seen as a critical shortcoming. The costs came in the form of lower productivity, both because of the exclusion of women from work and also because less educated men might be selected for jobs that better educated women could do. The study also noted that a mere 1 percent increase in secondary school enrollments for girls would be associated with a 0.23 percent per annum increase in economic growth. A big effort today in this sphere could have increasingly beneficial effects in 20 to 30 years' time, when labor force growth in Asia stops, or starts to decline.

It is not possible to say with any confidence how gender discrimination will change in the future. That it should isn't the point. It is a question of whether it will. The economic commentator Will Hutton estimated that Asia suffers from a deficiency of 100 million women as a result of the use of scans to detect early the sex of unborn infants and of consequent abortions.[5] This prediction, originally made in 1990 by the economist Amartya Sen, was later revised to about 60 million and attributed by some to the proliferation of Hepatitis B, which apparently tilts sex at birth toward baby boys. Regardless of the numbers and the causes, however, the gender gap and gender discrimination are real and of great significance. Apart from the moral and economic issues, Hutton also points to the consequences of the social, criminal, woman-trafficking, and political leanings and inclinations of dispossessed, displaced young men with no or little prospect of finding a partner. In China by 2020, it is estimated that 10 percent of men between the ages of 20 and 45 may not be able to find a wife. China, of course, isn't unique in this regard, and similar developments are likely to occur in parts of India.

China—Middle Kingdom, middle age

The popular perception of China—a rapidly growing emerging market expanding at 10 percent per year with regional power status and aspiring global power credentials—is not misplaced. It was, not so long ago, a socialist, wholly centrally planned economy, closed to the outside world, dogged by inefficiency and vulnerable to famine. In the Great Leap Forward of 1959–61, some 30 million people are thought to have died prematurely and another 33 million babies were either lost or postponed. Today it is a mainly state-run market economy that is either beacon or competitor or both, more or less integrated into the global economy, one of the most dynamic societies in the world and rapidly catching up to Western economies. In one crucial respect, however, China is an outlier in the pathology of great economic and political powers. It is aging rapidly, probably faster than any other country in the world, and its working-age population will start to decline around the same time as in Germany. China's demographic dividend is pretty much exhausted. This is bound to have significant implications for China's economy, for its society, and for public policy.

China's median age of 33 years is far above India's 24 years and Vietnam's 25, and not so far behind Australia's 37 and South Korea's 35. By 2020, China's median age of 38 will only be slightly lower than South Korea and on a par with Australia. By 2050, at nearly 45 years, China's median age will be the highest in Asia, except for South Korea and Japan. China's old-age dependency ratio of 11 percent is lower than South Korea,

(13 percent) and Australia, and New Zealand's (19 percent) but it will grow to 17 percent by 2020 and almost 40 percent by 2050. At midcentury, measured this way, China will be five years older than the United States and about the same age as northern European countries.

In fact, between 2005 and 2025 more than 70 percent of China's population increase of 133 million (from 1.31 billion to 1.44 billion) will be in the over-65 age group. Between 2025 and 2050, China's population is expected to drop by close to 40 million, but the number of over-65s will rise by a further 136 million. By 2025 China will have nearly a quarter of the world's over-65s, and by 2050 it will be home to a quarter of the world's over-80s. It is true that a relatively large proportion of over-65s stay on at work, but this is predominantly manual and agricultural labor, and, not surprisingly, their productivity tends to drop away very quickly. In the future, China will have to pay more attention to both the social security of rural citizens and to the kind of work and workplace that older urban citizens may want, and the skills and education they will need to be of value.

One-child policy

China's well-known one-child policy, introduced in 1980 when 80 percent of Chinese lived on the land, compared with 60 percent nowadays, has clearly been a significant factor in lowering China's fertility rate and accelerating its aging process. Chinese Communist Party leader Deng Xiaoping introduced the policy at a time when it was believed that the population was growing at an unsustainable rate, that China risked impoverishment as a result, and that strong initiatives were required to help China break away from being one of the poorest nations on Earth. It is somewhat ironic that despite long-standing and widespread criticism of this policy, China's fertility rate today is higher than in Italy, Greece, Japan, Russia, Hong Kong, and Germany, but the intrusion of government in this way, into the reproductive decisions of couples, has been and remains unique. In 2006, the policy was reconfirmed as "basic national policy," but the authorities are no longer quite as rigid as in the past, now that they are attempting to find solutions to aging and rising old-age dependency. One factor they might have a real problem with, though, is trying to correct the gender imbalance. Partly for cultural reasons and partly because of the one-child policy, China has an extreme ratio of about 120 boys for every 100 girls. The global average is about 104 per 100 girls. Left unchecked, it is possible that by 2020, there might be 35–40 million Chinese men of marriage-age, mainly in rural areas, unable to find a bride. As in other places where gender imbalance has intensified, the excess of males is spawning deep social problems including a booming sex industry, a rising incidence of rape, and the abduction and sale of young girls as wives.

To a significant extent, authority over the policy rests with provinces and cities, and some have relaxed it. In fact in 2007, the vice-director of the National Population and Family Planning Commission, Wang Guoqiang, stated that China no longer followed a standard one-child policy. That is, the policy tends to apply more to urban dwellers and those living in the developed and more affluent coastal provinces. Elsewhere, for example, couples whose first child is a girl are allowed to have a second child, as are parents who are single children. Nevertheless, a system of rewards and punishments remains in force. Couples with one child get a certificate, entitling them to benefits such as cash bonuses, longer maternity leave, better childcare, better schools, and preferential housing assignments.

On the other side, while the more coercive means of forced abortions and sterilizations are no longer sanctioned, financial penalties are common. In fact, it was reported in 2007 that in the southwestern province of Guangxi, local population control enforcement had resulted in violent clashes between police and residents. The incidents began with mandatory health checks for women and, according to newspaper reports, obliging women pregnant with a second child without approval to abort their fetuses.[6] The local authorities had also imposed fines, the reports said, of RMB500–70,000 (US$65–9,000) on violations of birth control measures since 1980.

One of the main effects of the one-child policy and the other factors that have contributed to China's low fertility rate has been the steady rise in older women who have borne no sons. Currently, it is estimated that about 10 percent of women aged over 60 have had no sons. This is rather important in a society where social insurance is limited and weak, and where filial support is a long-standing part of cultural life, especially in rural areas. Nicholas Eberstadt has drawn attention to the coming "son deficit" facing prospective retirees over the next 20 years.[7] Because of local traditions, according to which sons are normally relied upon to support aged parents, he believes this deficit will become socially critical. By 2025, about 30 percent of Chinese women aged 60 will have had no sons. For tens of millions of people this promises growing hardship or the necessity of having to labor well into old age to support themselves. Since about four-fifths of China's elderly workers are employed in agriculture, where work requires stamina and muscle-power, their prospects in particular look rather poor.

Even with a slightly more relaxed interpretation of what is still a basic policy nationally, though, China's demographic picture isn't going to change much. China's employed labor force is going to start falling between 2009 and 2011, and its working-age population will peak around 2015. After that, it will fall by 10 million by 2025 and by nearly 140 million by 2050. China will have 300 million pensioners by 2025 and nearly 450 million by 2050. This means that while there are 6.5 workers per pensioner today, there will be 3.4 workers per pensioner by 2025, and less than two by 2050.

For a while, it will remain possible for China's urban workforce to keep growing as a result of migration from the countryside, but the government is concerned about some of the social and congestion issues this is raising, and it adopted policies in 2007, for the next five years, in which it wants to redress the imbalances between rural and urban expansion and incomes. There are other reasons why migration may not be rocket fuel for the urban labor force in years to come. Most migrant labor is young—and the young age cohort is exactly where the largest declines in population are going to occur in the next decades.

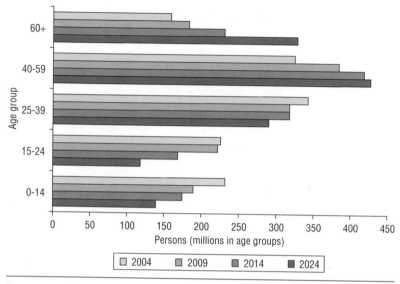

Figure 7.2   China: Changing size of age groups
Source: Global Demographics.

Running out of cheap labor

The demographic projections for China over the next 16 years, let alone the next 40, indicate clearly that the younger age groups, up to 39, are predicted to decline especially sharply while the over-40s and over-60s show vigorous increases (see Figure 7.2).

Will this sharp change in the structure of China's population lead to labor shortages, much as Western countries will? On the face of it, the answer for a while at least should be "no," because a country with 450 million people of working age living in rural areas should be able to draw on this pool of labor for quite some time. That said, this is a bit of an oversimplification. There is a floating migrant population of between 80 and 120 million. Most of the women in this pool are young, not least because the simplest manufacturing companies tend to hire mainly women aged 18–26. They are seen as less troublesome, more dexterous, and willing to work longer hours. Many men end up on construction sites, and one could imagine that the typical age might be 25–35. It isn't surprising then, that a large proportion of migrants go back to the countryside in their late twenties or early thirties, where the inducements include more equitable land distribution, fulfilling the role of parental care, especially if the migrant is an only child, and, of course, the chance of receiving lifetime gifts or inheritance bequests.

For China and for the world economy, however, the main issue in the next five to 10 years is not about whether China will run out of workers, but whether it will run out of cheap workers. For many years, most of China's rural migrants, being young and single, have been willing to travel far, work six- or seven-day shifts, and live in overcrowded urban dormitories where they have formed a cheap "reserve army" of labor willing to work for poor and relatively stable wages. But now, because of the one-child policy and other demographic changes, the pool of young rural labor, aged about 18–30, is starting to decline—and this is putting upward pressure on the wage rates paid to rural migrants. Rural migrants typically earned about RMB400–600 per month (US$50 or a bit more at the then prevailing exchange rate) until about 2001, but the average is now running at or above RMB1,000 a month. In effect, this means that rural migrant workers have not only had bigger wage increases in the last three years than for over a decade, but that their annual increments have been running at more than 12 percent a year.

Jonathan Anderson, at UBS Investment Bank, has argued that the math for China in this respect is compelling.[8] First, the supply of young rural workers, aged 20–29, is starting to drop below 120 million and will halve by 2030. Second, they aren't going to be replaced because today's 10- to 19-year-old group is declining just as quickly. Third, more than 100 million migrants are already working off the farm, and they have to "reboot" or expand every five to six years as some migrants return to the countryside and as urban needs increase. In this sense, China is running out of workers who must or want to work at rock-bottom wages. The implication, that demographic changes are pushing up wages in China, is therefore one of enduring significance for the living standards of

Chinese workers and especially rural migrant workers. It is also of long-term significance for the cost structure of Chinese companies and the prices they charge to both domestic and foreign customers, unlike other more cyclical or temporary factors that may influence costs and prices.

More expensive labor may, of course, tend to push up China's inflation in coming years, and many will worry that this will, in turn, push up global inflation since the fall in the prices of China's exports—from toys to textiles and advanced technology goods—will be reversed. In fact, after falling almost continuously between 1998 and 2004, the prices of China's exports have since started increasing. This does not turn China overnight into a source, let alone a major source, of global inflation. There is a myriad of other factors to consider, including trends in China's productivity, its exchange rate, and its influence on oil and basic material prices. But it is an indication that things are changing in China. And to the extent that China faces more inflationary headwinds in the future, the global economy should also be prepared for a rather less benign inflationary environment as well.

Economic consequences

Gradually, as shortages of cheap, and possibly skilled, labor become more widespread and as the old-age dependency ratio rises more quickly, economic growth will slow. Jonathan Anderson has estimated that since the economic reforms of the 1960s, the fall in the dependency ratio has contributed between 15 and 25 percent of China's economic growth and accounted for between 5 and 21 percent of the country's savings rate.[9] Clearly as the dependency ratio rises, these contributions will go into reverse, though it is not easy to estimate the effects. It is enough to note that the effects are likely to start appearing soon after 2010–11 and that they could knock 2 percent per year off China's long-term growth rate over coming decades. Further, some of the support for China's productivity growth might also fade over the medium- to longer-term as a direct result of aging, lower savings rates, and lower rates of investment growth.

Consider that between 1980 and 2003, as China's total dependency ratio fell from 67 percent to 43 percent, the resulting demographic dividend accounted for about a quarter of the increase in the growth of GDP per head. As this dividend becomes exhausted by roughly 2015 and the dependency ratio starts rising again toward about 50 percent by 2030 and 64 percent by 2050, savings are predicted to decline.[10]

Moreover, rising urban wage costs and lower growth rates could impair China's competitiveness, especially at the lower end of the (labor-intensive) manufacturing food chain. In that event, China's magnetic effect on global foreign direct investment flows, for example, could suffer. In 2006, according to preliminary data from the United Nations Conference on Trade and Development, China attracted about 5.7 percent of worldwide foreign direct investment, or about US$70 billion, from an estimated global total of US$1.23 trillion. This was the fourth-largest inflow after the United States, United Kingdom, and France, but since these flows (in 2005–06) had been boosted significantly by the record boom in mergers and acquisitions, it would be better to consider China's position in 2004 when its share was about 10 percent and second only to the United States. In other words, given China's demographic profile and without changes in population policies, China will have to improve its investment and competitiveness environment, perhaps via more significant financial, legal, and institutional reforms. Failing that, though, China's growth rate might look quite pedestrian several years from now.

The point was made earlier about how rapid aging in developing countries is occurring at much lower levels of income and development than has been the case in industrial countries. China's current income per head[11] is about US$6,600. The United Kingdom and Japan reached China's current median age in 1970 and 1980, respectively with income per head at about US$10,000 and US$9,000. The United States had income per head of US$23,000 in 1990 when its median age was the same as China's today. South Korea had China's current median age in 2000 when its income per head was about US$16,000. There's no question that China's economy will continue to grow quickly, but pressures to moderate the pace of expansion and pay more attention to the quality and impact of expansion are quite widely discussed against a background of rapid aging, rural-urban tensions and inequalities, and the effects and costs of addressing climate change.

Growing social policy agenda

China's major problems arising from aging are liable to be social and political, rather than economic—for the time being at least. Because adequate social support and affordable healthcare are in short supply, rising discontent in China's aging, urbanized workforce is quite likely. Because most people in China still do demanding physical work, either on farms or in cities, getting older will probably entail growing hardship. Because of rising incomes and a change toward Western consumption patterns, China is already experiencing rising demand for healthcare because of dietary changes, leading to obesity, hypertension, and smoking-related illness.

An editorial in the *British Medical Journal*, for example, noted that it was not even China's 20 percent share of the world's 1 billion overweight or obese people that caught the eye as much as the speed with which these conditions were growing.[12] The number of overweight and obese children aged 7–18 years increased by 28 times between 1985 and 2000. About 17 percent of the population is thought to be overweight or obese, which is a lot lower than in the West, but China is only just developing the bad aspects of modern life associated with these conditions. Last but not least, because of economic growth and the drive to realize a better quality of life and national economic strength, the effects of environmental pollution are also contributing to rising demand for healthcare. It is thought that two-thirds of China's population live in cities with bad or very bad air quality and that three-quarters of the water in China's seven most important rivers is unfit to drink. This is quite apart from China's shrinking water tables and drying rivers. Remember that China, with 20 percent of the world's population, has only about 7 percent of its arable land

and a long history of alternating periods of feast and famine, flooding in the south, and desertification in the north.

On top of all these things, finding the funds to address pension and healthcare needs for an aging Chinese society will be demanding, but by no means impossible, partly because the coverage and benefits of both systems are low—at least for now—and partly because China has much of its wealth tucked away in very uncommercial places. The official retirement age is 60 for men (50–55 for women) though the actual national average is just a little over 51, considerably below the world average, but China has no unified national pension system. Pensions are managed mainly at the provincial level, where funds are held in accounts at state-owned commercial banks. While the numbers participating in basic pension schemes have risen in recent years, the beneficiaries are overwhelmingly concentrated among urban workers and their families. As Professor Robert Ash points out, in 2005 only 43.6 million rural residents—or 9 percent of the total rural employed population—were covered, compared with about 50 percent for urban residents.[13]

The precise scale of China's pension deficits is not known but the difference between pension assets and liabilities has been estimated at between two and three trillion dollars—or close to 115 percent of GDP. Looked at another way, Ash notes that 2006 pension payouts to 46 million retirees, for example, had cost the government RMB500 billion, or roughly 2.4 percent of GDP. Yet if all those aged 60 and above had been paid an equivalent pension, the payout would have been three times as large. This can only become more costly and troublesome, given that the number of retirees (at the current official retirement age) will rise to more than 420 million over the next 40 years. The time to worry, is now—and not in 15 years, even if the ratio of retirees to working-age people only starts to rise more sharply then. However, this all depends on the working-age population growing as demographers predict in the next 10–12 years.

Pension deficits could be reduced by a variety of measures, and in any event it is not as though the People's Republic doesn't have wealth from which it could derive significant returns. Income from investment, changes to the pension system, higher taxes, the sale of state assets, and ultimately higher government borrowing could all be deployed over time. China owned about US$1.75 trillion in foreign exchange assets at the end of June 2008, and this pot was growing at about US$30 billion a month, thanks to China's continuing large trade surpluses and capital inflows. Most of the money sits in very low yielding US Treasury bonds, but the government has also set up a new agency (China Investment Corporation), with funds transferred from the central bank's reserves, with the task of investing them to realize higher returns. The initial size of the fund of about US$200 billion will doubtless grow over time. This appeared to be one of the first and most significant changes in the management of China's foreign exchange assets as the country resolved that they should in fact be managed in the long-run interests of the country. What better deserving cause, for example, than helping to finance, in part, the consequences of China's populous and aging society? That said, China's current and future pension liabilities constitute an exceptional charge, especially on what is still basically a poor country.

In any event, although national savings and wealth can pay bills in the future, no such solutions exist for the social, family, care, and kinship dislocations arising from the one-child policy; the gross distortion in the sex ratio; the high levels of female mortality at young ages; and the extremes in rural-urban living and population conditions. None of these will go away any time soon, and they will probably become more important in the next decade or two. On current trends, the uneven economic performance of China's cities and coastal regions, relative to the countryside, will exact a macabre backlash. In 20 years, China's urban population will be as old as that of Japan or Italy today with 20 percent or more of the population aged over 65, while in rural China, this won't happen until 2050.[14] Just when China needs the savings of its middle-aged citizens, the "haves" in the cities may be starting to run them down and the "have-nots" in the countryside didn't have much anyway.

India and its human capital

India's arrival on the global economic scene in recent years, and its achievement of almost Chinese-style economic growth rates, has been remarkable. In 1947, when India achieved independence, its population was about 350 million, life expectancy was about 29 years, and the country was desperate for food and financial aid. Today, it has over one billion people, life expectancy is 65 years, and it exports wheat. For decades, the country's growth rate was very ordinary, rarely straying far from an underlying 3 percent annual rate and often weaker or negative. At the beginning of 2007, the Indian economy was growing at over 9 percent.

India is widely recognized as one of the emerging market giants in the world. It is not a manufacturing power such as China, nor an energy power such as Russia. Instead it is a services power, with service-producing industries accounting for more than half of GDP. These industries include information technology, banking, finance, media, and entertainment. It is in fact ideally positioned for the world's twenty-first-century information economy: English language is common, labor is cheap, and its many well-educated people are steadily being incorporated into the global economy directly via India's own corporations and also indirectly via the outsourcing phenomenon. For India this is a US$25 billion business, employing over 1 million people and contributing about 5 percent to GDP.

All of that said, India is still classified as a low-income country with income per head estimated at about US$730 measured normally and US$3,500 in terms of purchasing power parity (based on the idea that, adjusted for long-run exchange rate values, a basket of goods should cost the same everywhere). About a quarter of the population is thought to be living at or below, the poverty line, only about half its roads are paved, hundreds of villages barely have ready access to drinking water, and there is widespread malnourishment, especially among children. The literacy rate is relatively high at 61 percent, and primary school enrollments are very high, but 40 percent of primary school children drop out of school before the age of 10. Sanitation is often poor, and overall healthcare provision is low. These constitute the darker side of India's current global status.

The contrast between what India has achieved in the last 10 to 20 years and its integration into the world of technology and information alongside the existence of poverty and deprivation give cause for hope and worry at the same time. It is possible that over the long term, India's growth and prosperity prospects are better than those of China and other countries in east Asia, not least because of its youthful demographic characteristics and the suitability of younger people to the tech world. In addition, India's total dependency ratio is still falling and will continue to do so for a couple of decades at least.

An Asian America?

India's relatively youthful demographic features certainly make for a sharp distinction with those of China and lend much support to those who believe that India might even be the new China. India's population is second only to that of China, but India's fertility rate is twice as high (about three children per woman), and it is just a matter of time before India's population catches up, in about 2025, and then surpasses China.

India's median age is just less than 24 years, and this is projected to rise to about 30 years in 2025 and 38.6 years in 2050. So, there is no escape from aging in India either, but the process is not happening nearly as quickly as in China. The great advantage that India will enjoy, regionally and globally, lies in its current youthfulness and the implications for the working-age population (or labor supply) in the future. About a third of India's population is aged under 14 years, some 54 percent under 24, and only about 5 percent over 65. The population aged 15–64, currently estimated to be in the region of 680 million (60 percent of the population), is expected to rise to 922 million by 2025 (64 percent), and 1,020 million by 2050 (62 percent).

By 2025 India's very young (0–14) will have fallen by about 15 million, and by 2050 the decline will amount to 72 million, at which point they will only represent 18 percent of the population. At the other extreme, the over-65s will grow by 56 million by 2025 and 185 million by 2050, at which point their share will have risen to almost 15 percent.

India's total dependency ratio is still quite high at 61 percent, but it is heavily weighted toward youth (53 percent). By 2025 it is expected that the ratio will have fallen sharply to about 48 percent, comprising youth dependency of 37 percent and old-age dependency of 11 percent. It is only by 2050 that India's dependency ratio will turn up again and with a rapidly growing old-age contribution. It is predicted that by then the total dependency ratio will be about 49 percent, but with youth dependency at 27 percent and old age at 22 percent. India then has ample opportunity to try to realize much more from its demographic dividend. *Opportunity* is the key word for, as I have emphasized before, turning the opportunity into successful outcomes does not come naturally.

India's demographic advantage is not the only reason for optimism. Unlike other Asian economies, including China, India's path to development has had a much more domestic, as opposed to export, focus. If Western economies were to cool down under demographic pressures in the next several years, India would not be as exposed as, say, China. Moreover, India's more domestic development pattern has emphasized personal consumption, services, and high-tech (as opposed to low-skill) manufacturing. So, this young, consumer-oriented, and service-based economy looks remarkably like that of the United States. In fact, India's demographic profile in 2050 will look very much like America's today. By then, India's median age will be 38 compared with America's current median age of 36. Life expectancy will be over 75 in India compared with America's 78 years today. India's total dependency ratio will be 49 percent, the same as America today. India's working-age population will also rise over the next 20 to 30 years to peak at about 69 percent of the total population, compared with America's peak at this level, expected around 2010. Could India become an Asian America?

India can expect to continue to grow quickly and make strides to improve the quality of life for more of its inhabitants. Its demographic trends should produce a rising tide of new savings and investment that will add to future growth; and continuing movements of people from the countryside to India's cities and towns, and expected improvements in literacy and completion of secondary and university education will doubtless bolster productivity growth. For this rosy scenario to materialize, however, there is one important component that must fall into place: job creation, or more specifically, the avoidance of a youth bulge with not enough jobs to go round.

Jobs and skills are what India needs

An Asian America in India, at least in terms of economic and demographic structure, is a tantalizing thought, and hinted at by headlines of economic success and the increasingly reported global aspirations of some of India's largest corporations. Nevertheless, the truth is that now India is a poor country with GDP per person not too different from Angola and Bolivia. About 55 percent of people earn less than US$1,970 a year, little more than US$5 a day. Its democratic political systems and institutions have, in the past, sometimes been characterized by weak or populist policies. Of course, India is also a regional power in a part of the world that is volatile, to say the least.

If adequate job creation proves impossible or only partly successful, much of the optimism will fade quite quickly. The outside view of India is of a country teeming with English-speaking and highly qualified workers, comprising a major source of labor for the technology, health, and finance sectors, and as a magnet for foreign direct investment, but this perception is flawed. The country has a 39 percent illiteracy rate and only 10 percent of 18- to 24-year-olds are enrolled in higher education; and because of a chronic shortage of qualified and skilled workers, wages have been rising rapidly, up by over 14 percent in both 2006 and 2007.

But will India's youthfulness be enough, not only to overcome the existing manifestations of backwardness, but also raise prosperity levels for all? India's working-age population of 704 million is expected to increase by more than 300 million to 1,070 million by 2035 and 1,100 million by 2050. Although the officially measured unemployment rate has fallen from about 12 percent in the 1980s to about 8 percent at the end of 2006, job creation has fallen from 2.5 percent a year to about 1 percent a year. Over the next 25 years, the working-age population will be growing by 1.7 percent a year on average. This bodes poorly for employment prospects. Moreover, because of widespread poverty, many of those in employment may not earn enough to sustain themselves and their families. A fast-growing, young labor force in which unemployment and underemployment become more pronounced will not produce any demographic dividend.

Future governments of India will have to manage the economy and deliver an economic expansion to realize two goals: first, improvement in the lot of people who are counted as being in the labor force but who are, to all intents and purposes, poor or living below the poverty line; and second, the creation of 12 million new jobs a year until 2025, especially skilled jobs, and at a rather slower but still demanding pace after that.

Fundamentally, the problem for India is that one of its great strengths, the services sector, is also its great weakness. In the first place, it isn't a big job machine. Modern technology and information processing type activities are not especially labor-intensive. Second, much of India's services and outsourcing boom is in the southern part of the country, which is demographically quite different from northern India. In a nutshell, IT and outsourcing hubs such as Bangalore and Hyderabad belong to a part of the country that is highly literate and educated but also relatively older. Agriculture, on which 60 percent of the Indian population remains dependent, and which accounts for barely a fifth of GDP, is not only failing to create jobs, but is adding to labor supply, congestion, and unemployment or underemployment in towns and cities.

Manufacturing remains small by comparison and has, if anything, only recently reversed a long period of shedding jobs.

While the reported unemployment rate in India has fallen in recent years to about 7 percent in early 2007, the actual number is probably a lot higher, taking into account underemployed people, unemployed people who aren't registered, an army of day laborers and temporary workers, and the still substantial population "employed" but maybe not really working (much) in agriculture.

Although economic reforms since the 1990s have been hailed as instrumental in India's economic progress, labor laws remain rigid. Without change, India's unemployment tally could rise significantly in the coming years. One estimate by an Indian recruitment company estimated that on current (that is, slow) trends of employment creation, India's unemployment could rise to 211 million, equivalent to about 30 percent of the active population.[15] It noted that the problem of unemployment was especially severe for younger people aged 15–29 years and that an employment or unemployment crisis in coming years could only be averted if labor laws were overhauled.

The growth of new jobs for men in this age group has fallen from about 2.5 percent per year between 1987 and 1994 to 0.7 percent per year for rural men and 0.3 percent per year for urban men between 1994 and 2004. Yet this is an age group that is growing by about 1.3 percent per year and with high recorded unemployment rates. Essentially, the argument is that current laws force employers to cut jobs in the organized sector (which is to say, regular, contractual, and hired labor) and create them in the "unorganized" sector where wages are low and benefits and working conditions are poor. Unofficial estimates suggest that of India's 450 to 500 million labor force only about 7 to 10 percent work in the organized sector, and two-thirds of those are in the public sector.

Demographers, such as Nicholas Eberstadt, also point out differences between northern and southern India.[16] The north is and will remain very young for the next 20 years while the south is aging rapidly. Southern Indian cities, for example, including Mumbai, and Chennai, have below-replacement fertility rates, as do large parts of rural southern India. The fertility rate of the half a billion or so people in the north is about twice as high as for the quarter of a billion in the south. Eberstadt refers to two Indian states that have contrasting demographic characteristics: Kerala in the far southwest and Bihar in the northeast, sandwiched between Nepal and Bangladesh. Kerala boasts India's highest educational achievement in contrast to Bihar, which has the lowest. By 2026, almost everyone in Kerala aged 15–64, most of whom will be in their forties, will have had some schooling and qualifications. In Bihar, on the other hand, those in their twenties will be the dominant group but, fewer than a third of the 15-64s will have finished school, and more than two-fifths will be illiterate.

The implication, of course, is that India's more populous, less literate and educated north will be growing quickly and aging slowly, whereas the better educated and less populous south will be stagnating in a demographic sense. Notwithstanding India's deserved high reputation for its modern economy professionals—doctors, chemists, engineers, scientists, and programmers—India lags behind China, South Korea, and some other Asian countries in educational achievement. Secondary school enrollments are lower than in China, perhaps reflecting to some extent India's greater concentration of people in rural areas, and the growth in enrollments in higher education is half the rate of China. For India, then, educational opportunities—creating and capitalizing on them—are a priority for the coming decades.

The only way that India will be able to generate enough jobs in the future and simultaneously facilitate the movement of employees into the organized sector is, as many academics and professionals believe, by expanding access to education, reforming labor laws, and encouraging much more labor-intensive manufacturing. Japan traveled this route first, followed by the Asian Tigers (Hong Kong, Singapore, South Korea, and Taiwan), and then China. India looks to be trying to skip this stage and jump from a low-income, agrarian economy to a prosperous, service economy. It is doubtful that this is possible in the long run or for a low-income country of more than a billion people. Youthfulness will be on India's side, but it will not be enough without significant investment in human capital to reap the demographic dividend.

Russia—a failing petrostate?

Russia today has reverted in some respects to what it was at the beginning of the twentieth century. By European standards of the time, it was a rapidly growing but relatively poor and autocratic country, rich in natural resources and a natural trading partner for the more sophisticated economies of the West. But Russia, as history shows, became a failed state, succumbed to violent revolution and civil war, and was the first country to establish (its version of) the dictatorship of the proletariat.

Following the demise of the Soviet Union, Russia's economic story has been nothing, if not volatile, but it has become a new kid on the power bloc because of its petrostatus. Thanks to the combination of its vast hydrocarbon, mineral, and forestry resources, and the high prices for oil and gas and basic materials in recent years, Russia is unquestionably one of the world's major energy powers, its oil production rivaling that of Saudi Arabia. Its oil and gas industry accounts for about 20 percent of GDP and about 65 percent of its exports, with mineral resources accounting for a further 13 percent of exports. Its gas reserves of 48 trillion cubic meters are the largest in the world, accounting for nearly a third of the world's estimated total. The confidence that this petrostatus has given the Russian state, not least in its foreign policy dealings, has not been lost on leaders both inside and outside the country.

After the economic crisis in 1998, in which Russia defaulted on its external debt, the ruble collapsed, and inflation surged to over 80 percent, the nation's economic recovery has been remarkable. It has again become one of the darlings of the emerging markets and much loved by international investors. Its growth rate has been in the region of 6–7 percent per year in recent years, and its gold and foreign exchange reserve assets had grown to over US$560 billion by the end of June 2008.

At the same time, Russia's successes are overshadowed by exceptionally poor demographics, the effects of which are visible today, and which will surely become increasingly significant in years to come. Without an extensive and focused program by Russia's leaders to address serious weaknesses in the structure of its population, fertility, and mortality, there is a high risk the country will encounter economic as well as social and political turbulence in the years ahead. High energy prices will, of course, favor Russia but not forever, and, in any event, the so-called resource curse applies in many respects to Russia.[17]

And even if the country's economic viability is basically sound, demographic and health problems would still pose a series of risks to the pattern and pace of economic development and to the country's ability to maintain cohesion. It is in this latter sense that Russia might again become a failing state. With strong and flexible democratic institutions, tackling demographic problems will be hard enough, as discussed in the case of the West. Without them, solutions might well entail more dramatic political outcomes. This would, of course, be of great significance not only to Russians but to the country's relations with other states in central Asia, eastern Europe, and, of course, the United States.

Demographic decay

This is the fourth time since 1900 that Russia's population has been in decline. On previous occasions—the First World War and subsequent civil war, the famine and repression of the 1930s, and the Second World War—the causes were nondemographic, and the duration of decline was temporary. This time, it is different, not as violent or dramatic, but more sustained and difficult to reverse. The threats to Russia arise from chronically low fertility, high mortality among working-age males in particular, HIV/AIDS, poverty, and possibly the growing influence of non-Russian ethnic populations.

According to the 1937 census, Russia had about 162 million people. The total was later revised to 170 million after the organizers of the census had been arrested and executed.[18] However questionable the data may have been then and until roughly 1989, Russia's population in the early 1990s was about 150 million. Today it is about 142 million, and with current trends, it might be no larger than 80–90 million by 2050. In fact it is falling in spite of the high rates of immigration from the former Soviet republics.

Russia's population decline really began in the 1970s when infant mortality started to rise and adult life expectancy started to decline in ways that were unusual in peacetime. The main causes, even then, were weaknesses in Russia's health-care system, alcoholism, and a zealous use of abortion as a means of birth control. In the last decade of the former Soviet Union, the deterioration in the country's demographic position accelerated. The fertility rate was still just over two children per woman in the 1990s, but by 1999 it had fallen to 1.17, before rising again to about 1.25 in the last three to five years. The UN prediction is that it will continue to rise to 1.51 by 2025 and 1.71 by 2050, but this is by no means assured, and in any case, it won't really help in the next 10 to 20 years.

Russia is now at the tail end of the decline in its total dependency ratio that started in the mid-1960s, but it is hard to argue that Russia has enjoyed or is enjoying the demographic dividend. In many countries and regions, the fall in fertility and dependency is associated with rising prosperity and favorable structural economic and social change. In Russia, there is an eerie feeling that fertility trends are just one sign of serious social and economic problems.

Today's dependency ratio of young and aged citizens is about 41 percent, and a further small drop is expected before 2010. But after that, the dependency ratio is likely to rise to 48 percent by 2025 and 63 percent by 2050, as the working-age population falls and the number of elderly increases. Russia's working-age population of about 102 million is predicted to decline by 15 million by 2025 and by a further 21 million by 2050. That's a fall of more than a third. Meantime, the number of over-65s is forecast to rise from just over six million to almost 20 million by 2025 and 26 million by 2050. In other words, there are about 5 workers per elderly citizen today but this will drop to 4 by 2025, and 2.5 by 2050. By European standards, this is not radically different, but what Russia has that Europe does not, is a serious health crisis among its working-age people, which threatens to aggravate all the consequences of aging societies and undermine the country's potential to tap higher productivity as a partial solution.

Fading fertility

Declining life expectancy and rising mortality rates in Russia are really what make the country stand apart. Successive generations in most of our aging societies can look forward to improvements in both, but in Russia there has been no improvement comparing generations born before the Second World War and those born in the 1970s. Poor or declining standards of health and welfare will potentially rob Russia of the human capital on which aging societies will depend more and more. Deprived of human economic potential, the country's growth rate and productivity could suffer. The chances of being able to raise labor force participation, as other countries might, would be slim in Russia's case.

In 2006, President Vladimir Putin, noting that population was declining by 700,000 a year, told the Russian parliament[19] that Russia's demographic problem could not be solved without a change in attitude in society as regards the issues of family and family values. To this end, he promised, among other pronatalist cash incentives, the state would pay 250,000 rubles (US$9,000) to women who had a second child in the form of vouchers to be spent on accommodation, children's education, or their own pension once a child had reached three years of age. He also vowed that the government would tackle premature deaths related to alcoholism, car accidents, and heart disease. All very well, and encouraging women to have more children by means of financial incentives might seem quite a reasonable policy, except for two problems. First, it hasn't been especially effective anywhere. Second, by keeping women out of the labor force for longer, in the absence of Scandinavian-type childcare facilities and employment practices, Russia might become increasingly dependent on immigration on an absurdly large scale.

If the slow motion decline and then sudden collapse of the old Soviet Union and of the fertility rate went hand in hand, then might the more recent economic and political renaissance of Russia be accompanied by higher birth rates, as the United Nations predicts? A number of reasons have been advanced as to why this should not be taken for granted. First, poor or declining health patterns in reproductive health are producing a serious rise in female infertility that could be affecting up to 15 percent of married couples. Second, the use of abortion as a means of birth control, even though not as widespread as in the past, is leading to high rates of secondary sterility and sexually transmitted diseases. Incidentally, this ignores HIV/AIDS. Russia has one of the worst epidemics in the whole of Europe. The UN's estimate, at the end of 2004, was about 850,000 infected persons, of which 60 percent were in the 20- to 39-year-old age group and two-thirds of whom were men. By 2006, the total number of cases must have risen to well over a million. Despite some recent improvements in treatment and detection, the epidemic could reduce Russia's working-age population by three million by 2025 with quite adverse consequences for the economy. Third, a decline in two-parent families and a corresponding rise in single mothers have reduced the attraction and raised the costs of having children. Young Russians are increasingly less likely to marry—and more likely to divorce if they do—while close to 30 percent of children are born outside marriage.[20]

Mounting mortality

It is not just at the young end of the age spectrum that Russia's demographic problems are concentrated. According to World Health Organization (WHO) data, Russia has one of the highest mortality rates in the world at 15 per 1,000 people per year, compared with a global average of nine. The probability of dying between the ages of 15 and 60 per 1,000 of population is given as 470 for men, the highest in the WHO European area, and for women it is 173 per 1,000, the highest in the region except for Kazakhstan. Life expectancy is as low as 59 for men, a full three years lower than in 1955, and 72 for women, about the same as in 1955.

As in most countries, noncommunicable diseases including cardiovascular disease and cancer are the most common causes of death, but the mortality rates from the former, for example, are between five and eight times what they are in western Europe. The high incidence of, and mortality related to, tuberculosis (TB), for example, have been alarming. Russia actually lost more people during the First World War from TB than it did on the battlefield, but by the 1960s, Russians were pretty confident about its eradication. Nowadays, the infection rate is about 88 per 100,000 of population compared with an average of 4 in Europe and the death rate from TB is now higher than at any time since the 1960s, at about 20 per 100,000 (excluding the much more highly affected prison population), with most cases occurring among the working-age population. Moreover, Russia has comparatively high numbers of injury-related deaths (from murder, suicide, road deaths, and violent causes), smoking and alcohol-related illnesses, intravenous drug use, HIV/AIDS, and the effects of pollution.

Alcoholism is the third highest cause of death. Twenty percent of Russia's annual 36,000 road deaths are the result of drunk driving. Russia is the world's third-largest market for tobacco products after China and the United States, despite having a population that is 10 percent of China and half that of the United States. The murder rate in Russia is about 25–30 per 100,000 of population per year, which is the fifth highest in the world after Colombia, South Africa, Jamaica, and Venezuela, and compares with about four per 100,000 in the United States and 1–1.5 in European countries. The interconnections between these causes of death are of course self-evident, one telling example of which appeared in a research paper in 2005. It comprised a report of family health in Izhevsk, a medium-sized city in the Ural Mountains. The researchers had carried out a survey of 1,700 cases of death in males aged 25–54 and claimed that 38 percent of deaths, including those related to cardiovascular illness and injury of one form or another, had been linked clearly to alcohol abuse at the time of death.[21] It has been suggested, moreover, that of today's 15- to 19-year-olds, only 54 percent are likely to collect pensions at the age of 60.[22]

Manpower, military, and immigration

Poor health, low fertility, and high mortality then are rampant among a population that is in decline. While these may be masked or suppressed to some degree by the beneficial implications of high oil and gas prices for as long as they last, the social and political implications of Russia's demographics are going to become more acute. In the face of demographic decline, moreover, Russia's population structure is shifting from being Russian- and Slav-dominated to one that is slowly but increasingly characterized by diverse ethnic and religious groups, foremost among which are Russia's 14.5 million Muslims (10 percent of the population in the 2002 census). In addition, immigrants from China, central Asia, and other developing countries figure prominently in Russia's migrant numbers.[23]

Immigration poses a variety of challenges for all countries, but in Russia's case higher immigration carries strong political and social as well as regional undertones. Net immigration to Russia in the period 1995–2000 was about three per 1,000 of population or 439,000 people per year. By the following five years, the rate had fallen to 1.3 per 1,000 of population or roughly 183,000 per year. By 2006–07, the United Nations estimates, it had fallen to 0.4 per 1,000 or less than 50,000 people. At 20 times this rate, it might start to make a difference to the expected changes in the working-age population over the next few decades, but this is, of course, pure fantasy. Ethnic nationalism and xenophobia are already rife in Russia, despite Putin's public statements about the need for tolerance. The resurgence of right-wing and antidemocratic movements has fed on popular feelings of insecurity and also stirred stronger anti-Western feeling in Russia, by tapping the support of fearful citizens who cannot use political force or pressure in open opposition to the Russian government.[24]

Harley Balzer has highlighted the manpower shortages that loom, not least for the Russian armed forces, whose conscript pool will shrink, become ethnically more diverse and non-Slav, and be populated increasingly by less fit and less well-educated young men. It is possible that as many as 40 percent of draftees are being rejected on the grounds of being physically or mentally unfit. Balzer argues that everyone of draft age by 2022 will have been born by 2004, more or less the peak for 18-year-olds in Russia. Their numbers will drop by 100,000 a year from 2007, and the numbers reaching draft age each year by 2015 will be about 650,000, which is about half the number recorded in 2005.[25]

There is also what some, and many in Russia, regard as a growing regional and military dimension to Russia's demographic problems. One military analyst wrote in the main journal of the Russian General Staff in 2001 that depopulation in the Russian Far East in particular (given existing demographic pressures) was liable in the future to create conflict over the declining Russian ethnic presence in a region rich in natural resources. The perceived or actual Chinese threat to Siberia is not new, but it has acquired a new demographic angle. Siberia has lost 1.3 million Russians since 1989. In 2004 alone, it admitted more than 800,000 people from China legally. Russian newspapers regularly comment on the degree to which the Chinese population in Russia's Far East has grown to close to 10 percent of the population and about how fast the region is attracting China's unemployed and unskilled (whereas the West allegedly gets China's educated and skilled emigrants).

Historically, Russia has often voiced concerns and played up threats from China in the Russian Far East when there was—and is—no obvious or imminent demographic or military danger, but the existence of a threat is not really the issue. Perceptions matter more, for example, as to whether Russia and Russians are losing control of strategic parts of the Motherland, and political groups may choose to exploit such issues as cover for, or diversion from, other socioeconomic issues.

Think about the disintegration of Yugoslavia and the eruption of religious and ethnic conflict in the Balkans that accompanied it. There is little question that demographic trends reinforced interethnic tensions, which were exploited to inflame anti-Russian/Slav and anti-Muslim sentiments. This is not to suggest for a moment that the lesson of the most recent Balkan wars—and ongoing instability—is that Russia is next. This would be too extreme. Instead, the lesson is that demographic shifts can be highly destabilizing if ethnic and religious factors collide with weaknesses in the state and state institutions, poor social and economic conditions, and nationalism. Professor Niall Ferguson of Harvard University has argued powerfully that the extreme violence of the twentieth century, in the 1940s in particular, and in central and eastern Europe, Manchuria and Korea was the product of ethnic conflict, economic volatility, and empires in decline, concluding that "they are forces that stir within us still."[26]

The implications of demographic trends and developments in Russia and its surrounding regions are not inconsistent with Ferguson's "forces," though there may be other more likely candidates today. Nevertheless, by, say 2017, a hundred years after the Russian Revolution, could Russia again be at risk of becoming a failing state? Hydrocarbon and mineral endowments aside, demographic change is about whether population pressures, income inequalities, and poor health could collude to produce one or a series of crises in the next two decades with inevitable shocks running through domestic politics and foreign policy.

Africa and the Middle East, banking on the dividend

The global population will grow by about 2.7 billion between now and 2050, and half of these will be born in Africa and the Middle East. These regions include some of the poorest countries in the world and many that are at the center of regional or global political instability. The working-age population in Africa and the Middle East is going to rise by nearly a billion people, and both regions will experience a pronounced decline in their overall dependency ratios, with modest increases in old-age dependency swamped by the substantial decline in child dependency. Apart from India, if there were parts of the world that should be able to bank what seems like an enormous demographic dividend, then sub-Saharan Africa and the Middle East and North Africa should.

So this concluding section on emerging and developing countries asks if they are likely to do so. If they do and become persistently high-growth economies with better-off societies and mature, efficient political institutions, the local benefits will be self-evident. It is the beneficial effects this might have on global economic welfare and international relations that make it such a mouthwatering prospect, however.

Against this, the volatile social and political conditions, and high unemployment that characterize much of the Middle East and North Africa actually make the area's demographics unstable. According to the Human Security Centre at the University of British Columbia, there were roughly 30 state-based armed conflicts each year between 2002 and 2005.[27] About half were in Africa and the Middle East. There were 25 cases of nonstate armed conflict in 2005, of which 17 were in these regions, as were almost all of the 590,000 people who are reported to have died globally in such violence between 1989 and 2005. In sub-Saharan Africa, the worst examples currently are in Somalia, Sudan/Darfur, Chad, the Democratic Republic of Congo (unresolved civil war), and Nigeria (armed rebel groups in the oil-based Niger Delta). In the Middle East and North Africa, the trouble spots are well known and revolve around oil and gas, clashes between regional and global powers, and the threat of terrorism. While Iran, Iraq, Israel, Lebanon, and the occupied Palestinian Territories are rarely out of the news, it is worth noting that from Algeria to Egypt and across to Syria, Jordan, and Saudi Arabia, there are continuing concerns that periodic political violence might develop in ways that threaten both incumbent governments and international relations.

So what chances do the continent of Africa and the Middle East stand of banking their dividends in the next 40 years?

Africa: a distorted dividend?

If you look at sub-Saharan Africa as you might have done in geography at school, it is not obvious in some respects why it has been called the "lost continent." It has 10 percent of the world's proven oil reserves with an estimated lifespan of 30 years. It has 12 percent of the world's arable land (though it produces only US$85 of produce per hectare, compared with US$436 in Asia and US$185 in Latin America). It is rich in reserves of metals and mineral ores, including gold, copper, nickel, diamonds, cobalt, and phosphate rock, and it is a big exporter also of agricultural produce such as cocoa, tea, tobacco, and coffee as well as fruit, vegetables, and flowers. As noted before, Africa's dependency ratio is falling steadily as fertility rates decline (in many though not all countries), as the working age population rises strongly and before there is any marked increase in old-age dependency.

These conditions conform precisely to the type and pattern that are associated with economic advancement and success. For all this, however, the roughly one billion people in the whole of Africa produce a GDP that is less than that of Spain, Russia, or Brazil.

Africa has been through long periods of growth spurts and set-backs, but to bank its demographic dividend, Africa is going to

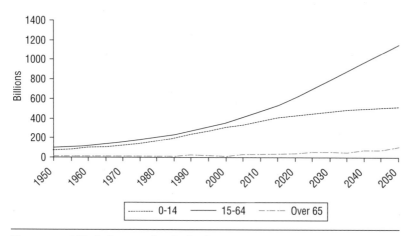

Figure 7.3 Africa's demographic dividend
Source: United Nations Population Division.

have to concentrate on the spurts and reduce the setbacks. The demographic dividend can only be realized if political instability becomes exceptional and if HIV/AIDS can be controlled so that young adult men and women can grow up to participate fully and properly in economic and social life. Sadly, there is precious little good news as regards the latter, and the outbreak of violence and instability in Kenya after a contentious election in December 2007 was especially disturbing because the country had been hailed for several years as a model of political stability and resurgent economic growth.

Although Africa's economic potential actually looks rather better nowadays than for many years, there are structural or noneconomic factors that may yet work to the continent's disadvantage and prevent it from taking full advantage of declining dependency. HIV/AIDS (and other communicable diseases) may already be undermining the decline in dependency by robbing Africa of too many young and healthy working adults.

Reasons to be optimistic regardless?

Looked at over long periods and ironing out the spikes and the troughs in growth, sub-Saharan Africa has been growing faster since 2000 than at any time since the 1970s. In 2007 the growth rate may have been almost 7 percent. For the region's oil exporters, notably Nigeria but also Angola, Sudan, Gabon, Equatorial Guinea, and the Democratic Republic of Congo, performance has been even stronger. The strong increases in commodity prices between 2004 and 2008 gave Africa a much-needed shot in the arm and curiously, for a variety of reasons, Africa's commodity dependency may work to its advantage for a while.

First, for African oil producers, higher energy prices may actually be sustainable because of concerns that the world is reaching geological limits to the production of conventional oil. Second, climate change and extraordinary weather patterns may have mixed outcomes for Africa. The conventional view about climate change in Africa is that a continent that is already subject to long, hot, dry seasons, drought, and rising temperatures will become drier and hotter. For some countries and regions, though, the consequences of climate change and of climate change policies could be to boost food and agricultural prices.

Third, Africa's growing relationships with China and, to a degree, India offer opportunities that have not existed before. Historically, China has always had commercial and political interests in Africa. For most of the period following the Second World War and before modernization really began, China's interest in Africa was mainly to support anticolonial and liberation movements opposed to colonial or dictatorial governments. China's newer economic interests are in building and developing Africa's farms, industries, resources, and infrastructure in what some see as a resurrection and extension of the former Silk Road—a network of trade and caravan trails that stretched from western China to the Middle East and Europe before the birth of Jesus Christ and until the seventeenth century.

African exports to Asia have tripled in the last five years, making Asia Africa's third biggest trading partner (27 percent of exports, compared with 29 percent to the United States and 32 percent to Europe). It is clear that China's industrialization and modernization are generating enormous demand for materials that Africa exports, such as cotton, food, processed commodities, light manufactures, hydrocarbons, raw materials, and tourism. For example, more than 60 percent of African timber exports are now destined for east Asia and 25 percent of China's oil supplies are now sourced in the Gulf of Guinea region. That these commercial and economic ties will grow is beyond doubt, probably to Africa's advantage.

Fourth, Africa has benefited from the adoption of the Heavily Indebted Poor Countries (HIPC) and Multilateral Debt Relief Initiative (MDRI) programs, the basic goals of which are to allow African countries to allocate more export revenues to economic development instead of having them leak out of the country to pay debt. For about 50 African countries, the average stock of foreign debt has fallen from 50 percent of GDP in

1999 to about 30 percent in 2006. (HIPC, launched in 1996 and enhanced in 1999, aims to offer speedy debt relief and has so far amounted to more than $60 billion. MDRI, launched in 2006 and amounting so far to nearly $40 billion, aims to further reduce the debts of HIPC countries and provide additional resources to help countries meet the Millennium Development Goals.)[28]

Last, Africa could benefit substantially from the successful adoption and implementation of new technologies. Before the large-scale adoption of cell phones, for example, vast swathes of Africa were communication voids with few landlines and all the financial and physical difficulties of building and maintaining the relevant infrastructure. Africa's three landlines per 100 citizens compare with 40 in Europe. But there are now about 100 million cell phones in Africa, 12 times the number in 2000, and equivalent to one for every nine Africans. In some countries, though, Kenya for example, the ratio is one for every three. The benefits for Africa's farmers, fishermen, and traders, as well as small and larger firms, are clear. They can check prices and market conditions in multiple locations, obtain inputs from the cheapest sources, call for assistance or supplies, and generally improve productivity, real incomes, and economic efficiency.

Stronger institutions, too much HIV/AIDS

The possibilities, including high energy and food prices, the extended Silk Road, financial relief, and technology will help Africa realize its demographic dividend, and they certainly constitute a more favorable background than has existed for the last several decades. It is no more than potential, however, for Africa has an important deficiency and a tragic excess. The deficiency concerns its institutions; the excess is the incidence and impact of HIV/AIDS. Of 62 highly affected HIV/AIDS countries in the world, 40 are in sub-Saharan Africa.

Sound institutions are generally regarded as a *sine qua non* for successful economic development and advancement. In their absence, economic development will be slow or retarded, political instability is likely to be the norm, societies tend to experience high rates of unemployment and crime, and the elderly and infirm face a miserable existence. They cover a multitude of factors that facilitate the ability and willingness of people to trade, save and invest, accumulate and deploy wealth, and develop flexible and harmonious societies. They include such things as the rule of law, openness, political freedom, the efficiency and accountability of bureaucracy, intolerance of corruption, freedom of speech, freedom from having property expropriated, political structures that encourage infrastructure development, and a formal labor market with unions and laws to protect employers and employees.

The significance of sound institutions and their relevance to banking the demographic dividend was examined recently in a research project that concluded that some countries—Ghana, Ivory Coast, Malawi, Mozambique, and Namibia—had a high potential to profit from demographic change in the next 20 years. South Africa and Botswana were also considered as beneficiaries because of their institutional strengths, rather than their demographics, which are rather poor. Some countries such as Senegal, Cameroon, Tanzania, Togo, and Nigeria, however, which will experience strong increases in their working-age populations, have work to do to strengthen their institutions. Among the policy recommendations were measures to improve the quantity and quality of education for girls, incentives to encourage girls to postpone marriage into their twenties (when they are likely to have fewer children and stay for longer in the workforce), and policies to encourage more job creation and job mobility.[29]

Apart from conflict, drought, poor education and health standards, and limited financial infrastructure, Africa's potential is compromised most by infectious diseases: malaria, tuberculosis and, of course, HIV/AIDS. Malaria and HIV/AIDS account for three to four million of Africa's annual deaths of some 10 million. Between 1985 and 1995, four million people died of AIDS. By 2005, the death toll had risen to 15 million, mostly teenagers and young adults aged 15–29. The effects on Africa's working- age population are crippling from an economic standpoint, not to mention highly destabilizing from a family and societal point of view.

The HIV/AIDS epidemic is generating demographic changes that are quite different from those in other developing countries, specifically falling life expectancy and rising mortality. If these trends are not reversed soon, child dependency may start rising again, perversely, because of the devastating impact on young working-age people, especially women. Aside from the human cost of the disease, the economic and social costs are high and pervasive. It wrecks family life, education, and employment, is both a cause and a result of poverty, and has many disruptive effects on the workings of society and government.

Once a household member is infected, income will fall as he or she eventually becomes too ill to work. Further income losses will occur as other family members stay at home to look after the victim. It isn't uncommon for a father to have died, a mother to be infected, and for children to drop out of school and stay at home to care. Again, the human tragedy aside, on a national scale, this degrades human capital formation, skill formation, and literacy. It is also inextricably mixed up in a vicious circle with poverty and malnutrition as the already stressed family budget is diverted away from food and clothing and basic medicines to more expensive forms of healthcare. Once a company or small enterprise finds growing numbers of employees infected and falling ill, the life of the company itself is at risk. Costs rise, productivity slumps, new staff have to be found, recruited and trained, and markets can suffer as customers or suppliers relocate or move abroad. The costs of HIV/AIDS in terms of GDP growth can hardly be measured in any scientific sense but are thought to lie anywhere between 1 and 4 percent per year.

In Africa, HIV/AIDS is the primary cause of death, accounting for about a fifth, which is about twice the rate for malaria and 10 times for deaths attributable to violence and war. On average, the prevalence of HIV among 15- to 49-year-olds was about 7.5 percent in 2003, but it was more than 20 percent in half a dozen countries and more than 30 percent in Botswana and Swaziland. For the worst affected countries in sub-Saharan Africa, HIV accounts for more than 90 percent of deaths among 15- to 39-year-olds. As recently as 1985–90, deaths in east Africa were concentrated in young children and older adults so that the 20- to 49-year-old group accounted for 16 percent of deaths. By now, this proportion has become 29 percent. The result is drastic decline in life expectancy in some countries in the last 20 years, so that it is no higher and in some cases lower than it was in the 1950s. For example, in Botswana, male life and female life expectancy is about 45.7 and 47.4 years respectively, compared with rates of more than 61 years in the 1980s. In South Africa, average life expectancy is 49 years, compared with 61 years about twenty years ago. In Zimbabwe, women can expect to live to 39.7 years on average compared with 64.5 years between 1985 and 1990, and 50 years between 1950 and 1955.

As a result of the epidemic and especially its ravaging of women, the number of orphans has soared to about a fifth of the youth population in badly affected regions. It is estimated that more than a third of children infected by mother-to-child transmission die before their first birthday, and 61 percent die by the age of 5. If you bear in mind that in rich countries, child mortality before the age of five is about nine per 1,000 births, just think for a moment about child mortality in South Africa where it is 66 per 1,000 births, or Zimbabwe where it is 104, or Swaziland where it is 135.

Twenty-seven years or so into the HIV/AIDS epidemic, there is little confidence that it is stabilizing, let alone declining, in spite of the effort being made to increase the use and efficiency of antiretroviral drug therapy. It is not disputed that this hangs as a dark cloud over Africa's economic prospects and the opportunities that Africa could seize as its demographic change evolves and as its dependency ratio continues to decline. Higher raw material prices could work to Africa's advantage over the next several years, greater involvement with China and other developing countries will certainly assist, and debt relief will help the poorest. The slow moving but inexorable benefits of education and technology, and modern communications constitute a favorable background against which to make economic and institutional changes work.

The magnitude of the task in many countries should not be underestimated, and it will be some time before we can be more confident that some of today's more auspicious factors will take root and flourish. One thing is for sure, though. Unless the trends in HIV/AIDS incidence can be reversed, Africa's demographic dividend is all too likely to be distorted and distributed far too unevenly.

Middle East and North Africa—rage, religion, and reform

The Middle East and North African countries are also expected to have the potential to benefit from demographic change as their overall and working-age populations rise strongly in the coming decades. The overall population of the region was just over 100 million in 1950. Today it is about 430 million, and by 2050 it could rise to 700 million. Until now, however, the population has been growing faster than the number of people in work, with the result that the unemployment rate across the entire region is about 25 percent, the highest of any major region in the world. In fact, in the Middle East, the employment rate—that is, the share of people in work relative to those who could work—is a staggeringly low 47 percent. Some estimates put the number of new jobs that will be needed at 100 million by 2020. If the bulk of the population growth in the next decades is going to occur among young people and younger adults, and job creation and educational attainment do not improve, it is not difficult to see why many observers of the region say the biggest issue there is who will be able to mobilize and engage the aspirations and energy of the youth bulge most successfully and to what political ends.

Basic population characteristics

Figure 7.4 shows the population of several countries in the region, the numbers inside the bars representing the

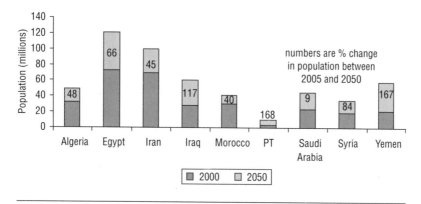

Figure 7.4   Middle East and North Africa population change (millions)
Source: United Nations Population Division.
Note: PT stands for Palestinian Territories.

percentage change between 2005 and 2050. Some of the sharpest population increases are expected to occur in Yemen, the Palestinian Territories, Iraq, Saudi Arabia, Syria, and Egypt.

The change in the structure of the population can be seen in Figure 7.5. Although the 0- to 14-year-old age group will continue to expand a bit until about 2030, and we can also see the start of a rise in the population of over-65s, the dominant change is the doubling of the 15- to 64-year-old age group. The working-age population in the region is expected to grow by 40 percent between 2000 and 2010, and by a further 40 percent by 2020. As many people will be looking for work between 2010 and 2020, as were doing so during the four decades to 1990.

This bulge in the region's working-age population will, for the next 20 years or so, be dominated by the increase in young adults. Today, 40 percent of the region's population is aged between five and 24 years (see Figure 7.6). By 2025, of course, they will have become twenty-, thirty- and early-forty-somethings, with the fastest growth expected to occur in Iraq, the Palestinian Territories, and Yemen.

The child dependency ratio (0–14 year olds in relation to 15- to 64-year-olds) is about 53 percent today across the region and is expected to drop to 30–32 percent over the next two to three

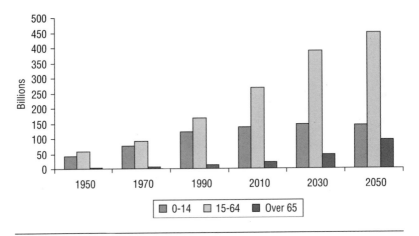

Figure 7.5   Middle East and North Africa—rising age structure
Source: United Nations Population Division.

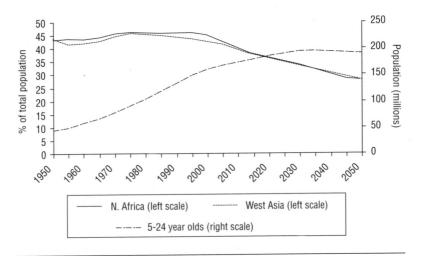

Figure 7.6   Middle East and North Africa—a still expanding 5- to 24-year-old age group
Source: United Nations Population Division.

decades. This decline will more than offset the gradual rise in old-age dependency, so that total dependency will carry on declining for a long time. This trend is being reinforced by the decline in fertility rates, which in the whole region averages about three children per woman compared with seven in 1960.

The highest rates, between three and six children per woman, are to be found in Iraq, Jordan, the Palestinian Territories, Syria, Saudi Arabia, Yemen, Libya, and Egypt. As a consequence of higher fertility rates, the under-15 age group in Iraq, Yemen, and the Palestinian Territories accounts for more than 40 percent of the population. But in some countries, for example Lebanon, Iran, Morocco, and Turkey, where the current fertility rates are relatively low at between 2.04 and 2.24 children and where the trend is toward further declines, the fall in child dependency will be especially marked. The share of 0- to 14-year-olds in total population in these four countries will drop from about 28–30 percent today to about 21–23 percent in 2025 and 17–18 percent by 2050.

The population aged 0–24 in the entire region was about 60 percent of the total in 1950 and is now about 53 percent. It is expected to fall to 44 percent by 2030 and 35 percent by 2050. The actual number of people in this age group will continue to rise nonetheless. Today they number about 214 million, more than three times as large as in 1950. By 2030, they will peak at roughly 240–245 million, of which about half will be aged 15–24 years. Thereafter, the numbers in absolute terms, as well as their share in total population, will start to drop but this means, of course, that for the next 20 to 25 years at least, demographic pressures will intensify.

Angry young men in an unstable region

The population of the Middle East and North Africa is relatively small, certainly compared with sub-Saharan Africa. Simple population measures are wholly disproportionate to the economic and political significance attached to the region by the rest of the world. The reason of course is oil. The political—or rather geopolitical—reasons for the significance of the region—apart from the continuing impasse between Israel and the Palestinians—emanate partly from oil and partly, of course, from two important demographic characteristics. The first is that the region is overwhelmingly Islamic, even though there are important differences between countries and, indeed, between the major powers of Iran, Turkey and Saudi Arabia. In the current environment, of course, the evolution of economic performance, of government stability and of social tensions in the region will be watched with great interest and some angst. The second, which follows directly, concerns the prospects for social and political stability in a region, troubled by fear (of political oppression or unrest) and characterized by large numbers of young unemployed men.

The changes in population structure and characteristics in the region are precisely what demographic dividends are founded upon, but the reality of course is more complicated. The region already faces a daunting series of tasks to accommodate peacefully and constructively the inexorable growth in total population—working age adults and young workers especially. In the future, these challenges are likely to become more pressing. Not only are jobs hard to come by now but even those mostly oil-rich countries that have high per capita incomes tend to have inequitable arrangements when it comes to income distribution, education, and opportunity. Like sub-Saharan Africa, the quality of the institutions is below what is necessary for fast and sustainable economic growth that is not dependent on oil prices rising forever.

Banking the demographic dividend in the Middle East and North Africa is going to require a multitude of economic, political, and social reforms, difficult though these may be to implement. As in sub-Saharan Africa, population growth and the change in age structure are going to raise the demand for more and better infrastructure, especially in respect of health, transportation, urban services, and above all education. While both secondary and higher education attainment levels have increased in the last decade or so, overall levels are almost 30 years behind those of east Asia. Too many people emerge from schools and higher education poorly equipped for a knowledge-based economy. Too many people are still classified as illiterate, or they drop out of school early. It is estimated that Egypt, Iraq, and Yemen are home to about three-quarters of the 10 million illiterate youth in the entire region.[30] Many girls have inadequate schooling and tend to marry and bear children at a young age. This deprives the labor force of women who could work, leaving aside for a moment the issue of cultural and religious restraints over female employment, and works to perpetuate a cycle of low education, large families, and poverty.

The region is plagued already by one of the highest unemployment rates, about 25 percent. Country rates vary from more than 40 percent in Algeria and the Palestinian Territories to less than 8 percent in the smaller countries in the Gulf. The share of youth in unemployment varies a lot between countries, but at an average 26 percent or so, the region's youth unemployment rate is higher than in sub-Saharan Africa and Latin America and southeast Asia (16–18 percent) and three times as high as in east Asia. Curiously, most of the region's unemployed are not the uneducated or highly educated but those with some skills and some education. In one or two countries, though, unemployment among highly qualified university graduates is a serious issue, for example in Egypt. This is partly attributable to the run down in employment growth in the public sector in that country, which hasn't been offset by the private sector. Women, of course, continue to experience widespread discrimination as regards their rights and access to employment, a serious handicap to full economic development, not to mention other issues this raises.

None of the above is to suggest that the region is stuck in a time warp and that nothing is changing. In the six countries that make up the Gulf Co-operation Council (GCC), Saudi Arabia, Kuwait, United Arab Emirates, Bahrain, Qatar, and Oman, GDP has risen so fast (to over US$750 billion) that this area has become, in effect, the seventh-largest emerging market, about the same size as Mexico or South Korea. Many people have become familiar with the skyline of Dubai and other parts of the Gulf, and ultramodern airports competing for regional hub status as well as new and old tourist destinations. The real story goes a lot deeper.

GCC oil and gas revenues are running at about US$350 billion a year, three times as high as at the turn of the last decade. The bulk of these revenues end up as foreign exchange reserves that are invested overseas by the local central banks and by so-called Sovereign Wealth Funds (SWFs), which are government-owned investment agencies given the role of investing assets abroad either for a rainy day or to pay dividends to future generations of citizens. Around the world, SWFs own assets worth about US$3,000 billion. The Middle East is home not only to the largest SWF in the world (Abu Dhabi Investment Authority) but to about a third of the total assets owned by SWFs.

During the oil price boom that began in 2005, government spending has been much more restrained than in the 1970s and more wisely allocated to development goals. Public and private borrowing has been cut back substantially in all countries, and private sector firms have become much more prominent in spearheading the estimated US$1 trillion of infrastructure projects that are due to be completed over the next 10 years. Saudi Arabia, the biggest GCC member by far, has joined the World Trade Organization (WTO), liberalized tariffs, introduced privatization, reformed corporate governance and regulations, embarked on a program to build new cities and economic zones, and encouraged private sector firms to lead the investment surge planned for the oil and gas, petrochemical, infrastructure, real estate, telecommunications, and health sectors. The non-oil part of the economy has been growing almost as fast as in China in 2006–2007. In 2007, Saudi Arabia announced that it wanted to endow a new state-of-the-art science and technology university at Thuwal on the Red Sea to the tune of about US$10 billion, designed to provide educational infrastructure for the non-oil sector of the economy. It also said it wanted to almost double the number of 18- to 24-year-olds in higher education and to guide students away from humanities and religious studies. Not far from the university, the US$27 billion King Abdullah Economic City is being built.

All these developments are, of course, encouraging, but what is important is who will take up the challenge of adequate job creation and contribute toward shifts in the region's political status, a long-term and massive task. Since 1997, GCC private sector companies, for example, created about 55,000 medium- and high-skilled jobs a year, but this figure is going to have to rise five times to about 300,000 a year over the next several years, and at higher wages than private companies pay today.[31]

The need for reform

All things considered, change isn't happening fast enough, and the timescale within which relevant economic, political, and social reforms can be made in a relatively peaceful environment is surely shortening. Reforms would alleviate unemployment, create jobs for tomorrow's worker bulge, and improve the region's economies if governments were prepared to tackle at least four major weaknesses, in addition, that is, to the educational shortcomings noted earlier.

First, dependence on oil and gas does of course bring great monetary benefits when prices are rising, but they may be fleeting if and when oil prices drop again, even if only for short-term or cyclical reasons. More than this, though, countries that rely on commodities are often thought to be vulnerable to both economic distortions, as their exchange rates rise too far and too fast, and to corruption. Often in oil producing countries, there is a large energy sector that is publicly owned, a large public sector where most of the jobs and protected wage benefits can be found, and a small or struggling private sector.

As it happens, two-thirds of Arabs live in countries without significant oil exports. They depend on agriculture and manufacturing, which is the major source of jobs. However, manufacturing exports for the Middle East and North Africa are lower than for almost all Asian countries considered individually. Consider Egypt, the region's most populous country, with almost 73 million people, of whom about 54 percent are aged less than 24 years. Egypt's exports of manufactured goods per person some 40 years ago were roughly the same as for the Asian Tigers, such as South Korea and Taiwan. Today, Egypt's manufactured exports in a year equate to what these ex-Tigers export in three days, according to Marcus Noland and Howard Pack.[36] The Philippines' manufactured exports are 10 times as large as Egypt's. The entire Arab world exports fewer manufactured goods than does Thailand, which has a quarter of the population.

Second, the region's countries are not well integrated into the global economy. Oil and gas exports and investment give the region's energy producers a special role in the world economy, but this does not compensate for the benefits that might follow from a more open and diversified trading relationship with partners in Europe, the United States, and increasingly in Asia. These include not only gains from trade but also benefits in terms of the transfer and diffusion of technology and information. China's diversified commercial assistance in construction and other industrial projects in the last few years in Saudi Arabia and Iran make for an interesting new development, but what China wants is access to the very products on which many such countries are too reliant. Apart from oil and gas, the participation of Middle Eastern and African countries in world trade and in world direct investment flows is extremely low.

Third, the quality of the region's institutions is poor, and its reputation for local political unrest and terrorist threats is not only central to geopolitical affairs, it can also retard or reverse economic development.

Last but not least, the social and political arrangements that prevent women from realizing their full economic potential are a major weakness. To a degree, this reflects the difficulties that some countries have with modernization. Many societies face the challenge of how to balance better the conflict between the needs and workings of a productive economy on the one hand and local or cultural traditions and customs on the other. In the modern economy, the Internet, chat rooms, satellite TV, and cell phones have accentuated this conflict, generating both rising aspirations for change from some and growing hostility by more conservative groups.

The fuller integration of women into work and society is now recognized in many countries as not just a moral right but also as a source of economic strength. In the case of the Middle East and North Africa, the significance of the contribution that women can make in economic terms as well as in public life has been recognized. However, the Arab Human Development Report 2005, for example, concluded that for women, better social and economic prospects would require first that they be afforded full opportunities to acquire essential health and knowledge on an equal footing with male counterparts and then that they be allowed to participate in all types of activity outside the family on an equal footing.[33]

Believing, not belonging

So why are reforms too little or too slow? The answers are complex. Many people think that Islam itself is the obstacle to progressive and sometimes radical reforms, but this may be as much about rhetoric as it is about reason. Islam and the creation of Islamic institutions have not been an excessive drag on growth in the predominantly Arab world. Nonetheless, it is important to understand why private and public institutions have failed to adapt and tackle the discontent that more fundamentalist or radical religious followers express about local politics, globalization, and engagement with the rest of the world. Countries in the region have, after all, recorded respectable economic growth rates in the past, but there is a strong perception that they are falling behind relative to other middle-income nations and that the willingness and ability of governments to address poverty, unemployment, and other social ills is lacking. The issue here is not Islam as a faith or Islamic institutions but the authoritarianism of those who rule and deny freedoms to citizens, and those who rebel in similar fashion.

In surveying the region and considering its economic possibilities, it is also necessary to distinguish religious beliefs that people hold as a guide to self-conduct and social values, and religious belonging that people may emphasize to express identity, security, force, power, and protection against enemies. Although making this distinction is difficult, the argument is that believing rather than belonging best serves economic progress and flexibility.

The debate about religion and economic progress is not new. Max Weber's writings about the influence of religion on social and economic development are well known and have spawned extensive and continuing argument.[34] Weber saw religion as a key factor behind the different development of cultures in the West and in the East, and he stressed the significance of particular aspects of Protestantism in the development of capitalism, bureaucracy, and the nature of the state.

The debate resonates, especially in the Middle East and North Africa today, and scholars from many disciplines have their pet theories on the topic. There is nothing simple about how religion is related to economic growth, which we assume here to be a proxy for economic and social progress. There are, after all, many strands that run between economic and political developments, religious beliefs and participation, and the development of political institutions. For instance, one study that attempted to look at this relationship in an empirical way concluded that church attendance and religious beliefs were positively associated with advances in education, which is a spur to development. They were negatively associated with urbanization, however, which in developing countries especially is a key feature of development.[35]

Ultimately, religious belief and practice can and do have both good and bad effects on economic growth. If they encourage openness and positive interaction with strangers and foreigners, it is probable that advances in trade, investment, and technology transfer will be greater. If they emphasize a work ethic, thrift, fairness, and social values, it is likely that education and health provision and standards will be higher. On the other hand, if they are associated with fear, terror, insularity, and exclusion, then prime economic drivers, such as capital accumulation, growing worker participation, the payment of profit and interest, and innovation may be blunted or subdued. In extremis, of course, they might encourage or be associated with violence, which is unequivocally negative.

The importance of shifting the balance away from religious belonging to religious belief as a means of improving the possibilities of economic advancement can be seen in the three major challenges the region faces in the next 10 to 20 years. First, it must expand labor-intensive manufacturing and service activities to create jobs. Energy intensity is not going to help, and it may even hinder, to the extent that it underpins the resistance to change and reform.

Second, it needs to import, much more heavily, goods and services related to new technology and equipment and intermediate raw materials, which it can process and re-export. This would provide a robust stimulus to productivity growth. It also needs to attract much more in the form of foreign direct investment in activities aside from energy, construction, and tourism. The trouble, so to speak, with these cures for economic malaise are that they all require greater openness and stronger willingness to integrate into the global economy, and both of these clash with established practices and customs.

Third, the type of liberal reforms to trade, governance, labor markets, and education that are popular in the West may not suit or fit societies in the Middle East and North Africa the way they do elsewhere. However, reforms will be essential if the economies of the region are to develop and bring future prosperity and if they are to grasp its demographic dividend to good effect. For that kind of reform effort, though, you have to have dialogue and engagement, and religious belief delivers this more effectively than religious belonging.

Even then, economic efficiency is not assured. Two small anecdotes, by way of conclusion, illustrate the last point. According to a recent report, "the influence of Islam or the anthropology of Arab culture may have many effects on local institutions and practices but they cannot explain why it takes fifteen times as long to enforce a contract in Egypt as it does in Tunisia,"[36] and starting a business in Saudi Arabia supposedly takes three times as long as it does in Morocco.

Don't hold your breath

In whatever ways, religion and economic development are viewed, two conclusions remain. First, serious weaknesses in the availability of jobs and education could cause the area's demographic dividend to become increasingly distorted. Second, the Middle East and North Africa is likely to remain a troubled region, as a result, for the foreseeable future.

If there is good news, it is that some countries are expanding more quickly, thanks to high energy prices. Outside the energy sector, light manufacturing, telecommunications, food processing and the especially fast-growing tourism sectors offer indications of broader development as well as the gradual rebalancing, in some nations, of the roles played by the government and private sectors. As global economic and political power shifts continue to roll through the world, there is a fair chance that the countries in the region could slowly become more integrated. On this basis, absorption of the next 100 million job seekers might get off to a reasonable start, but it will require widespread and continuous reforms to work.

It is therefore becoming increasingly pressing that the region's economies be diversified away from energy and that education and employment opportunities, especially for women, be broadened. Moreover, stronger, fairer, and more peaceful societies stand more chance if policymakers seek to build and reinforce sound institutions that support openness and the rule of law as well as other essentials discussed in the previous section.

On the surface, some might dispute that becoming better off makes for more peaceful societies. It is often said that hungry people beg. Better-fed, better-educated people fight—for rights, jobs, power and so on. But if rising education, income per head, and improved all round income distribution help more people to reason rather than rage, to produce rather than plot, and to re-engage with rather than disengage from the global economy, then their significance cannot be understated. The alternative would be chronic political instability, external conflicts, and economic progress that is too slow and too piecemeal. The demography of the region is becoming too dangerous to rely on hope alone.

Endnotes

1   This is not to denigrate the initiatives and activities, per se, of debt relief for some of the poorest countries of the world or the transfer of moneys for the relief of famine or to help spur local economic development. But long-term prosperity for Africa, as for everywhere else throughout history, is going to be about fundamental domestic economic and social factors, relevant and efficient institutions, and a nurturing set of global rules on trade and capital flows.

2 Singapore, Malaysia, Hong Kong, and, to a more limited extent, Thailand have established state funds, based on compulsory savings, that finance housing, education, medical care as well as retirement income, even though the replacement rates (of wage and salary income by pension income) are only 20 to 40 percent of earnings. South Korea, the Philippines, Taiwan, and Thailand have PAYG pension schemes, though again there are still big gaps as regards low replacement rates and limited coverage of the working-age population. China has been obliged to reform its social insurance, partly in response to the fragmentation of, and decline in, the old pension insurance system run by state-owned enterprises. These provided state-supported, cradle-to-grave security, retirement at age 60 for men (55 for women), and pension replacement at 80 percent of earnings. Nowadays, China maintains a three-pronged pension structure comprising a defined benefit, PAYG-type system along with a mandatory defined contribution scheme, and a voluntary scheme. Its weaknesses include low coverage (50 percent of urban workers, less than 25 percent of all workers), noncompliance by employers, and other irregularities.

3 Rakesh Mohan, "Fiscal Challenges of Population Aging: The Asian Experience." Global Demographic Change Symposium, Jackson Hole, Wyoming (August 26–28, 2004).

4 Economic Survey, UN Economic and Social Committee for Asia and the Pacific, Bangkok (April 2007).

5 Will Hutton, "The Calamity of Asia's Lost Women," *The Observer*, (March 18, 2007).

6 "Chinese villages riot over limits on births," *International Herald Tribune* (May 22, 2007).

7 Nicholas Eberstadt, "Old Age Tsunami," *Wall Street Journal* (November 15, 2005).

8 For the background to rural migrant wages, see Jonathan Anderson, "The End of Cheap labor (Period)." *Asian Focus*, UBS (August 9, 2007).

9 For subsequent references see Jonathan Anderson, "How To Think About China Part 2." *Asian Economic Perspectives*, UBS (February 7, 2005).

10 Cai Fang and Dewen Wang, "Demographic Transition: implications for growth." Garnaut and Song eds., *The China Boom and Its Discontents* (Canberra: Asia-Pacific Press, 2005).

11 Measured in terms of purchasing power parity, which corrects for exchange rate distortions, according to the theory that a given basket of goods should cost the same anywhere. However, to citizens of China (as elsewhere) this measurement must seem entirely alien. They earn and spend money in market prices, not purchasing power parity prices. According to a report in the *People's Daily*, "What it

means to have a per capita GDP of US$2000," April 11, 2007, GDP per head was about US$2,000 in 2006.

12 Editorial, *British Medical Journal* (August 19, 2006).

13 Robert Ash, "China's Harmonious Society—Daydream or Reality?" *DSG Asia* (December 5, 2007).

14 Feng Wang and Andrew Mason, "Demographic Dividend and Prospects for Economic Development in China," UN Expert Group Meeting on Social and Economic Implications of Changing Population Age Structures, Mexico City, July 25, 2005.

15 Cited in "Unemployment explosion to hit India by 2020 if current trends continue," *The Hindu*, (August 15, 2006).

16 See, for example, Nicholas Eberstadt, "Growing Old the Hard Way: China, Russia, India." *Policy Review*, Hoover Institution (April/May 2006).

17 The "resource curse" describes the paradox under which enormous wealth and power arising from the ownership of natural resources sooner or later affects economic growth in a negative way (because of excessive exchange rate appreciation and lack of competitiveness), increases the volatility of revenues derived from the resource sector, and lends itself to bigger economic mismanagement and/or corruption.

18 Catherine Merridale, "The 1937 Census and The Limits of Stalinist Rule," *Historical Journal* 39, No. 1 (1996).

19 Reported in *Izvestiya*, May 11, 2006.

20 Nicholas Eberstadt, "The Russian Federation at the Dawn of the Twenty-First Century: Trapped in a Demographic Straitjacket," *NBR Analysis* 15, No. 2 (September 2004).

21 London School of Hygiene and Tropical Medicine, "Izhevsk Family Study Interim Report" (2005).

22 Steven J. Main, "Russia's 'Golden Bridge' is Crumbling: Demographic Crisis in the Russian Federation," Conflict Studies Research Centre (August 2006).

23 Given Russia's land mass, the country's historical affinity to "land" and the diversity of everything from population density to ethnic diversity, regional population and immigration patterns in Russia are of great significance. A comprehensive and informative insight can be found in Jessica Griffith Prendergast, "A New Russian Heartland? The Regional Consequences of Russia's Demographic Crisis," Department of Geography, University of Leicester (July 2004).

24 "A benign growth," *The Economist* (April 7, 2007).

25 "The Implications of Demographic Change for Russian Politics and Security," Conference on Health and Demography in the Former Soviet Union. Harvard University, Davis Center for Russian and Eurasian Studies and the Weatherhead Center for International Affairs (April 30, 2005).

26 Niall Ferguson, *The War of the World* (London: Penguin Books, 2006).

27 Human Security Brief 2006, Human Security Center, The University of British Columbia, Canada.

28 The Millennium Development Goals and targets come from the Millennium Declaration, signed by 189 countries in September 2000 under the auspices of the United Nations. It has as its primary target development and the elimination of poverty but also incorporates goals and targets (many specified by 2015) related to universal primary education; gender equality and the empowerment of women; child mortality reduction; maternal health improvement; the reversal of the incidence and spread of HIV/AIDS, malaria, and other diseases; environmental sustainability; and a variety of other initiatives to encourage stronger and more sustainable growth and development.

29 David E. Bloom, David Canning, Gunther Fink, and Jocelyn Finlay, "Realizing the Demographic Dividend: Is Africa Any Different?" Program on the Global Demography of Aging. Working paper No. 23, Harvard University (May 2007).

30 Ragui Assaad and Farzaneh Roudi-Fahimi, "Youth in the Middle East and North Africa: Demographic Opportunity or Challenge?" Population Reference Bureau, Washington, DC (April 2007).

31 Kito de Boerand and John M Turner, "Beyond Oil: Reappraising the Gulf States," www.mckinseyquarterly.com (January 2007).

32 Marcus Noland and Howard Pack, "The Inward East," *Newsweek International* (October 29, 2007).

33 United Nations Development Program, Regional Bureau for Arab States, New York, 2006.

34 Max Weber, *"The Protestant Ethic and the Spirit of Capitalism"* (1904).

35 Robert J. Barro and Rachel M. McLeary, "Religion and Political Economy in the International Panel," NBER Working Paper 8931 (2002).

36 Farzaneh Roudi-Fahimi and Mary M. Kent, "Challenges and Opportunities – The Population of the Middle East and North Africa," Population Reference Bureau, Washington, DC (June 2007).

Chapter 8

Where globalization and demographics meet

> *The most challenging issue raised by globalization is how we can all get along with each other in our race against time.*
> —Li Ka Shing, interview with Bloomberg, December 22, 2002.

So far we have looked at demographic change largely from the standpoint of individual countries or groups of countries. But in a world undergoing rapid globalization—in some respects on an unprecedented scale—we need to look too at the global context in which these things are occurring. Think of globalization and demographic change as the overlapping circles of a Venn diagram. What, for example, are the implications for populations when markets, as opposed to institutions, drive greater interaction between countries and people? Why is there so much hostility to globalization, and does it matter? Is globalization cause or cure for the poverty and epidemic diseases such as HIV/AIDS that can rob people of their demographic dividend and well-being, and turn it into "ill-being?" What difference does it make to Japan or to other rich countries to be a fast-aging nation when they trade goods and services and exchange capital with slower-aging and rapidly growing developing countries?

Globalization has had profound effects on economic and social progress but it has also generated considerable concern about "haves" and "have-nots" at all levels—from the global economy down to local communities. In trying to combat its more negative effects, individuals, organizations, and governments have argued that globalization needs to be tamed or managed better so as to further extend its benefits.

We will therefore look more closely here at globalization and ask how it matters to demographic change and aging. Globalization, after all, doesn't happen in a vacuum, least of all in a population vacuum, and the footprints of population change and movement can be found on the route map of globalization.

Globalization is the death of distance

The word *globalization* is both ambiguous and contentious. Some use it as a byword for economic progress that has to be either left to markets or much better managed. Others see it as signifying threat and injustice, and arguments about the United States as the villain of globalization are common. But this is to get ahead of ourselves. Globalization is simply the "death of distance"[1]—in other words, a process in which geographic space and distance are compressed across a broad range of activities, including travel, communication, commerce, and the movement of capital and labor.

Mankind's natural propensity is to trade and barter. When this combines with comparative advantage related to geography, resource endowment, and skills, for example, our history reveals the generation of powerful forces to integrate. There are many instances of civilizations that have sought to bring distant peoples closer together through the use of force, law, communication, and transport—sometimes with beneficial results, sometimes not. Alexander the Great and the Romans tried. From before the birth of Christ and until the early years of the nineteenth century, Asia represented, in a way, an archetypal force of globalization, with China and India at its hub. For a variety of reasons, this Sinocentric world disintegrated, to be replaced by a Eurocentric world. The period from 1870 to 1913 is generally regarded as the first phase of real globalization, a period of profound and extensive economic integration that grew out of a number of what we would now call "levelers" or distance-compressors. These included sailing and steamship technology, railroads, the telegraph, and the telephone, as well as revolutions in scientific discovery.

In this first major globalization, the revolution in transportation, the decline in transport costs, and the distance-
compressing effects of the construction of the Suez Canal (1869)
and later the Panama Canal (1914) created spectacular economic
effects. The price differences between the United States and the
United Kingdom and between Europe and Asia, of a whole array
of agricultural goods such as wheat, cotton, and jute, and metals
such as iron, copper, and tin, were largely eradicated as a result
of the expansion and liberalization of trade. Labor shortages in
the United States led to rising wages and waves of immigrants,
while price declines in Europe for agricultural products contributed to economic hardship and a flurry of willing migrants
to the new worlds of America and Australia.

With the collapse of globalization between 1913 and the late
1940s, the interplay with demographics took on a much more
sinister and shocking form. This time, instead of the facilitation
of labor movements and the search for new opportunities, col-
lapsing globalization led to mass unemployment, deep-seated
insecurity, financial crises, severe restraints on trade and immigration, fragmented and disconnected markets, and ultimately,
war—and waves of poor, stateless refugees.

Our contemporary version of globalization, unlike the concept of a century ago, features unprecedented integration of
(free) trade and capital movements. For most of us, this integration manifests itself in an array of factors such as the ready
availability of cheap made-in-China toys and textiles, the proliferation of ever-more-sophisticated and cheaper technology
goods, the outsourcing phenomenon, and the year-round availability of every kind of fruit and vegetables. But when it comes
to labor and immigration liberalization, it has been slightly
more restrained. For instance, identified capital flows between
1945 and 1975 were little more, and often less, than about
1 percent of world GDP. Between the mid-1970s and 1997,
they averaged about 5 percent of world GDP. By 2005, they
amounted to about 16 percent of world GDP or close to US$7
trillion.[2] But immigration is no higher and mostly much lower
than it was in the nineteenth and early twentieth centuries.
Between the 1860s and the 1900s, it was not uncommon in the
British Isles and other parts of Europe, the United States,

Canada, and Australia for migration rates to be as high as 4 to 10 people (or higher) per 1,000 of population compared with rates of about 2 in Europe today, 4.5 for the United States and Canada, and 6 for Australia.[3]

Today's distance-compressors are the computer, the Internet, and the cell phone. Tomorrow's may be the deepening and broadening of "connectivity" on a scale we can't yet fully contemplate. Around the world, we are all conscious about the death of distance, the shrinkage of time in communications and transactions, and the disappearance of boundaries and borders—all of which are linking peoples' lives more intimately and immediately than ever. And yet, in this world of relatively free trade and capital flows, and of labor movement in and out of companies and factories, numerous contradictions and criticisms have emerged.

Put another way, there have been few problems with the globalization of markets, companies, and finance. If anything, there has been spectacular success. The tricky bit is how to get people and labor markets to integrate globally as the counterpart. Successful globalization will require richer and poorer countries to interact without resort to barriers and protectionism. In other words, the successful transition to aging societies will require Western countries to reach some kind of understanding with emerging nations about labor and capital transfers.

Solving the globalization problem via institutions

Nineteenth-century imperialism (forcibly) opened up previously closed societies and integrated them into global markets of the time according to then prevailing institutions and rules. But the end result was a tragic failure to deal with the consequences of the globalization of the time. While the causes have been debated ever since, they certainly included political and institutional failings, ethnic conflicts and demographic trends, and economic weakness. To address these failures, considerable attention was paid by many thinkers in the 1930s and 1940s to the role of institutions in the integration of markets in goods and services and of capital and labor. Institutions are essentially political, and if they become dysfunctional or if the political and social willingness to adapt or adjust to the costs and challenges of integration fails, then no matter how powerful the technologies of the day, the capacity to deepen and maintain support for economic integration will fail.

The great British economist, John Maynard Keynes, understood this. He recognized that institutional weaknesses, which characterized the first wave of globalization, contributed to its downfall. He drew attention to the absence of policy measures to create and sustain full employment and the relative ease with which the world succumbed in the 1930s to trade wars and protectionism. But he also believed that "great moderation" was required and that economic integration should not be pressed too far. He asserted that the institutions, rules, and policies needed to maintain stability in the world economy were more complex and difficult to set up than earlier generations had believed. Partly under his guidance, the Bretton Woods[4] system was established after the Second World War with a view to balancing the desirability of economic integration on the one hand and political acceptability on the other. This was done under the auspices of strong institutions, specifically the International Monetary Fund (IMF), the International Bank for Reconstruction and Development (World Bank), and the General Agreement on Trade and Tariffs, whose functions were taken over by the World Trade Organization in the 1990s. These institutions brought together sovereign nations that negotiated and subscribed to a rules-based code governing trade and monetary affairs.

This system survived until the early 1970s, when the economic and financial strains arising from America's domestic economic policies, for example, the Great Society social and civil rights spending programs and its conduct of the Vietnam War (so-called guns and butter programs) collided with the economic interests of the then-new powers: Japan and Germany. The Bretton Woods monetary system went into terminal decline and finally collapsed in 1973. The economic and political powers of the day had to come to a new *modus vivendi* with the help of the multilateral institutions in which they clearly still had strong vested interests, not to mention voting power.

But international monetary and economic relations changed, and the role and strength of multilateral institutions waned in the wake of the political and economic shift to the right from the late 1970s onwards. The "Washington Consensus" was a phrase initially coined in 1989 to describe specific economic policy prescriptions that countries in economic crisis should pursue in exchange for assistance by the IMF, World Bank, and the US Treasury. But it has come to mean something more ideological and therefore much more contentious, namely a set of policies, geared toward the role of market forces and limits to the role of the state. In more recent years, new economic powers have emerged, especially China, India, Russia, and Brazil, most of which have different perceptions about the way the world should work and which are not properly or adequately represented in the highest policy-making bodies in international institutions. The Group of Eight (G8) countries, for example, comprise the United States, Japan, Germany, France, the United Kingdom, Italy, Canada, and Russia, but not China or any of the other major emerging markets.

The globalization "trilemma"

The dominance of market forces and solutions in a sort of unfettered globalization, the weakness of global and national institutions, and a lack of proper representation for emerging markets are now real matters for concern. Professor Dani Rodrik of Harvard University has powerfully sketched the balancing trick that faces us.[5] He says there is a political "trilemma." You can have deep economic integration. You can pursue national sovereignty and self-determination. Finally, you can assert democratic politics. But at best you can only ever have two of these.

For example, deepening economic integration involves some sacrifice, either of national self-interest or certain aspects of democratic government or both. The only way to reconcile these three goals is by ensuring that global markets are subject to proper governance. He says that what made Venice the epicenter of international trade and finance until its decline in the seventeenth century was the quality of its public institutions. The same went for London in the nineteenth century and New York and London subsequently. Further, he says the reason for the success of the original Bretton Woods system was that its architects subjugated international economic integration to the needs and demands of national economic management and democratic politics.

As markets in goods, services, and capital have become increasingly globalized and market outcomes have been the preferred way of resolving economic problems, Rodrik insists that the domain of domestic political debate and spheres of authority have narrowed. Have you ever wondered why it has become so hard to differentiate between the economic programs of ruling and opposition political parties, why it so often feels like choosing between Nike and Adidas trainers?

In essence, deep economic integration has the effect of crowding out much political debate and action. You can't really have an effective debate about tax and public spending policy or about education and demographics-related policies when the current version of globalization restricts the power of the state, for instance. The one area where governments have maintained much of their sovereignty, notably under pressure from their domestic voters, is the one where the least integration has occurred, namely the free movement of labor. In theory, a genuinely free market in labor might do as much, if not more, for global welfare than free trade and capital movements. But the reality is that, for good or bad reasons, this will not be possible for the foreseeable future because of the social and political issues associated with—though not necessarily caused by—immigration.

The search for proper global governance is likely to become an increasingly important and urgent one, to which we can only hope political leaders will be alert. We certainly have the so-called architecture. Though the subject of much scrutiny and debate today about their functions, the IMF and the World Bank now operate alongside other international institutions such as the United Nations, the International Labor Organization, the World Trade Organization, and a proliferation of sometimes very powerful nongovernment organizations (NGOs) and even multinational companies with global power and reach. All the world's economic powers should be properly represented in appropriate bodies and subscribe to codes of behavior, action, and enforcement that are relevant to our times.

Elsewhere, the European Union exists as an integrating force not just for Europe but also to countries beyond its original (western European) boundaries. America's North American Free Trade Association fulfils similar, though much less ambitious, functions. The same applies, on a much smaller scale to other regional institutional arrangements in Latin America, the Middle East, Africa, and Asia. How these institutions succeed in addressing the contradictions of globalization is important as they tackle a host of issues that include fair (not necessarily free) trade and access to markets; labor market, social security, and healthcare reforms; education and healthcare systems as aging advances; anti-immigration sentiment; income inequalities; job and financial insecurities; and national security concerns.

It is, after all, better that global issues are tackled at a genuinely international and multilateral level than according to the randomness of national self-interest. It is also better that they, in turn, should consider issues of global trade, capital flows, employment swings and roundabouts, climate change, and aging in a structured way than according to the whims of the market alone. The concern today is that in our current version of globalization, Western countries especially may be at or close to a point where institutions become dysfunctional or appear irrelevant, where resentment against markets becomes irrational, and where populism and nationalism emerge from the shadows of political debate to threaten in undesirable ways. That would certainly affect large parts of the world's population adversely and make the adjustment to aging societies much more complex and costly.

Negative sentiment

A growing chorus of resentment about globalization or aspects of it can be heard, mainly in Western countries. Antiglobalization protests are commonplace whenever the leaders of the major industrialized nations meet and are all too easily blamed on the exuberance of youth. But what exactly are they protesting about and why? Is the antiglobalization movement really campaigning to arrest global economic development? For some perhaps, but for most clearly not. While there are some people for whom *globalization* is simply a catchall term to rail against the United States and "Western" domination of the global economy and culture, most people blame the current version of unfettered globalization for leading to outcomes that are either unfair and/ or threatening.

More and more people, even if they don't take to the streets, think the protestors have a point. They worry about the impact of globalization on the poorest countries in the world, on jobs, financial security, migration flows and their communities, security and crime, and on social insurance. People have become increasingly anxious about "welfare," not just in the sense of transfers to the poor and disadvantaged within societies and between countries, of course, but in the sense of general "well-being." Globalization, as we know it, is perceived to be driving us toward more integrated markets, smaller government, lower taxes, deregulation, and open labor and capital markets. Yet, many issues today, including climate change and the implications of aging societies, are creating pressures for more active public policy.

The more mobile labor becomes, the stronger might be the downward pressure on wages, especially of low-skilled workers. The relocation of production to emerging countries has curtailed the bargaining power of workers and trades union in many industrialized nations. The opening of markets for goods and, increasingly, of services, has squeezed companies, many of which face growing pressures to cut costs continuously or accept lower profit margins with consequences for employment. It's not too fine a point to ask whether there is at least a contradiction between the consequences of increasing economic integration on the one hand and the demands—including of course those related to aging—of contemporary societies, on the other.

For the most part, global surveys of attitudes toward globalization have found majority support but with large and growing minorities expressing reservations about, or opposition to, a number of the consequences of globalization. There seems to

Table 8.1   Support for globalization by age group (%)

	18–29	30–49	50–64	65+
N. America	43	35	35	27
W. Europe	41	37	40	36
E. Europe	39	30	30	7
Latin America	36	36	44	45
W. Africa	75	66	58	61
E. and S. Africa	59	51	48	31
Conflict Area	50	50	45	39

Percent responding "very good" to "How do you feel about the world becoming more connected through greater economic trade and faster communication?"

Conflict Area includes Egypt, Jordan, Lebanon, Pakistan, Turkey, and Uzbekistan.

Source: The Pew Research Center, A Global Generation Gap (February 24, 2004).

be an age dimension, moreover, to these attitudes. Older people are patently more anxious. In a Pew Research survey,[6] it was suggested that older Americans and Europeans were more likely than their children and grandchildren to have concerns about globalization and their way of life. Perhaps unsurprisingly, this generation gap was not nearly as sharp in eastern Europe, Asia, and Africa. For most people in these regions, the demographic dividend is alive and well.

That said, the survey results indicated that in America and Europe, even within the 18- to 29- and 30- to 49-year-old age groups, less than 50 percent responded with great enthusiasm to the question. Moreover, the survey also drew attention to the finding that people of all ages everywhere are proud of their cultures but that in the West pride is markedly stronger among middle-aged and older people. This may not be entirely benign, however, since it is quite possible that underneath this pride lie feelings of nationalism that may well be related to the insecurities referred to above. In another survey conducted by the polling company Harris for the *Financial Times*,[7] a majority of people in the United Kingdom, Italy, France, Spain, Germany, and the United States felt globalization was having a negative impact on their countries. In the United Kingdom, the United States, and Spain, less than a fifth of respondents thought globalization was beneficial. Most people wanted governments to do something. In Latin America, despite more than four years of strong economic growth and, mostly, low inflation, several countries reported disillusionment with the globalized market economy. A poll by Latinóbarometro, published by *The Economist*,[8] reported that popular support for democracy had declined, the largest falls occurring in Argentina and Chile as well as in Honduras and Costa Rica. Across 18 countries, only 37 percent of respondents said they were satisfied with their democracies, and no more than half said that a market economy was best for their country.

It is not just middle-aged and older citizens who feel anxious. A significant number of younger people also have growing reservations about globalization, albeit for possibly different reasons. Thomas Friedman, in his best-selling book, *The World Is Flat*,[9] has described and analyzed how and why the world is becoming "samey," for want of a better term. But this is precisely what seems to concern people: They don't like a world that has become flat. And while flatness has clearly brought great gains for the world and for business, flatness also goes to the heart of a serious contradiction in the way we approach the organization of society and the global economy. It is a contradiction, in fact, that carries considerable implications for the role of the market and the individual in the triangle of the welfare state, national interests, and democratic politics. By way of illustration, let us take a look at the question of globalization and health, specifically the case of HIV/AIDS in many of the world's poorer countries.

The point is to highlight how the fight against this epidemic needs to embrace a wide-ranging social and cultural agenda, rather than just the deployment of doctors and medicines, if it is to be successful. Globalization can help us pursue that agenda, but at the same time, it is clear that the two often come into conflict.

Globalization and well-being: the case of HIV/AIDS

Faster and deeper economic integration, rapid urbanization, and immigration mean more and more people are living in close proximity. Health issues are an important part of these developments and as such globalization may be part of both the problem and the solution. Cities, for example, require the harnessing of food, water, energy, and materials on a scale that is beyond nature. Globalization helps us to do this effectively. But then what do we do with the waste we generate in the form of the refuse, sewage, and pollution of air and water? Mostly, these become the responsibility of communities and national governments to sort out, often ineffectively. To take another example, globalization helps us to deliver cheap and processed food on a mass scale around the world, but when this becomes associated, as now, with a global epidemic of obesity, the solutions have to be sought locally and nationally.

So even the word *health* has a double meaning. In Western parlance at least, health means something quite personal. We value it as individuals. We pay for it, we insure it, and we focus on diet and exercise as ways of improving it. Pharmaceutical firms supply medicines and treatments into markets that essentially function around this core concept of health. But health also has a broader meaning, too, in the sense of public health, something that goes beyond individual well-being and the supply of drugs and treatments that cater to our ailments. If you consider high public health standards as a worthy goal, you must, in effect, consider a wide range of policies that focus on the avoidance of poverty specifically and on the social and community aspects of globalization and health-care in general. Epidemics such as HIV/AIDS, after all, don't occur in isolation.

Think for a moment of SARS, or severe acute respiratory syndrome. Between November 2002 and July 2003, according to the World Health Organization (WHO), there were 8,096 known cases of SARS and 774 deaths. The ease and the speed with which it spread disrupted travel, tourism, economic activity, and social interaction, and even though the disease was brought under control fairly quickly and efficiently, it served as a timely reminder that globalization could be both a cause and a victim of adverse human developments. A bird flu pandemic and its possible mutation into a highly contagious and dangerous infection of humans remains a major global health risk. The human and economic costs would probably be substantial and imperil globalization, for a while at least. It wouldn't just be tourism and travel that would be affected, however. If high proportions of employees were infected, not to mention died, attendance at work and the operation of industrial, energy, utility, and service companies, among many others, would be affected in ways that would most likely include both strong recessionary impulses and rising prices.[10]

The focus on bird flu risk is important, but just as important are the economic, social, and agricultural circumstances under which viral diseases like this are liable to occur and spread. This applies equally to HIV/AIDS, the biggest health issue to have accompanied and challenged globalization. Agencies such as the World Bank and the WHO, spearheading the fight against it, have sponsored much laudable work and encouraged donors and governments to become involved in their programs of reform and public investment. But they aren't beyond criticism as to methods and effects and many focus on the emphasis on individual health and market solutions as opposed, for example, to other critical public health policies aimed at preventing and containing the epidemic.

HIV/AIDS reached public attention as an affliction of gay white men in parts of the United States, but it now affects about 33 million people worldwide, including 2.5 million children. Every day, 6,800 people become infected and 5,700 die as a result of the disease. Globalization has come to be seen as both a facilitating force in the spread of the disease as well as potentially a major source of control.

The former speaks for itself while the latter speaks to the ability of multilateral and charitable institutions to harness the resources, modern communications technology, and medical science to combat a global epidemic. Yet the spread of HIV/ AIDS continues and is, of course, a source of grave concern. If the nation-state is widely believed to be inadequate to the task of combating a global epidemic, it is curious, to say the least, that with global and supposedly trustworthy international bodies progress is slow. New data from the WHO, published in the AIDS epidemic update in 2007, which utilized new estimation and measurement techniques, revealed a fall of seven million in the number of people believed to have been infected. It now appears that the rate of new infections has been slowing from the peak rate of 3.4 million, or 9,318 per day, in 1998, but this should give us no cause for complacency. It remains the leading cause of death in Africa and the fourth-leading cause globally. It is widespread in India and growing in China, Vietnam, and Indonesia, and common in Russia and parts of eastern Europe. The slower expansion of HIV/AIDS infection that underlies current expectations is only an assumption, not a prediction and a failure to reverse the trend of infection decisively renders us vulnerable to some re-acceleration in the future.

The spread of HIV/AIDS, in particular in sub-Saharan Africa, has been facilitated by the success of globalization in opening up and providing access to new forms of communications and transportation. If anything, globalization has driven an even bigger wedge between the many countries that have benefited from its effects and the many, mostly poorer, countries that have been left behind. Sadly, globalization is not a tide that lifts all boats. As national and regional markets become more integrated, it has become easier for HIV/AIDS infection to spread between countries, cities, towns, and villages. Increased migration from the countryside to urban areas becomes more possible, and, in extreme but not unusual circumstances, the flight of refugees from areas of drought, hunger, and war becomes a more lethal transmission mechanism.

Clearly there are many other causes, including weaknesses in public health systems, difficulties of communication, and access—especially in rural areas—and the ineffectiveness of HIV prevention campaigns. And then, of course, there are the problems associated with gender imbalance and sex inequality.

These are not matters of globalization, of course, but the problems with which they are associated highlight the challenge of using the power of globalization to combat the disease. Where once polygamy protected populations from the effects of poverty and helped sustain population development, for instance, in the modern context the practice of multiple

sexual partners has precisely the opposite effect and con-
tributes to the spread of HIV/AIDS. It is common in some cultures for the wives of men who have died to be "inherited" by
their brothers-in-law. If the cause of death is AIDS and the
widow had become infected, this practice adds to the conditions for the spread of the disease. The practice of polygamy is
declining partly for this reason but also because of the spread
and intensification of poverty associated with it.

Discrimination against women has also been identified as an
important problem that lies at the heart of the HIV/AIDS pandemic in Africa. The United Nations Secretary General's special
envoy for HIV/AIDS in Africa, Stephen Lewis, has written
poignantly on the subject. He says the pandemic is compounding
the premature death of thousands of productive people, especially women, and wrecking the livelihoods of millions more,
while at the same time sowing the seeds of future famines. He
argues that the assault of HIV/AIDS on women in particular has
no parallel in human history, and, highlights the significance of
women as the pillars of the family and the community, the
"mothers, life-givers and farmers."[11]

The HIV/AIDS epidemic, then, is not only a human tragedy that
saps the social and economic strength and potential of communities and nations. It distorts family structures and increases dependency on unaffected family members and on public authorities. It
undermines productive capacity and labor volume, thereby lowering household incomes and aggravating poverty and vulnerability. No one yet knows quite how HIV/AIDS will interact with other
threats such as climate change, water shortages, and food insecurity, if and when these threats become more evident.

If this sounds bleak, it is. But surely globalization gives us the
tools to do something about it if—and maybe only if—organizations and governments emphasize a wider social and economic
context. Individual treatment and market-based solutions have
important functions, but too many people just cannot gain access
to the resources they need. Properly managed and structured,
globalized healthcare solutions could help spread advances in
medicine and provide better access to immunization and birth
control programs, to protection against disease, and to childcare

facilities. By exploiting the decline in transport costs and the spread of cell phones, globalization could also enhance the effectiveness of such programs and increase local medical treatment, care, and monitoring.

Not least because of these factors, the demographic gap between richer and poorer countries in terms of birth, mortality, and life expectancy rates has been narrowing and will continue to do so. All this is occurring under the auspices and guidance of numerous institutional structures that are well regarded and respected, including the WHO, the World Bank, UNICEF (the United Nations Children's Fund), the United Nations Development Program, the Food and Agricultural Organization, and the World Food Program, as well as the voluntary sector, including such entities as Oxfam, the International Committee of the Red Cross, and Medecins sans Frontieres. These institutions offer global programs to fight disease and illness, raise life expectancy, and combat infant mortality. Getting a grip on and finally controlling HIV/AIDS and lifting Africa out of poverty and recurring famine should be within the capacity of human endeavor. In conjunction with improved and more sustained education (that is, fewer dropouts, especially girls who leave to tend to sick parents) and enhanced employment opportunities, the fight against poverty and deprivation in many areas could be pursued far more successfully.

If the quality of health improved, family life became more stable, and children didn't drop out of school or higher education, the building blocks for faster and more sustainable economic growth in Africa could be laid into the decades ahead. But it needs sound and respected institutions working at local, national, and international levels in comprehensive ways that only globalization, not nationalism, can provide. As I showed in the more detailed examination of Africa's demographics in Chapter 7, these are essential if the continent's existing demographic problems are to be resolved and its potential realized.

For richer, for poorer: marriage by globalization

Rich aging countries and poorer younger ones have become increasingly interdependent with rapid globalization. Rich countries are well endowed with capital, poorer ones with labor. Accordingly, capital and labor should flow in opposite directions. It was probably fair to say that 100 years ago, in 1908, the world actually worked like that. In 1958 it worked that way too. In 2008, it doesn't. Nowadays, capital tends to flow relatively freely and copiously from supposedly capital-scarce emerging and developing countries to richer countries, mainly the United States (except Japan, which is a capital exporting nation), while labor also tends to flow, under restrictive legislation, into richer countries from poorer ones. At least the direction of labor flows is what might be expected. But the directional flow of capital is an anomaly—and one of several reasons for this curious development is the phenomenon of aging societies.

It might help to offer a quick reminder about two essential accounting relationships in economics. The first is that countries' balance of payments transactions with the rest of the world must always balance (by definition). That is, current account (trade plus income transfers) surpluses and deficits are always matched by capital (physical and financial) outflows and inflows. The second is that savings must always equal investment. If they don't, changes in interest rates and capital flows, for example, will occur to restore balance. From these principles we can observe that in open economies, current account surpluses occur in countries where there is excess saving, and deficits occur where there is inadequate saving. Table 8.2 shows the structure of savings and investment and the balance of payments in key countries and regions in 2006.

Even if you're not a finance professional, I hope the key concepts are clear. The United States saves less than it invests and, accordingly, runs a deficit on its external balance (the current account) with the difference borrowed overseas. To put this into a slightly clearer perspective, national income accounting shows that any change in investment spending is always matched exactly by a change in aggregate domestic saving. Since saving is the difference between income and consumption, it follows that when domestic saving is inadequate,

Table 8.2   Savings, investment and balance of payments 2006

	US	Japan	Euro Area	E Asia*	China	Oil export countries	Other emerging and developing
As % GDP							·
Savings	12.9	28	21.3	29	58.6	33.2	21
less							
Investment	19	24.1	21.3	23.4	50.2	21.4	−22.5
equals							
Net lending (+)/borrowing (-)**(= current account)	−6.1	3.9	−0.1	5.7	8.3	11.8	−1.5

Source: *World Economic Outlook*, IMF, Washington (April 2007).

*East Asia excluding China

** Net lending or borrowing and the current account balance are equivalent to one another, by accounting definition, more or less, after allowing for some differences in calculation and rounding errors. In effect, the difference between what a country/region saves and invests is reflected as an external current account surplus or deficit. If a deficit, the country has to import capital from overseas. If a surplus, it exports capital overseas.

income must have fallen short of consumption. Consequently, a balance of payments deficit is the consequence of too little savings and too much consumption, relative to investment. The opposite situation can be seen in the cases of the balance of payments surpluses of Japan, China, and most developing and emerging country groups.

Now consider that countries age at different rates and as a result, dependency ratios (of economically inactive to active people) differ and change at different speeds. In other words, faster-aging countries such as Japan, Germany, or the United States, which have a rising dependency ratio or may be close to a rising trend, should experience a decline in national savings. The main reasons are higher age-related spending by public authorities, which is reflected as a fall in national savings, and the lower-saving behavior of people as they age and then retire. If the savings fall (faster than investment), they will need to import more capital from overseas. As it happens, this describes the United States perfectly, but not faster-aging Japan nor Germany. The reason is that in both Germany and Japan, national savings have fallen, but investment rates have fallen even faster. So these two countries are still capital exporters, while America is a voracious importer of other peoples' capital. The United States borrowed more than US$740 billion from the rest of the world in 2007 or the equivalent of US$1.4 million every second. Other significant but much smaller capital importers were Spain, Australia, Greece, Portugal, the United Kingdom, France, and Italy.

Younger or slower-aging countries, such as China, India, Saudi Arabia, or Brazil are still experiencing declining dependency ratios and rising national savings. If savings rise faster than investment, they will have surplus capital, which will be exported. In almost all cases of emerging and developing country groups, this is precisely what has been occurring. National savings have been rising in recent years, but the scale of their excess savings has been bewildering and normally something to anticipate much later in their economic and demographic development.

To a degree, we can appreciate why this might be. Many emerging markets that haven't yet made it into the developed league have relatively immature consumer markets and relatively low incomes per head. In addition, resource-rich economies, such as those in the Middle East have relatively small populations. The surprising part is why, in fast-growing, younger economies, investment has been relatively subdued. The answer may be found in the economic development policies pursued in Asia and Latin America since the Asian financial crisis of 1997–98, and the Latin American financial crises that followed two to three years later.

These crises exposed the vulnerability of developing countries to economic strategies that relied on heavy imports of capital goods and on significant borrowing abroad in foreign currencies, especially when most of them had weak fixed exchange rates and very small international foreign exchange reserves. Since then, most major developing countries have adopted export-led growth strategies. As I have shown, countries that run big trade surpluses must, by definition, be accumulating large revenues that end up in the form of capital exports, often in the form of vast foreign exchange reserve assets, which are invested in the capital markets of advanced economies, mainly the United States. Of the world's total of about US$7 trillion of such assets at the end of April 2008, China alone had roughly US$1.7 trillion.

Economists believe that in the longer run, as China and other emerging markets develop, grow older (but not yet old), and become richer, they will develop into more consumer-oriented economies and that these surplus savings will diminish, much as one would expect as dependency ratios start to turn up. Though this could still be a considerable time away, it is sufficient now to prompt many people to wonder whether this might actually cause problems much sooner, not least because China's own demographic profile is about to start changing in the next three to four years. Therefore, if the West's need for capital continues to rise because of the age-related decline in savings and the developing country piggy bank (surplus savings) starts to empty much earlier than expected, could the world face a possible shortage of capital?

Put more directly, if China, one of the world's most prolific saving nations, sees its demographics begin to chip away at its high savings and no other country or region is in a position to compensate, then the world might face increased global competition for savings. This scenario has been sketched according to the provocative question: Is China going to eat our lunch? This would be reflected in higher world interest rates and greater domestic pressures for Western countries to raise taxes so as to plug widening age-related fiscal deficits. This would be a mirror opposite of the situation that has evolved in the last decade or so and that prevails today, that is, ample global savings (relative to investment), and generally low levels of taxes and long-term interest rates.

In other words, as China continues to develop and expand, its role in the world may change in very important ways, not all of which would be welcomed in the West. China is already changing from a nonthreatening consumer of goods and services to a potentially more threatening competitor in world trade. It is amassing foreign assets, and some observers wonder whether these might be deployed eventually for political and for competitive purposes via investments (overtly or otherwise) in strategic industries or companies.

But leaving such conspiracy theories to one side, the economic problem may arise if China's aspiring middle classes, along with rapid population aging and immature public pension system contrive to starve the world of the current supply of Chinese capital exports. In other words, China will consume or invest more of its own savings. Economists who deny this will happen argue that China might be inclined to apply strict limits on its public spending and that Chinese citizens could continue to maintain high savings rates and, by definition, relatively subdued consumption rates relative to (rising) income. I can't imagine for a moment why either of these should prove to be true over time. In any event, even though Chinese citizens' savings rates are currently high—in the region of 25 percent of income—it is also important to point out that a key reason for China's overall high savings rate of about 58 percent of GDP is the savings of Chinese companies. This is partly due to temporary and cyclical factors that can hardly be extrapolated too far. As China's economy becomes a more sophisticated economy, its overall savings flows and capital exports are likely to slow down or decline. China may not intend to eat our lunch, but we may find ourselves coming up short, regardless.

Conclusions

Several challenges confront the cozy and comfortable pattern into which the global economy seems to have settled in recent years. They include better management of globalization, wider distribution of benefits, strengthening of institutions, and improved management of age-related capital flows. Ideally, the good bits of globalization will survive and incorporate acceptable political ways of addressing the tensions and frictions we have discussed here. We need to emphasize a multilateral approach, with advanced and developing countries fully involved and represented, to address savings and investment-related financial imbalances and govern a fair and effective transfer of goods and services and capital and labor between countries and markets. The very real risks of a drift toward more trade and capital protectionism is one important reason to worry about the weakness of multilateral initiatives. Numerous examples of the latter have been evident in recent years. These include poor co-ordination by major industrialized countries in the management and oversight of foreign exchange markets and global current account flows. But there have been other worrisome trends, including the proliferation of bilateral trade agreements, acts of protectionism by the United States and the European Union in favor of their farmers and against China, and the failure to conclude the Doha Round of multilateral trade negotiations that began in 2001.

The costs of climate change and natural resource constraints are other reasons. Attempts to control and regulate carbon emissions will add to the costs of doing business and could undermine productivity. Attempts not to control them would result in substantially larger costs, concentrated mainly in poorer countries in tropical areas. The UK government-sponsored Stern Review on the Economics of Climate Change[12] has estimated the costs at 1 percent of global GDP per year. At the same time, the costs of exploring and ensuring adequate supplies of energy and water are rising. To repeat the point, demographic changes that lie behind global growth and increasing demand for resources could lead to greater instability in commodity markets, asset markets, and the global economy.

Different rules geared to the specific economic and demographic conditions of individual countries could be devised. This would be more effective and fairer than a single model based on markets and small government that is applied equally to a multitude of countries at different stages of development. A globalization run along these lines that allowed us more or newer degrees of freedom with respect to domestic policies on tax and welfare, education, employment, and productivity— not least related to the demands of aging societies—might at least begin with the priceless advantage of public support, even enthusiasm.

If, however, for all the wrong reasons, globalization were allowed to falter, all of this would become a pipe dream. Acts of terror or aggression, over and above those experienced so far this century, could cause us to lurch in this direction. We could succumb to internal or external pressures to swing too far toward overregulation, protectionism, and nationalism. If our policy initiatives or responses are weak, fragmented, nationalistic, or simply too slow, what we might end up with is the worst of worlds. We might find our societies growing old amid rising poverty and stagnating productivity. We might find rising inflation, aided and abetted by governments looking for the easy option to manage deteriorating fiscal positions. As a result, but also because of a flawed global financial system, a capital shortage or financial crunch could occur that would exacerbate the probable rise in interest rates. High-saving economies such as China, Japan, and Germany would not escape lightly, but countries such as the United States, Spain, and Australia, which are heavily dependent on foreign borrowing, might find themselves in a complex financial quagmire.

Demographic change and population pressures will ultimately force countries to adjust. If anything, they will have to depend on one another to an even greater degree—whether in relation to healthcare and the fight against disease, to trade, migration, savings and investment flows or to population and growth aspects of climate change. The last thing we must do is turn our backs on globalization or let it wither in the face of resentment and popular backlash. Globalization needs to be managed by sound and respected institutions working in all our interests. People need to feel they have vested interests in its success and that they are more beneficiaries than victims of its power. Globalization presents issues that can be addressed partly by using markets where appropriate, but in the context of a much stronger role for public policy and for social benefits and cohesion, not just those of the individual.

Endnotes

1   The term of "death of distance" may have been by Frances Cairncross in an article in *The Economist* in 1995 and later as the title of her book *The Death of Distance: How the Communications Revolution Will Change Our Lives*, (Cambridge: MA: Harvard Business School Press 1997). It describes aptly the dynamic process of globalization.

2 Capital flows comprise international flows of equities, debt instruments, physical investment and equity participations, and other corporate and government assets and liabilities. Here, they are quoted on a gross basis, that is, adding up only the capital outflows that can be identified of all countries reporting to the IMF. See George Magnus, "Capital Flows and the World Economy: Petrodollars, Asia and the Gulf," UBS Investment Research, Economic Insights—By George (November 2006).

3 Timothy J. Hatton and Jeffrey G. Williamson, "What Determines Immigration's Impact? Comparing Two Global Centuries," National Bureau of Economic Research Working Paper 12414 (July 2006).

4 The Bretton Woods conference took place in the rural resort that bears its name in New Hampshire in 1944 and resulted in the establishment for the first time of a fully negotiated monetary order designed to govern monetary relations among independent nation states.

5 Dani Rodrik, "Feasible Globalizations," National Bureau of Economic Research Working Paper 9129 (August 2002).

6 "A Global Generation Gap, Adapting to a New World," The Pew Research Center, February 24, 2004.

7 *Financial Times*, "Poll reveals backlash in wealthy countries against globalization," July 23, 2007.

8 "A warning for reformers," *The Economist* November 15, 2007.

9 Thomas L. Friedman, *The World Is Flat: A Brief History of the Twenty-First Century* (New York: Farrar, Strauss and Giroux, 2005).

10 The US Congressional Budget Office has released a report considering the possible effects of a serious or mild pandemic on the United States. The mortality rate could be between 1 percent and 2.25 percent of possibly 90 million infected persons, and the impact on GDP could be between −1 percent and −4.25 percent. See Congressional Budget Office, "A Potential Influenza Pandemic: Possible Macroeconomic Effects and Policy Implications," Washington, DC (December 8, 2005, revised July 27, 2006). The Asian Development Bank has looked at the possible consequences for the region in Asian Development Bank, *The Potential Impact of an Avian Flu Pandemic in Asia.* (Manila: November 2005). The effects, depending on severity, might involve 3 million or many more deaths and reduce regional GDP by between 2.25 percent and 9–10 percent.

11 Stephen Lewis, *Race Against Time* (Toronto: House of Anansi Press Inc., 2005), p. 136.

12 Nicholas Stern, *The Economics of Climate Change: The Stern Review* (Cambridge: Cambridge University Press, 2007) Part II, 3.2, p. 62.

Chapter 9

Will immigration solve aging society problems?

> *A more urgent problem is the bad population distribution around the globe. The unavoidable conclusion is that there will be massive pressures for emigration from the countries with very high birth rates to the rich countries.*
> —Eric Hobsbawm, in conversation with Antonio Polito, 1999.[1]

If globalization is a reflection of mankind's propensity to trade and integrate, migration is one of its most basic expressions, specifically of the human will to overcome adversity and prejudice or persecution in one location and seek a better life elsewhere. The arguments for and against immigration ebb and flow across many disciplines, but here I consider mainly economic issues for, as noted in Chapter 4, in many ways immigration can ease the pressures on aging societies.

In modern times, with the relatively low cost of transportation, the Internet, telephony, satellite television, and the ease of making financial transfers, you would assume that the scale of global migration would be unprecedented. Yet immigration amounts to only 3 percent of world population, a little lower than it was in 1900 and, in many countries, significantly lower. But it has been rising in recent years and, while the basic drivers of immigration do not change, the different speeds of aging around the world mean that an important new one is emerging. Human capital—labor—is migrating from poorer, younger countries where it is plentiful (and cheap) to richer, older countries where it is becoming increasingly scarce with higher wages as a consequence.

This gives rise to at least two questions. Does, and will, immigration benefit aging societies in the ways that economists say it should? And, even if it can be demonstrated that this is the case, will Western countries really encourage still higher levels of immigration in the future, given the increasingly skeptical or negative responses in many countries? This chapter will elaborate on the economic arguments for immigration from the standpoint of aging societies and show that they are not as persuasive as we're often led to believe. There is much, therefore, that governments can and should do to raise its effectiveness and, more than anything, its acceptability.

Rising hostility toward immigration

In countries around the world, immigration has fuelled resentment and in some cases a shocking backlash. Take Italy, where in November 2007, Giovanna Reggiani, the 47-year-old wife of a naval captain was found sexually assaulted, robbed, and dead in a ditch near the commuter station of Tor di Quinto in northern Rome, from which, apparently, she had been walking home. A 24-year-old Romanian immigrant was arrested for the offenses at his "home," a bivouac of makeshift shacks on the embankment of the River Tiber. This certainly was not the first shocking incident involving Romanian immigrants, of which there are about half a million in Italy, roughly half the number of Romanians living abroad. But it led to an eruption of latent hostility to immigration among Italians. Within a few days, racial violence broke out and the Italian government passed a tough decree, authorizing local authorities to expel Romanian immigrants in contravention of European Union Directive 38, which provides for the free movement of EU citizens.

Sadly, this is but one of many examples of Western societies experiencing a dangerous fusion of immigration, the emergence of mutual suspicions and fears between immigrants and host communities, and reactive government pandering to negative perceptions of immigration. This is a sorry state of affairs, moral issues aside, bearing in mind the way global demographics are changing, and the possibility that immigration can produce some economic benefits for aging societies. Governments will turn a blind eye to these issues at their peril.

In the years leading up to 2015, as the population of the advanced economies grows by just 30 million, the population of western Asia (basically the Middle East plus Turkey), North Africa, and Mexico is predicted to increase by 86 million (and by 202 million in sub-Saharan Africa). Between then and 2050, the populations of advanced economies will be static, while that of western Asia, North Africa, and Mexico will increase by a further 223 million (and 790 million in the rest of Africa). In advanced economies, the population aged 15–59 will fall by 115 million by 2050, while that of western Asia, North Africa, and Mexico will increase by 180 million (the rest of Africa 690 million). There will be no shortage of migrants looking for new homes and work overseas, especially in richer countries and if economic development efforts fall short in developing countries.

But even in countries such as the United States and Australia, which for the most part have a welcoming attitude toward migrants, immigration has aroused passionate arguments, not for the first time in Australia's case. Who should be admitted, for how long, on what terms? Under what circumstances will families be allowed to join? Should societies clamp down on immigration altogether and more forcefully?

In a Pew survey on global attitudes people in 47 countries in five continents agreed by huge majorities, mostly well over 60–70 percent, with the statement: "We should further restrict and control immigration."[2] There were a few exceptions. People in the occupied Palestinian Territories registered a 58 percent disagreement score and only 53 percent of Swedes agreed. For the most part, however, the results conform to anecdotes of fear or concern about high levels of immigration, if not outright xenophobia.

That the sentiment is predominantly about concern as opposed to xenophobia is borne out by the finding that people in Europe, for example, while more opposed to immigration than they were five years ago, are less likely to support tighter controls than they were five years ago. Rather, their concerns center on the types of immigrants granted entry permits and the countries from which they come. This boils down, simply, to skilled versus unskilled migrants. Moreover, Europeans and Americans have registered mounting concerns not specifically about immigration, per se, but about some particular aspects of immigrant skills that center on the ability to integrate into their new countries. Most people in the largest member countries of the European Union, for example, express very strong views about the need for would-be migrants to take citizenship and language tests. According to a *Financial Times*/Harris poll conducted in France, Germany, Italy, Spain, the United Kingdom, and the United States in early December 2007, such tests were supported by more than 80 percent of respondents in the United States, the United Kingdom, and Germany, and by more than 60 percent of Italians and French people.[3]

The official or government line in many advanced countries on immigration is normally comforting, if not enthusiastic. For example, in the United States, the Council of Economic Advisers, a White House think tank, is openly supportive of immigration and the benefits it brings to the country. It says that 40 percent of Ph.D. scientists working in the United States come from abroad, that the entrepreneurial activity rates of immigrants is 40 percent higher than for native-born individuals, that immigrants assimilate well, and that they improve the solvency of the pay-as-you-go benefit systems.[4] Several European governments have shifted their positions on immigration matters recently by emphasizing the desirability of skilled immigration. The UK authorities, for example, introduced a points system in late 2007, applicable to non-EU citizens looking to work in the United Kingdom and based on age, qualifications, and language skills.

The days are long gone when, for example, the United Kingdom and Germany had an open door policy to unskilled labor from the Caribbean and Turkey respectively. Nowadays, resistance is aimed specifically at more poorly educated and low-skilled migrants, who typically have accounted for almost half of immigrants to Europe, for example. Those with skills and education are most prevalent in the United States, Canada, Australia, and Switzerland, and are favored sometimes via a points system, examples of which have been introduced in the United Kingdom, Canada,and Australia. The European Union definitely lags in its ability to attract skilled migrants, with the possible exception of the United Kingdom. In the rest of Europe, France, Portugal, and Spain seem best able to attract such immigrants.

In 2001, the proportion of immigrants in the United States, Canada, Australia, and the United Kingdom aged over 15 with tertiary education was high and comparable to the native-born population. In most of western Europe, the proportion was low and often below that of the overall population. But the situation of immigrants aged over 15 years with less than secondary education compared quite differently to native populations. In nearly all members of the wealthy-country Organization for Economic Cooperation and Development (OECD), the proportion of immigrants in this category ranged from 30 to 55 percent and in most, the immigrant share was higher than for the native-born population. Only Canada, Australia, the United Kingdom, and Spain were exceptions.[5]

In advanced economies, more than half of young children go on to attend university or into other tertiary education. As the working-age population stagnates or falls, the overall educational level of the labor force over time should keep rising, but, as I shall show later, there are a few countries, including the United States and Germany, where a relative decline in educational standards casts doubt on whether this is happening. The main point, however, is unwillingness on the part of better skilled, native-born workers to take low-paid and more physical jobs, which end up being done by immigrants. These include manual jobs in retailing, cleaning, food services, the construction and allied trades, hospitals, public services, and the leisure, child and elderly care and catering sectors.

The skills or education gap between native and foreign-born citizens goes some way to explaining the shift in immigration policies in favor of more skilled migrants, but it may also reveal much about the reasons for negative attitudes in the population as a whole. Much of the hostility to immigration from the middle classes and the poor comes from a cross section of ethnic backgrounds and not only from white Americans and Europeans. This suggests that rather than race lying at the heart of the immigration debate, it is more likely to be economic and class factors. Working-class, and many middle-class families, whatever their racial origins or characteristics, may all have cause for concern about the social and economic pressures that immigration is perceived to bring to their neighborhoods, public services, and jobs. They are also likely to be in the front line, so to speak, where they may perceive and resent what they see as favorable treatment meted out to newly arrived neighbors from abroad.

It is not unreasonable, then, to sympathize with the unskilled or semiskilled worker in Sheffield, Düsseldorf, Marseille, or San Diego who becomes fearful or angry about losing his or her job or income and anxious about social conditions and public services. It is equally reasonable to sympathize with immigrants who may feel ostracized or isolated, either alone or packed into their own communities. Without support from a range of government, employer, and civil programs, some people find the consequences of immigration simply too much to handle on their own. It is hardly surprising that several Western countries now hear a growing chorus for more restrictive immigration legislation or control, along with the risk of right-wing, autocratic, and xenophobic political groups seeking to exploit the fears and perceived injustices of both native and foreign-born peoples.

Middle-income people who run local stores and businesses may sense that less well-off people don't tend to spend much on leisure, home purchase and improvement, eating out, and other activities that improve the prosperity and the look of towns and city neighborhoods. More affluent people probably become vocal when they see or fear the spillover of social and economic problems in poorer neighborhoods to (their) more prosperous parts of town.

A shift of mood in America—it is of no small importance that it is happening at all in the United States, of all countries—with a focus on Hispanic immigrants has become significant for two reasons. First, it rapidly became a key issue in the 2008 presidential election campaign. Second, the change of mood is not just taking place in the border states with Mexico. People in the Midwest, New England, and the Mountain states tell pollsters they are becoming more hostile about the numbers of illegal immigrants in the country—12 million with half a million entering every year—and losing faith in the country's formidable track record when it comes to both globalization and integration.

In an *Economist*/YouGov poll 55 percent of respondents said "yes" when asked if immigrants were a threat to traditional American values and customs. Nearly 70 percent agreed that immigrants take away jobs from American workers.[6]

Some anti-immigration groups associate the issue of immigration, especially regarding low skills and legality, with the policies of some of America's more southerly antagonists, such as Hugo Chavez in Venezuela, Evo Morales in Bolivia, and Andres Lopez Obrador in Mexico. They are also prone to point out, as did some of the 2008 presidential hopefuls, that when it comes to illegitimacy, school dropout rates and crime, the US-born children of Mexican immigrants have a track record far worse than past waves of immigrants, who also arrived without capital and education.

The main concern, from the standpoint of aging societies in the United States, western Europe, and even Japan, is not the accuracy or context of assertions such as these, but that they represent an increasingly intolerant mood in a volatile environment that works against any active use of immigration policy to address the implications of aging economies.

How many immigrants and where are they?

The biggest movements of migrant labor in history occurred between 1820 and 1914 when more than 50 million Europeans moved to the United States, Canada, and South America, and indentured Asian workers, mostly Chinese and Indian, moved to plantations and mines in tropical areas. As noted in the previous chapter, the collapse of globalization after the First World War, fragmentation of the world economy, and the closure of borders ended international migration until after 1945. Since then, immigration has again become a significant feature of the global economy, particularly with the rise of new destinations, especially in Europe and higher-income countries in the developing world.

According to the United Nations, the world's stock of migrants—that is, legal migrants, to the extent they can be

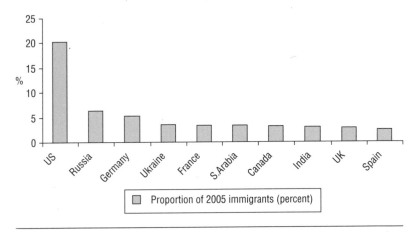

Figure 9.1   Immigrants by host
Source: United Nations Population Division.

counted accurately at all—rose by 36 million between 1990 and 2005 to 191 million. In 2005, 61 percent of migrants lived in advanced economies. Europe was home to 34 percent of migrants, North America to 23 percent, Asia to 28 percent, Japan to 9 percent, and Latin America and the Caribbean to 4 percent. But it is interesting to note that a fairly small sample of countries— 10 in all—hosted 54 percent of all migrants and 28 were home to 75 percent of migrants (see Figure 9.1).

Other countries with between 1 percent and 2 percent of total migrants (going from largest to smallest) included Australia, Pakistan, United Arab Emirates, Hong Kong, Israel, Italy, Kazakhstan, Ivory Coast, Jordan, and Japan. Some of these countries, as I shall point out, may have relatively small percentages of global migrants, but they may have very high numbers of migrants, in relation to their own populations.

Most immigrants move from the developing world to either advanced economies or to higher-income economies in the developing world. In 2005, the United Nations reckoned about 62 million people had moved from Southern countries (Asia, Africa and Latin America) to Northern ones (mainly the United States, Canada, Europe, and, for these purposes, Australia and New Zealand). An equivalent number had moved from and to countries within the South (61 million), while the third-biggest move was within countries in the North (53 million), including the rising flows of migrants from eastern to western Europe.

In the member countries of the OECD, the stock of immigrants in 2000 stood at 84 million, or roughly 7.5 percent of the OECD's population. The highest proportions of foreign-born individuals were to be found in Australia and New Zealand (about 20 percent), and in the United States (12 percent). In the European Union, this proportion then 15-member was about 10 percent. For much of the 1990s, Germany was the biggest European recipient of migrants but in recent years Spain has become the largest, accounting for about 30 percent of net EU immigrants. For example, Spain's 920,000 immigrants in 2000 accounted for about 2.3 percent of the population. By June 2007, the number of immigrants had soared to 4.5 million or about 10 percent of the population, of which about half were from outside the European Union, mainly from Latin America and Africa. Italy, Portugal, and Ireland have also switched from being traditional sources to being new receivers of migrants.

The United Kingdom has also been a big magnet for migrants. In fact, the largest wave of immigration in British history occurred in the decade after 1997. It was so large, that the British authorities were obliged to concede in 2007 that they had got their sums badly wrong. The official estimate that 800,000 immigrant workers had come to the United Kingdom was restated to show a flow of something closer to 1.5 million. Labor statistics subsequently acknowledged that more than half the growth in jobs in the economy in the previous decade had gone to foreign workers. The Office for National Statistics now reckons that net migration will contribute 2.1 million to the expected 4.4 million growth in population (to 65 million by 2016). The assumption is that net migration will average about 220,000 per year until 2011 and then taper to 190,000 a year. But in the United Kingdom, as elsewhere, public trust in such projections is low.

In the uproar that followed the government's admission on migrant numbers, there were the predictable shouts for immigration to be suspended or greatly restricted; but the abiding impression was that immigration had simply been treated in far too cavalier a way. The government didn't know how many immigrants had been admitted, didn't know where they were or who they were, didn't know how long they had come for or intended to stay, and clearly hadn't bothered to manage the consequences in local communities.

If formal data on immigration are suspect for one reason or another, no one really knows how many illegal immigrants there are. The United States is currently estimated to have about 12 million, and the growth in illegal immigrants prompted proposals for legislative reforms known as The Border Protection, Antiterrorism, and Illegal Immigration Control Act of 2005. Although it was approved by the House of Representatives in 2005, the Senate rejected it in June 2007 for the second time, and the bill died.

The legislation was aimed at resolving the status of existing illegal immigrants by giving many the eventual opportunity— after paying US$5,000 for a relevant visa—to apply for citizenship. It also sought to make it easier in future for foreigners to live and work in the United States, while tightening border controls to combat illegal entry to the country. During its passage, the bill drew both widespread protest and support, revolving around the proposed amnesty to illegal immigrants and the tightening of controls at borders and with regard to employers. In street demonstrations, those hostile to the bill hoisted Mexican flags on public buildings and burned them. Supporters sometimes demonstrated behind banners bearing the slogan "All Europeans Are Illegal On This Continent Since 1492."

The 27 member countries of the European Union are officially estimated to have roughly 20 million legal non-EU residents who arrived in three phases. The first, mainly guest workers, came during the 1950s and 1960s as part of Europe's reconstruction after the Second World War and then helped propel the ensuing economic boom. The second, emphasizing family reunification, developed during the 1970s. The third phase focused on asylum seekers, beginning in the 1990s. Net immigration to member countries of the European Union, rose from 198,000 per year during the 1980s to about 750,000 a year in the 1990s. By 2003, the rate of net immigration was running at two million, since that time it has dropped slightly to about 1.6–1.8 million a year. But illegal immigration also started to accelerate in the 1990s. The most recent official estimate of three million illegal immigrants (1998) will almost certainly have grown significantly, possibly to double that amount or more.

Accurate estimates of illegal immigration are particularly difficult in Europe as a result of the abolition of many passport controls within the Union. The European Commission has initiated a series of proposals in recent years to discourage illegal immigration, which it estimates at four to eight million people throughout, with about half a million new ones arriving each year. In 2005, the Commission asked member nations to implement common rules governing the repatriation of illegal immigrants and refugees who are denied asylum, and in 2007 it introduced a program to clamp down on would-be migrants who pass through Europe.

In Asia, some migration patterns are very old, for example from Burma to Thailand and from the Philippines and Indonesia to Singapore. But newer ones have been evolving. It is estimated that between 1995 and 2000, 40 percent of Asian migrant workers went to work in other Asian countries, compared with about 10 percent in the 1970s and 1980s. Asian migrants comprise a high proportion of workers in the Gulf countries of the Middle East, by some estimates between 40 and 70 percent. But there is also a high proportion of migrant workers in the labor force in both Singapore and Hong Kong.

There is no age-specific demographic need, however for Asian workers to migrate, except in the case of Japan today and South Korea and Taiwan soon. Japan has about two million non-Japanese living in the country, making up 1.5 percent of the population; about half are Koreans, many descended from those who arrived between 1910 and 1945 when the Korean Peninsula was under Japanese colonial rule. If ever a country needed to throw open its borders to immigrants from an economic and aging point of view, Japan is that country. Instead, it remains at best skeptical, and it has tried to deploy technology to address some of the issues of aging rather than liberalize its immigration policy. Much capital and effort have been allocated to robotics, for example, including devices designed to lift the elderly out of bed and act as companions to those living alone.[7]

It is also worth noting a new type of immigration: people fleeing their native countries for environmental reasons. Climate change, in so far as it is likely to aggravate the incidence of drought, soil erosion, desertification, and deforestation, is already having an impact on migrant flows. In 1995, a probably conservative estimate of 25 million people may have been environmental refugees in the Horn of Africa and in sub-Saharan Africa. The United Nations thinks that by 2010 there could be 50 million environmental refugees worldwide.[8] That would be equal to a quarter of the total number of migrants estimated in 2005.

By the time global warming is in full swing, disruptions to monsoons and other weather patterns such as drought and coastal flooding along with other environmental degradation could increase the number of environmental refugees to about 200 million, according to environmental expert Professor Norman Myers at Green College, Oxford.[9] That's about the same as the total number of immigrants estimated in the world today. Consider Bangladesh, which suffers floods regularly. One of the functions of this natural phenomenon is make the land very fertile, but floods also kill and displace people, and the growing frequency and intensity of flooding has been linked to climate change. Floods, resulting from a cyclone in 2007, for example, may have killed more than 1,000 people and displaced or marooned more than two million.

How sustainable is higher immigrant fertility?

The fact that most immigrants from the bulk of "sending" countries have higher fertility rates than Western "receiving" economies appears to be a sound reason to encourage immigration for demographic reasons. More children can help retain the youthfulness of the population as a whole and bolster the working age group in years to come.

Immigrant women are likely to have more children than native-born women, and they may actually bear more children than they would have done if they hadn't emigrated in the first place.

US Census data (2000) showed that the proportion of births attributable to foreign-born women stood at 20 percent in 1999 compared with 6 percent in 1970. And the US Center for Immigration Studies, looking at America's top 10 sources of migrants in 2002, for example, found that immigrant women had on average 2.9 children in the United States, compared with 2.3 in the countries from which they came. For example, Mexican women under the period of study had 3.5 children (compared with the then Mexican rate of 2.4 children); Chinese women had 2.3 children (1.7 in China); and Canadian women had 1.9 children (1.5 in Canada). In other cases, though, for example India, Vietnam, and the Philippines, immigrant women had fewer children than they might have had in their countries of birth.

The United Nations says that the biggest sources of migrants, with current fertility rates in parentheses, are China (1.7), Mexico (2.2), India (2.8), the Philippines (3.2), Pakistan (3.5), and Indonesia (2.2). All of these fertility rates, except for China's, are higher than in advanced economies—but not by as much as popular thinking would have us believe. The seven countries that the United Nations believes will be the biggest receivers of migrants over the next 40 years are the United States (2.05), Canada (1.5), Germany (1.36), Italy (1.4), the United Kingdom (1.8), Spain (1.4), and Australia (1.8).

In Europe, the Vienna Institute of Demography, comparing Austria, the Flanders region of Belgium, Denmark, England and Wales, France, Spain, Sweden, and Switzerland, found that in various periods from the late 1990s to 2003–04, immigrant women in every country had higher fertility rates than native-born women. Averaging the eight countries' numbers, the fertility rate for the latter was about 1.5, while for immigrant women it was just below 2.3. The only country where there was a relatively minor difference was Sweden. And it is clear that in Europe the proportion of births attributed to foreign-born women has been rising steadily. In the United Kingdom, the Office of National Statistics data reveal that this proportion was 21.9 percent in 2005, compared with 12.8 percent in 1996, and it is likely that the Europe-wide proportion is also in a range of 20–25 percent.

The argument about sustainable higher immigrant fertility, however, is probably more complex than it appears at first sight. While the initial and perhaps first-generation effects of immigration on fertility do appear to bear out popular percep-tions, there is no reason why this should remain true over time, indeed it has not, except in the case where cultural or religious factors lay great emphasis on larger family size.

In Europe, for example, where immigration is a significant and contentious matter, there is no common pattern that would help us to make the general association between higher immi-gration rates and higher fertility rates (and vice versa) and to conclude that there is a positive link to aging societies. Europe divides into three major groups: former East Germany, the Baltic countries, and eastern Europe have comparatively low fertility rates and low immigration. Spain, Italy, Switzerland, Austria, and former West Germany have low fertility rates but high immigration rates. Finally, the United Kingdom, France and Scandinavia have relatively higher fertility rates but also high immigration rates.

It may be that in the first instance when migrants move they already have large families, or that once settled, they tend to have more children. But this does not mean that they continue to do so during all of their childbearing years, and there is no evidence that second and third generations of immigrants, as a rule, maintain the same childbearing habits as their mothers and grandmothers.

Fertility rates of immigrant and native-born women tend to converge over one to two generations to the lower fertility rate of the two groups for a multitude of economic and social rea-sons that have little to do with race or country of origin. It also seems much more plausible that the fertility trends of these subsequent generations of immigrants are determined, as for everyone else, by educational achievement, marital status,

income, and career characteristics than, by anything associated with immigration or country of origin. The exception
might be among religious groups, where high fertility and large
families are encouraged as an integral part of the woman's role
in family and society. In other words, the economic effects of
initially higher immigrant fertility rates are all too likely to
fade over time, unless immigration continues to grow *ad
infinitum* so as to preserve its rejuvenating effects on society.

Economic arguments are awkward or weak

As labor or skill shortages begin to present themselves in western Europe and the United States, the intuitive appeal of
higher immigration is obvious. In some respects, this trend is
already evident. In the short term at least, immigration boosts
the supply of working-age people and, in theory, enables us to
slow down the rise in the dependency ratio and lessen the
financial burdens of aging. I will consider here both these
potentially positive aspects of immigration and the real or perceived negative effects, especially as regards lost job opportunities and lower wages for the existing population.

In reality, theoretical arguments about the long-run positive
effects of immigration on the dependency ratio, while persuasive when expressed algebraically, fall rather flat when the
implications for migrant flows are considered. The United
Nations population database estimates that the labor force in
advanced economies was roughly 800 million in 2000 and will
decline to about 740 million in 2050 with continued immigration at current rates (640 million without immigration). To
keep the labor force stable, then, would actually require mas-
sively higher immigration.

It has been estimated, for example, that in the United States—
a country with high immigration but with a demographic profile
that is quite favorable compared with western Europe and
Japan—an additional five million immigrants per year (four
times the current legal rate) would be needed to achieve long-term
financial balance in the Social Security trust fund that pays pensions. Measured another way, for America's old-age dependency

ratio to stay unchanged at a little over 18 percent until 2020 would require an additional 95 million migrants of working age. That's not that much lower than the entire population of Mexico.[10] As things stand, America's old-age dependency ratio is going to nearly double to 33 percent by 2040 and accordingly, the purely theoretical calculation is that to maintain stability in that ratio, the United States would need to more than double its working age population to more than 430 million.

To put it a different way, today there are about 142 people aged 20–24 potentially looking for work in developed countries for every 100 people aged 60–64 who are about to retire. By 2015, there will be just 87 people aged 20–24 per 100 aged 60–64. Additional migration could in theory reduce this deficit, but the scale of immigration required would be exceptional and unrealistic in most cases.

A comprehensive study of US immigration since 1980 found that its impact on the labor force, while not trivial, was fairly small. You would expect immigration to have a positive effect because immigrants are largely aged 15 to 64 years. But using the 2000 Census, the study found that within an overall labor force participation of 66.2 percent, the participation rate was 64.2 percent for natives and 81.9 percent for immigrants. Even if you stripped the data of immigrants completely, though, the overall participation rate would have barely differed.[11] In other words, immigration certainly increased the population and congestion but did not have a significant effect on the dependency ratio because immigrants arrived with dependants or acquired them once they had settled. And, of course, as they themselves aged, they became dependants.

Moreover, when the US Census Bureau projected different levels of immigration out to 2060,[12] it found that labor force participation in the far future varied between 58.7 percent and 60.8 percent. Labor force participation rates look likely to decline anyway, given current government policies, and while large-scale or very modest immigration would slow the decline, it would not do so by much.

This more skeptical perspective on the direct labor force impact of immigration is also illustrated in the European Union. In 2004, immigrants who arrived in the Union specifically to work only constituted between 10 percent and 35 percent of migrant flows in member states. The lowest proportions were in France and Sweden (10–15 percent) while the highest were in Denmark and Portugal (over 40 percent). Roughly half of migrant flows arose because of family reunification (40 percent in the United Kingdom, Germany, Denmark, and Portugal, and 70 percent in the Netherlands, Austria, Finland, Italy, France, and Sweden). Entries for humanitarian reasons among European countries accounted for between 2 and 23 percent of migrant flows, with Italy, France, and Denmark in the lower half of this range and the Netherlands, the United Kingdom, Sweden, and Austria in the upper half.[13] In the last two to three years, the flows of asylum seekers have been declining, partly because of tighter entry controls and partly because the flows of migrants from the Balkans and Afghanistan have tailed off. Iraq and Russia are now the largest sources of people seeking asylum in the European Union.

The most significant of these numbers are the 10–35 percent of immigrants who came specifically to work. The economic argument for immigration in aging societies assumes that mostly young migrants arrive and join the labor force where they will be economically active immediately and behave as economic theory suggests young workers should. If only a fifth to a third, say, arrive to work, then the economic argument is already flat on its face. If most immigrants are in fact not coming to work or don't work for one reason or another, then it would be improbable for those who do to contribute enough in the form of taxes, savings, and productivity to the national economy to make any positive difference. Looked at this way, you can see why many researchers find that the overall impact on labor force participation has been positive but by nowhere near as much as one might think.

Short-run effects positive but may not last

There is certainly an upbeat view about the short-term effects of immigration. In the United Kingdom, the Office of National Statistics has described immigration since May 2004 as "almost certainly the largest single wave of in-migration that the British Isles has ever experienced."[14] Anecdotal evidence testifies to the high profile of immigrants—in broad swathes of the economy including building sites and specialty trades, retail stores and restaurants, and public, office and domestic services—and not just selling flowers and washing car windows at traffic lights.

Public officials and private sector commentators have enthused about what they see as the positive impact of immigration on the United Kingdom's economic performance. The National Institute of Economic and Social Research analyzed the official data and revealed that the most recent wave of immigrants (since 2004) was overwhelmingly of working age: roughly 80 percent (88 percent for the newest EU member states, especially those in eastern Europe). This compared with an average 62.3 percent working-age population share for the United Kingdom as a whole. The study also showed that migrants at the low end of the wage spectrum and who arrived in 2004–05 received lower earnings than the indigenous population in all job grades surveyed. At the higher end of the wage spectrum, however, migrants who came from countries excluding the more recent EU member states earned more than native-born workers.

These observations suggest that apart from the positive effects on employment and population, immigration has not in recent years led to downward wage pressure on indigenous workers. It is also argued that immigration in the last few years was instrumental in raising the United Kingdom's fertility rate in 2006 to 1.87 children, the highest for 26 years.

But for a variety of reasons, many of these positive developments may have only a limited lifespan. In other words, they may be more cyclical than structural. In a report financed by the UK Home Office in 2003, the authors concluded that although fears about large and negative employment and wage effects on the resident population from immigration were not easily justifiable, there was not exactly enthusiasm about the long-term effects of immigration either.[15] The authors in fact drew attention to weaknesses in the available data and in the empirical work they themselves conducted. But from the perspective of aging societies, there were more important observations. Specifically, the main point was that the effects of immigration on labor markets depended crucially on assumptions regarding the flexibility of the economy and the degree to which it was integrated into world trade and investment structures. They argued that the greater the economy's flexibility and integration, the more insensitive employment and wages would be to immigration.

On this basis, several continental European countries may have more to worry about than the United States, the United Kingdom, Australia, or Scandinavian countries. For the latter group though, even the conclusion that they might avoid the negative consequences in the medium to long run doesn't go far enough. From an economic perspective, immigration should actually have positive effects in the long run in terms of fertility, working-age population size and dependency ratios. But the evidence is not compelling. Economic theory suggests there should not be any long-run effects on employment or participation while empirical evidence about the short run depends on the existence of very different skill levels between immigrants and the resident population. In other words, there will be positive short-term effects if immigrants, on average, have higher skill levels and vice versa.

Unskilled or semiskilled immigration issues

It seems plausible that low-skilled immigration does have negative effects on the job prospects of those with low educational achievement, especially where countries have high levels of insider job protection. In other words, employers who find it hard to fire existing workers (insiders) for legal reasons may increasingly try to recruit immigrant labor outside the formal labor market. Recruits are often not eligible for full employment rights and benefits. The implication should be not that immigrants are to blame for lost job opportunities but that employment laws offer too much protection to those with jobs and not enough to those without them. In the absence of changes to labor laws, employers looking for cheap ways of hiring or replacing workers are bound to want to hire immigrant workers.

Moreover, because many immigrants work in local and family businesses and small firms and are often prepared to work long hours for less than formal wage rates, immigration almost certainly does put downward pressure on local or certain (low skill) occupational wages, even if it doesn't lead to a fall in wage rates generally. If it were easier for native-born people to upgrade their education and skills, however, and move to new, higher-paid jobs, maybe elsewhere geographically, why would there be a problem? If governments continue to pay too little attention to education and the upgrading of skills, greater competition for work at the semi-skilled and unskilled levels will persist, with negative effects on jobs and incomes.

If employers are, in effect, given cost and convenience incentives to hire immigrants who have less protection and may work outside the formal labor market, it follows that there is little substance in two familiar arguments. The first is that immigrants do the jobs that native-born people won't do anymore. The second is that the latter regard as unacceptable the wages and conditions many employers offer. If employers are offering employment terms and conditions that local people find unattractive or unrewarding, it is hardly a surprise that they shun or won't apply for such opportunities. Immigrant labor, therefore, fills the gap, and wage rates in some areas or industries might be suppressed as a result. In order to address this anomaly between low-paid immigrant workers who take these jobs and low-skilled local people who can't or don't, there are two requirements. As previously mentioned, you have to make it possible and attractive for people to upgrade their skills and therefore their employment and pay prospects. You also have to create a shortage of cheap and low-skilled labor, for example, by an immigration policy that seeks to prioritize skills. If successful, such measures would force employers to pay higher wages in the unskilled parts of the economy.

For some, a brain drain into retirement

Immigration laws designed to encourage more high-skilled migrants, however, are not only a desirable way of managing immigration policy, they could even be thought essential in some countries. The main reason for this lies in our own backyard, as I shall highlight in a moment. In a few countries, including the United States, children are not being equipped with skills any greater than those of their boomer parents, and in some cases, skills are appreciably lower. In addition, this is happening at a time when skill enhancement in other countries, for example in China and India, is proceeding much faster than in the West. If the skill and education deficiencies in younger people are not corrected soon, several Western countries could find themselves in dire need of tapping the global market for educated workers.

Strange as it may sound, America is possibly one of the most seriously affected countries. One recent study published by the Petersen Institute argued that the United States was at risk of losing its status as the most skill-abundant country in the global economy, that it would require increasingly, over the medium term, foreign high-skilled workers, and that it would have to reform its immigration policies and processes to welcome the world's best and brightest and make it easier for them to stay in the country.[16]

The report conveyed two important points. The first is that the average skill level of the American workforce continued to improve until those now in their late-50s entered the workforce, that is, until roughly the 1970s. The population of graduates and those with advanced qualifications rose strongly relative to the population of unskilled workers. But the second point is that Americans now aged 25–54 are not better educated or skilled and there are some worrying signs that educational and skill standards may actually start to reverse. In 2006, there were more holders of master's, professional, and doctoral degrees among resident 55- to 59-year-olds than among the 30- to 34-year-old age group. Three important implications then follow.

First, unless the output of graduates starts to rise again quickly, there will be a decline in the resident US population holding graduate degrees and better. Second, this points to greater potential for earnings inequality and distorted job opportunities across the educational spectrum with benefits accruing only to those at the high-skill end. Third, those now in their fifties and sixties, who benefited enormously from the opening up of education opportunities and from the liberalization of markets and trade worldwide are, unsurprisingly, the backbone of liberal economic thought and policy. Their children and grandchildren may not be so happy to accept the core elements of globalization outlined in the previous chapter. That need not be a bad thing, if the result were a better-managed system of international economic governance. However, a lurch toward protectionism would be of great concern.

The emergence of a brain drain into retirement, so to speak, represents not only a deterioration in human capital but also a decline in competitiveness, because educational attainment measures among younger people are increasing more quickly in such countries as South Korea, Japan, Russia, France, Ireland, and Sweden. China, India, Malaysia, Thailand, and Peru are not so far behind. Note that in Germany, like the United States, 25- to 54-year-olds have comparable or lower educational attainment than the 55- to 64-year-old age group. For the United States and Germany, in particular, attracting and keeping migrants with high education and skill levels looks sure to be a key policy issue over the next five to 10 years at least. Maybe it will be just as critical a challenge for other Western nations but the urgency seems rather less.

Financial aspects of immigration are balanced

Higher immigration could help to finance aging societies if it boosted continuously the size of the labor force and, therefore, the amount of personal income, new sources of savings, and new sources of tax revenue to pay for pensions and healthcare. In theory, enough immigrants might lessen the problem about choosing between significant increases in taxation and cuts in social benefits. Once immigrants settle, work, and consume, they pay income and consumption taxes and possibly property taxes. If they arrive without children, parents, and other relatives, there are no benefits to be paid to

offset the taxes that are paid. Government revenues, especially social security receipts, clearly would be strengthened
as a result. But this argument is spurious.

If immigrants mostly move into lower-paid jobs, not only will
their tax payments be rather modest but also social benefits paid
to them will be higher, as you would expect since benefit
systems are designed to redistribute income to the lower
paid. Benefits to the lower paid tend to be higher as a result.
Moreover, as aging proceeds and lower-paid people retire, the
benefits paid to them during retirement are more likely to
exceed the tax contributions they made while at work, given
average longevity. But many immigrants have families, including both young and older dependants, who may also be eligible
for social benefits. They will all, sooner or later, become old, all
become part of the rising dependency ratio and all become eligible for benefits.

The tax-benefit tradeoffs are extremely difficult to measure, let
alone prove. You would have to account separately for foreign-
born people with larger and smaller families and dependants,
and you would certainly have to differentiate between skilled
and unskilled immigrants since they will have radically different capacities to pay taxes and receive benefits. You would have
to be able to calculate not only the taxes and benefits they
receive immediately or in their first two years, but over their
and their families' life spans. And you would have to balance
the financial benefits from immigration with the financial costs
of citizenship, job losses and replacements, changes in wage
rates, congestion, overcrowded housing, and much else.

Most models that try to calculate the fiscal costs and benefits
of current rates of immigration produce net costs or benefits of
0–0.5 percent of GDP in advanced economies, hardly worth
worrying about. While there may be some marginal positive
effects on the economy for a while, they are likely to wither
over time. In the end, the best answer may also be the simplest,
namely that the fiscal costs and benefits of immigration, looking at both skilled and unskilled, will eventually balance out.

The link between higher immigration and economic benefits
for aging societies is equivocal and perhaps much exaggerated.

Immigration may have temporary economic benefits but it seems not to have significant durable effects on the overall age structure, overall fertility rates, the labor force participation rate, dependency ratios, or the overall fiscal accounts of the government. Immigrants do, after all, adjust, certainly in economic ways. They also have dependants, they age, and they get sick. Some may also be especially vulnerable to unemployment, for example as a result of discrimination, low educational achievement, or when the economic cycle turns down.

Competition for migrants may be rising

Western economies won't be the only countries looking—or even competing—for the most skilled and educated migrants. China, as we have already seen, has a similar demographic profile to Germany, and its working-age population will start to decline in the next few years. South Korea and Taiwan are aging relatively rapidly and by 2030–35, many developing countries will be looking more actively for immigrant labor. This presumes, of course, that their societies become more open and receptive to immigrants. But if they do, and if China and other developing countries offer incentives and opportunities to attract the skilled and educated in richer countries, then skill shortages could be exacerbated quite significantly.

China and India are both looking to address possible skill shortages in the future. The Peterson Institute study cites Chinese official data that indicate only a quarter of the more than one million Chinese students who went abroad to study between 1978 and 2006 returned to China. As a result, China has begun to try to attract more of its educational émigrés home. In March 2007, new guidelines were issued to encourage roughly 200,000 Chinese scientists, engineers, and executives overseas to return by 2010.

Singapore intends to expand its population by two million to 6.5 million by 2025, principally by increasing immigration of skilled workers from China and India. These will be the people whose parents and grandparents originally turned Singapore from an equatorial swamp into a global financial center. Singapore already has Asia's largest population of foreigners as a proportion of residents. They account for more than a quarter of the population and a third of the labor force.

In the future, though, migrants from the Philippines, Indonesia and Bangladesh, who dominate immigration into Singapore and end up in low-paid jobs in construction and domestic service, may find it harder to enter. The government of Singapore intends to prioritize higher levels of education as entry requirements for migrants who can adjust readily to work in sectors in which Singapore excels, for example, private banking, finance, biotechnology, and education. This is not a policy without risk, because Singapore has already encountered a bit of a backlash as residents worry about the effects on congestion, local wages, and the implications of even greater population density for food and water supplies, housing, and urban services. Moreover, although issues surrounding Singapore's social balance between Chinese, Malays, and Indians are never far from the surface, it remains to be seen how this balance evolves under pressure from further large immigration. In any event, while this is a management and social challenge for Singapore, it is an economic and competitive challenge for Hong Kong, other Asian countries, and, by extension, for the global economy.

Conclusions

Immigration enriches society and culture, and it provides an important support, if not solution, for a country's skills development and the economy. If rich countries are to take advantage of immigration to try to address, at least partly, the consequences of aging societies, they must educate people far more about its benefits and tackle, over a sustained period, its social and community consequences as well as the attendant issues of citizenship and integration. In other words, they must manage the consequences of immigration and be responsible and accountable for the success of integration, long after the immigrants first arrive.

No matter how many think tanks and government departments in many Western countries are formulating numbers and commissioning research to support immigration, ordinary people in many countries appear to be losing patience with what they see as either incompetent government, or an abrogation of responsibility by government, over the policies and consequences of immigration. These matters merit close attention because it is arguable that the consequences of immigration are too serious to be left to immigrant and native-born communities to sort out on their own. If governments simply pass laws and agree to directives without providing adequate programs and resources to both migrant and local communities to assist cohesion in the community, these social and political tensions will grow. At some point, these could spark much more serious unrest and division.

In good times, when unemployment is low, jobs are plentiful, and local government authorities have money to spend, immigration-related friction may occur but rarely to anyone's real alarm. Even in recent times, however, with low unemployment and manageable inflation and satisfactory economic growth, those tensions have been increasing. Recessions, on the other hand, exceptional though they may be, can normally be relied upon to trigger social and ethnic tensions. As the West's banking and housing crises of 2007 evolve with probably negative consequences for economic growth and employment in 2008 and for some time to come, the way these tensions develop and are managed will become critical. But they will also affect the climate of opinion as aging societies evolve alongside them. To continue along this path with an overtly negative and restrictive approach to immigration would almost certainly be self-defeating for individual countries and would ultimately weigh on the global economy. If ever there was a case for a stronger role for the government and public authorities in a crucial area of public policy education and implementation, immigration demands it.

Endnotes

1   Eric Hobsbawm. In conversation with Antonio Polito, 1999. *The New Century*, (London: Little, Brown and Company, 2000).
2   The Pew Global Attitudes Project, "World Publics Welcome Global Trade—but not Immigration" (October 4, 2007).

3   FT/Harris poll on Nationality and Identity (December 14, 2007), http://www.harrisinteractive.com/news/FTHarrisPoll/HLFinancial Times_HarrisPoll_Dec2007.pdf.

4   Council of Economic Advisers, "Immigration's Economic Impact," June 20, 2007.

5   J. C. Dumont and G. Lemaitre, "Counting Immigration and Expatriates in OECD Countries: A New Perspective," OECD, Paris (2004).

6   Poll conducted December 10–11, 2007, available at http://www.economist.com/media/pdf/econ10dec2007_tabs.pdf.

7   David Pilling and Kathrin Hille, "The New Melting Pot," *Financial Times*, July 9, 2007.

8   Statement released to mark UN Day for Disaster Reduction by United Nations University, Institute for Environment and Human Security, Bonn (October 12, 2005).

9   See, for example, Norman Myers, "Environmental refugees: a growing phenomenon of the 21st Century," *Philosophical Transactions of the Royal Society B*. Biological Sciences, London (April 29, 2002), Vol. 357 (1420), 609–613.

10 Sarah Harper, "Global Aging, Migration and Workforces," Paper presented to the Australian Association of Gerontology, Sydney (November 2006).

11 Steven A. Camarota, "Immigration in an Aging Society," Center for Immigration Studies (April 2005).

12 Three scenarios were used: low immigration (100,000–200,000 a year), medium (900,000 a year), and high (1.6 million a year until 2015 and then 2.7 million a year).

13 N. Diez Guardia and K. Pichelmann, "Labor Migration Patterns in Europe: Recent Trends and Challenges," European Economy Economic Papers No. 256, European Commission, Brussels, (September 2006).

14 John Salt and Jane Millar, "Foreign Labor in the United Kingdom: current patterns and trends," Office of National Statistics http://www.statistics.gov.uk/downloads/theme_labour/LMT_Oct06.pdf.

15 Christian Dustmann, Francesca Fabbri, and Jonathan Wadsworth, "The local labor market effects of immigration in the UK," Home Office Online Report 06/03 (2003), http://www.homeoffice.gov.uk/rds/pdfs2/rdsolr0603.pdf.

16 Jacob Funk Kirkegaard, "The Acceleration in Decline in America's High-Skilled Workforce: Implications for Immigration Policy," Peterson Institute For International Economics, No. 84 (December 2007).

Chapter 10

Demographic issues in religion and international security

> *I hope 'I never get so old I get religious.* —Ingmar Bergman, reported in *International Herald Tribune*, 1989.

The economic and social consequences of demographic change in both advanced and developing nations, and its relevance to globalization and immigration, have been the focus of this book so far. Now I want to turn to two important areas where demographic change has significant implications—religion and global security—and where the connections with demographic change are rarely addressed.

The significance of religion or religious belief to demography has to do with the higher birth rates that are often associated with people who have strong religious affiliations and beliefs. As things stand now, certainly in faster-aging Western societies, low or falling fertility has been the main driver of changes in age structure and dependency. If there is a close association between higher fertility and more religious people, however, and the balance between secular and religious trends in society are changing toward the latter, it is important to consider what the implications might be.

Moreover, demographics and religion are important parts of the backdrop to international relations. Several sources of tension in the world, especially in the Middle East, revolve around the relationships between faster-aging, richer, secular countries on the one hand and more youthful and relatively poorer societies, where religion plays an important role, on the other. There have also been some notable examples where demography, religion, and politics have become more closely intertwined. Consider, for example, the Iranian revolution of 1979, the election of George W. Bush, a man of strong religious convictions supported by the so-called religious right, to two presidential terms in the United States in 2000 and 2004, the comprehensive election victory of Turkey's Justice and Development Party (AKP), which has strong Islamic roots and connections, in 2007, and the spread of religious conflict in Nigeria and the territories of former Yugoslavia.

This fusion of demographic characteristics, religious tendencies, and political outcomes also raises the question of linkages between demographic change and global security—and not only because of the observations referred to above. Aging societies in particular face other major issues. Possible shortages of fighting-age men and women and increased competition between the military and civilian sector for skilled personnel are likely to lead to big challenges for the armed forces and security services. Aging societies may be far less able or willing to engage in conflicts, let alone go to war. While this may be no bad thing as such, history offers no reasons to suggest human beings will abstain from either. Even aging societies may have to fight, but demography is fast becoming a constraint.

The secular-religious pendulum swings back

The world has become more secular over time, aided and abetted by scientific discovery, economic progress, and the social and political functions incorporated into the welfare state. As recently as 1989, when the Berlin Wall came down, people trumpeted—wrongly as it has turned out—the triumph of capitalism and the "end" of history and ideology.[1] In Europe, traditionally seen as an increasingly secular continent, hordes of tourists snake their way through the Notre Dame in Paris or Milan's Duomo, bypassing roped-off areas of pews for mostly older worshippers. Abandoned or derelict churches or church halls, abbeys, and monasteries have become prime sites for development into discos, spas, and sports bars. America has long been seen as a rather more religious place than Europe, and opinion polls regularly reveal much higher proportions of respondents who profess some religious affiliation and belief in God. According to an FT/Harris poll conducted in December 2006 in the United States and five European countries, 73 percent of Americans said they believed in God, compared with just 27 percent of French people, for example.[2] But this snapshot in itself does not really capture the still-strong secular strands of American society.

Even so, the influence and articulation of religious belief in policies and politics has undoubtedly increased in the last 10 to 20 years in Western countries. There are many examples of the hoisting of the religious flag, so to speak, to appeal to many peoples' senses of fear, insecurity, and prejudice nowadays—regardless of whether they follow literally the teachings of the *Bible, Talmud*, or *Koran*. For example, four months after the American-led invasion of Iraq in 2003, President George W. Bush, referring to the operations in Afghanistan and Iraq, was reported to have told an Israeli-Palestinian summit at the Egyptian resort of Sharm el Sheikh that he was driven by a mission from God.[3] And in February 2008, the head of the Church of England, the Archbishop of Canterbury, Rowan Williams, delivered a controversial address in which he said that the adoption of some aspects of Sharia, or Islamic, law in the United Kingdom was unavoidable. Whatever the Archbishop sought to convey with his remarks, the resulting controversy epitomized the heightened concerns over the relationship between religion and secularism in modern times. The reasons for these concerns are closely associated with the repercussions of globalization and the crucial shifts in global power, as discussed in Chapter 8 and also with the demographic dynamics of fertility, population movement, and immigration.

The Pyrrhic victory of secular capitalism

The fall of the Berlin Wall in 1989 defined not only the end of the Cold War but much else besides. America, as a modern, secular democracy, "won" in so far as it remained the world's sole superpower. Capitalism "won" to the extent that the way was then clear for the further advance of unfettered globalization with the entry of billions of people into the global market economy. It was believed widely—and still is by some—that economic success would advance the spread of secularism and act as an agent of change to lessen the influence of religious belief. In effect, the powerful drivers of growth, technology, and globalization, would reduce economic and social problems to the management of incremental improvement and progress, consigning spiritual and existential issues to the periphery.

Neither of these victories, so to speak, ushered in a new era for secular capitalism, however, and the religious-secular pendulum has at the very least faltered in its swing toward the secular. Almost 20 years after from the fall of the Wall, insecurity and injustice, perceived or actual, are rampant. The pursuit of wealth and the acquisition of material goods haven't become sources of comfort and satisfaction for individuals any more than our version of globalization has become the template for unqualified global economic success.

In Chapters 6 and 8, I explained how economic and financial insecurity and feelings of social unease in the West have developed or grown as a consequence of both population aging and globalization, respectively. It is at least in part against this background that new concerns about security, belonging, and identity have emerged. Inevitably, fear and prejudice lurk beneath these concerns. Such feelings are traditionally associated with soul-searching and tend to make people less trusting of secularism and possibly more amenable to what religious belief offers them. This can be in the form of identifying with like-minded people or being more receptive to the worldview of religious organizations.

Although mass religious protests against unfettered globalization and the secular West have been common in many developing countries for a long time, it is in the West that such incidents have become more common in the last 20 years. Christian fundamentalism is not new but was a small and insignificant force for much of the period from the 1920s to the 1980s. Since then there has been a resurgence, and, in recent years, Christian fundamentalists have organized demonstrations to protest the burden of Third World debt, the continuing famine and strife in Sudan, the spread of AIDS, abortion, international sex trafficking, and gay rights. Some religious protests have surprised or even shocked secular societies, none more so perhaps than the mass demonstrations, organized by Islamic groups in Western cities and around the Islamic world to protest the publication of cartoons depicting the prophet Mohammed in a Danish newspaper in 2005.

While these examples demonstrate the mobilization by megaphone of religious feeling, they differ from the more private adherence and respect for religious belief in which people may still mobilize but as self-consciously religious individuals. The main point is that, in both richer and poorer countries, more people seem to be looking to their version of God for the meaning and essential rules of life and for ways of addressing discontentment, injustice, or disadvantage.

Secular capitalism and laissez-faire globalization, then, have not calmed the sometimes turbulent waters between secular and religious society. On the contrary, secular capitalism has not brought with it the abandonment of bigotry and violence, and it has not encouraged people to abandon religious belief in the search for meaning and emotional security. If the world today provides fertile ground for religious alternatives to take root, the significance of demographic change, including population aging, becomes greater. This is for three reasons that I discuss below: the association of higher levels of religious belief with people who have lots of children; the links between stronger religious belief and age; and the tendency for people to pass on their religious beliefs to their children.

Will religion get us from here to maternity?

Mea Sharim is a densely populated district of Jerusalem that is almost exclusively populated by ultraorthodox Jews. Its crowded apartment buildings and narrow streets, filled with men wearing traditional black hats, white shirts, and religious adornments with families in tow, are in a stark contrast with the city's more secular quarters and districts. Mea Sharim is, of course, not unique. Religious quarters can be found in almost every city in the world where freedom to worship is respected. What these religious communities get up to in the privacy of their homes, however, preoccupies demographers and others who wonder what the future might look like.

Ultraorthodox Jews in Israel are growing about three times as fast as the rest of the Israeli population. Today they account for about 12–15 percent of the Israeli population and for about 10 percent of draft-age Israeli Jews. By 2019, it is thought they will account for about a quarter of draft-age people. The fertility rate of the ultraorthodox is six–seven children per woman, compared with 2.2 for nonreligious Jews, who represent 67–70 percent of the population, 2.6 for Arab Christians (16 percent of the population), and four for Arab Muslims and the Druze (about 2 percent of population). There are many reasons why Israelis are concerned about the fertility rates of their different subpopulations. The main concern is the viability of an Israeli state, bearing in mind the higher fertility of Arabs (in and outside Israel) relative to nonreligious Jews. Another is the possible polarization of Israeli society because of the higher fertility rates of both ultraorthodox Jews and Arabs. Polarization would make effective and popular government even more difficult and would hardly facilitate the already elusive search for peace and coexistence between Israelis and Arabs.

This is a small but illuminating example of an issue that we must all confront one way or another, especially in the West. For it is not only Orthodox Jews who have higher fertility than their less religious peers. The same applies to the devout of other faiths and can, as a rule, be seen in fertility contrasts between more and less secular societies. This proposition was supported by findings from the Baylor University Institute for Studies of Religion in Texas, which conducted a comprehensive survey of religion and religious attitudes in the United States in 2006.[4] So if a greater proportion of religious people tend to have more children than do secular people, will populations become increasingly religious and politically conservative in the longer term, in effect reversing decades, even centuries, of more liberal and progressive secular trends in society?

A proponent of this view, writer and demographer Phillip Longman, argued in an essay that religious belief is indeed a driver of larger family size and, consequently, of social trends. He noted that over time societies experience what he called "recurring tendencies"—we might say long cyclical patterns— sometimes toward declining fertility and sometimes to patriarchy. By patriarchy Longman means more than just "rule by men," but stronger religious belief that emphasizes the importance of larger families characterized by the exercise of strong roles by both parents in the education and rearing of children. He argues that patterns of religious revival tend to occur in the most secular societies and that advanced societies are becoming gradually more patriarchal.

Some of this reasoning is quite simply logical, given that childless couples and couples with one child are predominantly secular in outlook and that couples with a lot of children are predominantly more religious. Clearly childless couples do not reproduce themselves, and single children only replace one parent. Longman also noted that in the United States, the small proportion of baby boomer women who had four or more children, as opposed to those having only one, accounted for three times as many children born in the next generation. He concluded that members of society in the future will come mainly from parents who specifically rejected the social, and secular, tendencies that made childlessness or small families normal or acceptable. To the extent that there is a connection between stronger religious belief and larger families, Longman states that the large difference in fertility rates between more secular and more religious people augurs a vast, demographically driven change in modern societies.[5]

The argument that aging societies must become less secular and more religious by virtue of the differences in fertility patterns and social values between secular and religious people is contentious, however. At the very least, it could be construed as offensive to women and people of secular persuasion, who would object that it just panders to the subordination of women and to illiberal and possibly authoritarian societies. But what is at stake here is not the morality or justification of the argument. The key point is that the balance between secular and religious influences on societies will change significantly only if two propositions are true. The first is that people of stronger religious persuasion believe in the necessity or desirability of producing big families. The second is that this value system is passed on to subsequent generations.

In fact, the evidence to support these propositions is equivocal. The trend toward smaller families and secular beliefs in the United States (and western Europe) actually began a long time ago, when the role of religion in schools and in society was much greater. Today, the United States is the epitome of a modern society, spawning liberal cultural and arts movements and social initiatives, for example on gay marriage. So, what do we make of the revival of the religious right in recent years? Why do Mormons (members of The Church of Jesus Christ of Latter-day Saints) in the state of Utah, have a fertility rate that remains 25 percent above the national average? In addition, even though limited to some schools in the South and Midwest, what about the controversy over the teaching of creationism in schools?

Iran, a theocratic state, has a fertility rate that is about the same as the secular United States and much lower than that of India. But, unlike the latter two countries, religion in Iran governs much of life and pretty well all government policies. Ireland, a staunchly Roman Catholic state, had a fertility rate of nearly 3.5 children in the 1980s, but it halved to below replacement rate in the 1990s. If Ireland's fertility rate collapsed in less than a generation and the country has become more secular, however, how was it that a comparable decline in fertility in Northern Ireland was accompanied by the closest thing to (religious) civil war that the United Kingdom has seen since the seventeenth century?

At the very least, the relationship between fertility and religion transcends simple assertions about religious people having bigger families and secular people with smaller families ultimately driving themselves to extinction. Rather, the outlook for the religious-secular balance in society must take into account the demographic context in which religious belief is rising.

Religious belief in the ascendant?

The idea that fertility and religious belief have combined to have profound effects on human development and on history is not disputed. The spread and dominance of Islam in the world up to the thirteenth century owed much to conquest and to a number of features—a common language as well as a legal and moral code—that helped to underpin the creation and governance of commercial relations, trade, and trust. But there is little question that the demographics of Asia in general, and Islam in particular—though there are no reliable estimates for the latter—make up a large part of the explanation. According to data from Angus Maddison at the Groningen Growth and Development Centre in the Netherlands, the population of Asia more than doubled between AD 1000 and 1700 from 183 million to about 400 million, close to 70 percent of estimated global population.[6] Although no one was collecting fertility data at the time, the numbers testify to significant population growth, which must have aided and abetted military recruitment, the spread of political and religious influence, and the exercise of economic power.

Recall, also, from Chapter 2 that early Christendom boomed in the first three centuries of the first millennium to become the official religion of the Roman Empire. This phenomenon is attributed largely to the appeal of Christian beliefs and culture for nonbelievers, and because of their demographic characteristics. They cared well and extensively for their sick, which conferred a mortality advantage over pagans; and they emphasized male fidelity and marriage, which attracted female interest and converts, and this, in turn, gave them the additional advantage of higher fertility.

The intellectual movement in the eighteenth century known as the Enlightenment, in which English, German, and French philosophers argued the superiority of reason (over religion) to combat ignorance and tyranny, marked the beginning of a major, albeit glacial, shift in the religious-secular balance. The background to this was the cumulative effects of rising population growth and of the large-scale movement of young peasants from rural estates to towns and cities in search of freedom and prosperity. It spawned massive changes in the way a then Eurocentric world thought about social organization and the role of institutions other than the Church. The Enlightenment then inspired people—not least in British North America—toward what we might call modernity, which eventually became associated with declining fertility and infant mortality rates.

Thus, while higher fertility rates are associated with people who profess stronger religious belief, the balance between the religious and the secular in society can and does change, regardless, over long periods. Today, we may well be going through another shift for reasons, as I have discussed, that are related to the effects of globalization, feelings of insecurity or injustice, and perhaps a dislike or distrust of some of the contemporary manifestations of a secular and very commercial world.

Consider how the demographic map of the United States is changing and what the religious or secular makeup of the changing population might imply. There is an interesting section in the United States Census, conducted every 10 years, that locates the mean center of population—the point where "an imaginary, flat, weightless, and rigid map of the United States would balance perfectly if weights of identical value were placed on it so that each weight represented the location of one person on the date of the census." In 1790, the mean center was to be found in Kent County in Maryland. Since then it has been shifting south and west through Virginia, West Virginia, Ohio, Kentucky, Indiana, Illinois, and now to Phelps County in Missouri, which is about as far south as Washington, DC and slightly further west than New Orleans. Almost 80 percent of the movement to the south occurred between 1950 and 2000, reflecting both instate and external migration (particularly to Texas and southern California and neighboring states) and higher fertility ascribed to citizens in more southern and westerly states.

The shift in population is noteworthy because observers have attributed America's rightward political shift since the 1970s to the population shift away from the more traditionally liberal coastal states, where secular traditions and smaller families prevail, to the south and west, the Bible Belt, where religious traditions and higher fertility rates are more entrenched. In the 2000 presidential election, George W. Bush won in states where the average fertility rate was 2.11 children, compared with those won by Al Gore, where the rate averaged 1.89. In the 2004 election, Bush won in 31 states where the fertility rates varied between 1.75 and 2.5 children while John Kerry won in states with fertility rates ranging from 1.19 to 1.77.

These observations alone may not tell us nearly enough about exactly how election contests and domestic politics will unfold in the future. But to the extent they inform us about changes in population structure and attendant changes in fertility and measures of religious belief, they surely represent important pointers, not least for politicians.

Indicators of religious belief in Western societies have been compiled by Eric Kaufmann, a lecturer in politics and sociology at Birkbeck College in London. He found that people born after 1945 have lower levels of religious belief than those born before, but that there are signs that religious belief rises with age.[7] This is an important demographic observation in societies where rapid population aging is already under way. And it is not only religious belief that may rise with age. Voting at elections is something older people do more than young people. In the election Bush won in 2004, more than 70 percent of those aged over 55 and eligible to vote did so compared with 47 percent of those aged 18–24. Bearing in mind what I have already shown to be the substantial change in age structure expected over the next 20 years or so, the significance of simultaneous increases in age, religious belief, and political voice is self-evident.

In Europe, according to Kaufmann, there is a significant difference in indicators of secularism and religious belief between countries like France, the United Kingdom, and Germany, which set out on a more secular path more than a hundred years ago, and the Roman Catholic countries such as Ireland, Spain, Belgium, and the Catholic parts of the Netherlands, which started much later.[8] The secular trend in the latter group seems still to be advancing, despite high levels of religious attendance, whereas in the former, it appears to be more advanced but stalling, despite very low levels of religious attendance. In other words, in the most secular societies, there may be a lower limit to measures of religious attendance. But the data also suggest that religious attendance cannot be taken as a proxy for religious belief.

Kaufmann underscores the difference between religious attendance and religious belief in order to draw attention to two phenomena. First, even though the baby boomers and their children tend to have lower levels of religious belief than their parents and grandparents, there is a marked tendency for religious belief to rise with age. Second, religious belief is a powerful predictor of social behavior and more politically conservative attitudes and a more reliable predictor of fertility than education, income, and class. In fact, he claims this is particularly the case in developed countries.

To the extent this is so, population aging is going to have a potentially significant effect on the character of society in the future. If religious belief rises with age, then the tyranny of numbers suggests that a rising proportion of citizens may be expected eventually to have a higher level of religious belief. One survey, noting the difference in religious tendencies between very young adults and their elders, found that the proportion of American 18- to 25-year-olds who said they were atheist, agnostic, or nonreligious, rose from 11 percent in 1986 to 20 percent in 2006—twice the rate for over-25s.[9] But the relative, if not absolute, size of the 18- to 25-year-old age group— as well as those aged 25–39 years—is going to falter in the years ahead. The former group represents just over 14 percent of the population today, but its share will fall to 13 percent by 2025 and 12 percent by 2050. In the member countries of the European Union, in which overall population is expected to be stable or to decline, this age group will also fall from about

11–12 percent today to about 10 percent by 2050. In Germany, where the population is expected to fall, the proportion will decline to under 10 percent.

If religious families have higher fertility rates than zero- or one-child secular families, more and more of tomorrow's children will come from a religious background. The American comedian Dick Cavett once quipped, "If your parents never had children, chances are you won't either." But the serious point about children adopting their parents' beliefs and attitudes remains. The FT/Harris poll referred to earlier found that significant majorities of people had the same religious beliefs as one or both of their parents. Only a fifth to two-fifths of respondents answered that they did not share the same religious beliefs as either of their parents. Specifically, the percentages of respondents answering this way were 39 percent in the United Kingdom, 35 percent in Spain, 32 percent in France, 28 percent in the United States, 26 percent in Germany, and 21 percent in Italy.

In Kaufmann's view, the proportion of people who could be described as "religious" in most secular European societies is roughly 48 percent today. He thinks that by 2040–50, this proportion may have fallen a little in the aggregate to about 44 percent as a result of population developments in the countries that secularized later. By the end of the century, however, it will be higher than it is today. Clearly, this perspective is a purely demographic observation and does not take into account other factors that may stimulate or dull patterns of religious belief. Nevertheless, it points to the tendencies for religious belief to rise with age and for parental beliefs to be handed down to the next generation.

Last, immigration represents an important overlay on national religious, age, and fertility characteristics, in particular, because global migration trends have been rising and arousing growing concerns. The arrival of mainly east European, Asian, and North African immigrants in western Europe, and Asian and Hispanic immigrants in America is already playing a role in the development of local communities and regions, not least because of the religious affiliations they bring with them, and their beliefs and practices as they settle. Migrants who tend to be relatively poor and less well educated may struggle to adapt and thus experience financial hardship, social exclusion, and local hostility. Given this, they tend to look to religion and religious institutions for comfort and to satisfy their sense of belonging.

Kaufmann concludes that his evidence bears this out to an extent, but that it is also hard to generalize. For example, in the United Kingdom he found that Afro-Caribbean Christian immigrants tend to become more secular in the second generation (albeit with the same generational tendency for religious belief and age to rise together) but that Muslim ethnic groups exhibit very strong rates of religious retention. In other words, Muslims, who may account for about a half of non-European immigrants in western Europe in the next few decades, tend to show no strong secularizing trend from one generation to the next.

However, even this is debatable. A recent study about religion and fertility among European Muslims argued that Muslim immigrants do tend to have more children than other Europeans but that their fertility rates also tend to decline over time.[10] For example, Austrian Muslims and Turkish women in Germany still had larger families than native-born women in 2005, but over 20 years, their fertility rates had fallen much faster. So, while women who report high levels of religious belief do tend to have higher fertility than those who don't, the reason may have less to do with any particular kind of religious belief, and more to do with low marriage age, economic circumstance and social traditions.

In the United States another Pew survey, conducted among 35,000 people aged over 18 years, found recently that barely 51 percent of people reported that they were members of a Protestant denomination and that this proportion was most likely to continue to decline as the influence of largely Roman Catholic, Hispanic communities increases.[11] According to the survey, Latinos account for about a third of Roman Catholics, and their proportion is continuing to grow. There were also some interesting observations that brought age, religious belief, and immigration together. For example, Latinos account currently for about 12 percent of Roman Catholics aged over 70, but about 45 percent of those aged 18 to 29. As they grow older and have children and as new, younger immigrants settle, their role and influence within the Roman Catholic Church and in the country is liable to increase.

Secular balance can be sustained

Every now and again, once-in-a-lifetime human or global developments may alter the balance toward either greater secularism or greater religious belief. I have already noted the significance of the Enlightenment in seventeenth- and eighteenth-century Europe and the United States. Political revolutions alter the balance radically too and can go either way. The Bolshevik revolution in Russia and the establishment of Communism in China outlawed religion, in effect, but it was at the heart of the Iranian revolution.

In the absence of such movements or events, however, demographic change may still exert significant influence. In general, increased human security tends to lower both religious belief and fertility, but the reverse may now be the case in many communities and societies, reinforced by population movement and migrant flows. It is easy to overgeneralize, and we should note that some religious groups, including Jehovah's Witnesses, Seventh Day Adventists, and the Amish people in Pennsylvania, for example, don't exhibit the same (higher) fertility trends as, say Mormons and Muslims. Then again, Shia Muslim Iran, some other Muslim countries, and some in Roman Catholic Latin America have fertility rates that are relatively low and or are continuing to decline.

In the end, maybe the real significance of religion as a demographic and inevitably, political, phenomenon lies in its appeal when people question the ability of secular societies to meet their essential needs, whether these are for freedom from poverty or for social justice and access to education and opportunity. If the state cannot help them channel their aspirations and address their concerns, religious belief is liable to become more appealing. Indeed, it is quite possible that the revival of religious belief nowadays simply reflects a world in which identity and belonging matter more and more. Accordingly, it is not surprising that such people may find in religion the spiritual comfort they lack, or think they lack, as a result of alienation or exclusion from modern secular life.

Because of the presumed fertility differences between those of religious and secular dispositions, we may well find that over the long term the balance in society between the religious and the secular tilts further toward the former. To some, modern secular society is itself anathema, and nothing will prevent completely their intolerance of what they see as corrupt and deluded societies and their desire to return to some mythical, traditional order. There's no compelling reason, however, to believe that the fusion of extremist religion and politics must result eventually in a new Dark Age. It simply means that governments and institutions must address those features of modern society—alienation, exclusion, poverty, disadvantage—that lead to stronger religious belief in the first place and, more to the point, its politicization.

International security

Demographic change influences insurgency, ethnic conflict, terrorism, and state-sponsored violence. It does so because "youth bulges" increase social and economic pressures and expand the numbers of recruits to the armed forces, especially those out of school or work. As one author notes, "It is a formula that hardly varies, whether in the scattered hideouts of al-Qaeda, on the backstreets of Baghdad or Port-au-Prince, or in the rugged mountains of Macedonia, Chechnya, Afghanistan or eastern Colombia."[12]

Let us recall first some of our main demographic conclusions as a template for this discussion:

- The bulk of the world's population growth is expected to occur in less developed and emerging countries.
- More than half the world's population will live in cities by 2010 and about 60 percent by 2030. Of the world's top 10 megacities, that is, with population in excess of 10 million, only one—Tokyo—will be in a wealthy "Western" economy.

- "Youth bulge" will occur in many parts of the developing world, notably in Afghanistan, Pakistan, India, Colombia, Iraq, Yemen, Saudi Arabia, and the Palestinian Territories. No shortages of manpower for the armed services and armed groups here.
- The dominant trends in the West will be population decline or stagnation, population aging, and a growing risk of manpower shortages—at least as regards volunteer military recruits. The United States is different only in that its population will continue to expand in line with the world average, and it will gray somewhat more slowly than Japan and western Europe.
- The economic implications of aging societies may sap the financial strength of several Western economies to a greater or lesser extent, as discussed in Chapter 6. This could occur slowly and steadily over time or it may happen as a result of an international financial crisis.

How, then, will these factors shape global security issues in general and the outlook for violent conflict, in particular?

Demographic change and new forms of conflict

Recent experience of global conflict in Iraq, Afghanistan, and the wider Middle East has made us all more aware of the causes of global tension and of our strengths and vulnerabilities. Although demographic factors receive only scant attention in high intensity political and media coverage, they do constitute an inherent weakness of Western countries when it comes to international conflict and security, not least manpower shortages in the armed services and growing difficulties in attracting recruits. By contrast, the youth bulge in many developing countries, including those in the Middle East, merits no such concerns, especially when local economic and political conditions are highly unstable and repressive. If recent developments are anything to go by, these demographic contrasts are likely to become more important in the types of conflict we face in the twenty-first century—predominantly urban and between state and nonstate participants, or what some military theorists call fourth generation warfare, or 4GW.

According to those theorists, including Martin van Creveld and William S. Lind—who developed the 4GW concept—warfare changed with the Treaty of Westphalia that ended the Thirty Years' War in Europe in 1648. The treaty became a sort of constitution of the new system of European nation states, which were granted a monopoly on war, in effect replacing prior forms of conflict between tribes, families, religions, city-states, and so on.

First-generation warfare, from 1648 to about 1860, was based on the tactics of the musket and line-and-column formations. In second-generation warfare tactics, developed by France before and during the First World War, massed firepower replaced massed manpower. Third-generation warfare tactics, attributed to Germany before and during the Second World War, were based on maneuver and infiltration to bypass the enemy's forward units, rather than attrition.

In many ways, 4GW is a throwback to the time before the nation state was assigned its monopoly of armed force in 1648. Other informally and independently organized forces use a variety of tactics to attack the technologically superior state without real hope of conquest in the traditional sense of the word. Rather, the aim is to undermine the enemy's will to fight and to induce a sense of crisis in the state. Al-Qaeda and Hizbollah in Lebanon are prime examples. The distinctions between civilian and military, and between war and politics, diminish, and combat may take place anywhere—in urban or rural areas or even in third-party countries. The nonstate antagonist can wage total war within its financial and technological limitations, of course, and to a greater or lesser clandestine extent, depending on the terrain, as it were. For the state antagonist though, especially in the West, total war is not possible, mainly for moral reasons rather than because of capacity or ability, unless it is backed overwhelmingly by public opinion.

In other words, 4GW is waged by two very different protagonists. On the one side are state-organized and technologically advanced armed forces relying mainly, at least in the

West, on voluntary recruits for whom they are forced to compete with civilian sector employers. Already, they are running into manpower constraints in aging societies, which take a lot more persuading of the legitimacy and justice of conflict. On the other side are nonstate forces engaged in insurgencies and overt terror (as opposed to covert terror, which is what state actors are often accused of), including voluntary loss of life through suicide attacks. These forces deploy modern communications and information technologies, and cultural and religious appeals to recruit sympathizers, particularly among the younger generation. Seen this way, having a youth bulge on your side is a pretty formidable advantage.

Bulging youth populations are a necessary, but not sufficient, reason to expect a high potential for instability or violent conflict. Societies with growing numbers of young people may not be able or willing to provide them with the status, political freedom, employment, and education they expect. Resistance for many, peaceful or otherwise, is often the only form of expression they have left.

Context, as always, however, is important. Historically, six broad sets of circumstances have been associated with violent conflict. These are rising agricultural populations coming into conflict with feudal-type regimes; rising urban populations that become frustrated by insufficient economic growth or macroeconomic instability; increasingly educated populations whose opportunities are limited by repressive or reactionary governments; the confluence of large-scale immigration and existing ethnic tensions; the inability or unwillingness of existing world powers and institutions to accommodate the rise of new ones; and, last, competition over scarce resources, including land, energy, and, perhaps in future, water. In reality, sometimes a few of these are required, in conjunction with demographic factors, to trigger violent conflict. But there is no doubting the significance of the demographic ingredient.

It is believed, for example, that when 15- to 29-year-olds make up about a third or more of the population, violent outcomes to conflict are more likely, regardless of the underlying causes. Today, there are about 67 countries that fall into this youth bulge category, and 60 of them are involved in some kind of civil or other war in which large numbers of people are being killed.[13] To take a few examples, in 1985, Afghanistan had almost nine million people aged under 29. In 2007 that age group numbered almost 19 million, and by 2030 it is expected that it will be almost 40 million, still corresponding to 70 percent of the population. In Iraq, there are 20 million people in the same age group, also 70 percent of the population. While that age group will rise in number to about 28 million by 2030, it will actually represent a smaller, but still substantial, part of the total (58 percent). In the Palestinian Territories, today's 2.7 million under-29s are 71 percent of the population and are expected to grow to 4.6 million by 2030 (63 percent of the population).

Manpower shortages

In Western societies, although there are always groups or social classes that feel excluded or struggle against disadvantage, few choose to express their frustration violently, and fewer still think going to war is good, or justifiable. If more and more families have only one child in longitudinal-type family structures (three or more generations of living adults, no siblings and few, if any cousins, for example), they could become especially hostile to involvement in conflict and war for very personal reasons. If more and more families have only one child or no children as the rest of the population ages, manpower shortages for the armed services will become a more important issue.

Shortages have already become evident as American and British troops have become involved in operations in Afghanistan and Iraq, on top of existing commitments. The emergence of even larger manpower deficiencies in the future now begins to loom much larger. In the United States, Frederick Kagan of the American Enterprise Institute in Washington, DC, reckoned in 2006 that the size of US ground forces needed to be increased by at least 100,000 and possibly by as many as 200,000 active and reserve soldiers, marines, combat, and support forces.[14] Bearing in mind that America's permanent armed forces in all branches are currently about 1,365,000, this means they are 10–20 percent lower then what Kagan thought they needed to be back in 2006.

In the United Kingdom, the National Audit Office reported in 2006 that the armed services were 5,170 below strength, or nearly 3 percent on a total of nearly 181,000 people. Further, the House of Commons Defense Committee reported in the same year that a personnel shortage was already creating a clear danger that the military forces would not be able to maintain its commitments in the near future.

Analysts may argue over past policy issues regarding military spending, and even about strategic planning errors within the military, but only now is it evident that the armed forces face a difficult struggle with recruitment because of the combination of demographic change and because they have to compete for recruits with civilian employers and universities and colleges. Of course, in extreme circumstances, conscription among the unemployed or underemployed and even the prison population could boost the number of people that could serve in the armed forces. But extreme circumstances are not my primary focus.

Will manpower shortages crimp the willingness and ability of the United States and other Western nations to go to war? It is possible. At the very least, they will inhibit the ability, even if not the willingness. It should also be noted, however, that some forms of conflict, such as fighting protracted insurgencies and humanitarian intervention, would remain quite possible. These may well involve hearts and minds, rather than all-out military operations, and rely more on smaller, professional forces focused on expeditionary operations than the full-blown mobilization of large conscript forces.

Moreover, not all conflicts are alike. Where air and naval theater operations are the main focus, it's probable that some sort of balance of power is sustainable. Examples here might include the standoff between China and Taiwan and also between Greece and Turkey. Turkey's 20- to 39-year-olds outnumber those in Greece by more than seven to one (25 million against 3.3 million), and by 2030, the difference will be about 11 to one. Turkey's permanent armed forces of about 514,000 are about three times those of Greece. In the case of China and Taiwan, of course, the population and armed forces gaps are even bigger. Taiwan's permanent armed forces of 290,000 are but a ninth of China's. This is not to argue that there will never be deterioration in relations that might result in the engagement of land forces, but the smaller size of the populations of Taiwan and Greece do not seem an obvious weakness in their ability to sustain a semblance of balance against their larger neighbors.

The same sort of restraint or balance may, it is hoped, be maintained where one or both parties to conflict and dispute have or are believed to have nuclear weapons—for example, Israel, Pakistan, India, and, possibly soon, Iran. There are clearly some potential conflicts in which demographic disadvantage may not matter that much or at least it won't be the most important determinant of conflict. It is possible that for youth bulge to be the major determinant there would have to be contiguous land boundaries between antagonists at least, and for the most part, countries with vastly different demographics don't have such boundaries. Israel and her neighbors are, of course, a major exception; Russia and China may be another. As for France and Germany, let us assume they are not sufficiently different anymore to make a big difference.

But instability, with the potential to lead to conflict, could also arise in the future from uncontrolled and substantial movement of refugees, access to scarce resources including energy and water, the always unpredictable consequences of domestic unrest, and the consequences of failing or failed states. Think of the troubles in the Balkans in the 1990s following the disintegration of Yugoslavia. In Bosnia, Muslims were only 26 percent of the population in 1960, but they accounted for 44 percent by 1990. The Serb share of the population declined from 43 percent in 1960 to 31 percent in 1990. The shift in the structure of population composition was a crucial factor in the ethnic violence that was perpetrated, and also in the significant movements of peoples, often forced, throughout the region. The declining proportion of Protestants, Christians, and Serbs in Northern Ireland, Lebanon, and Kosovo respectively was also clearly an important factor in the conflicts in these regions.

In the end, though, the tragic events in these and other countries cannot be attributed to demographic factors alone, notwithstanding the fact that population and refugee movements over time were patently a catalyst or facilitating factor. Instead, we have to look to a combination of factors including policy mistakes, weak international institutions, social tensions, and, ultimately, chronically belligerent protagonists. Youth bulges in the developing world compared with an aging West need not, per se, produce conflict, but they might if other circumstances contrive to inflate commercial and economic tensions. As the demographic realities sink in, perhaps our attention needs to be drawn even more to managing those potential causes of conflict in future.

The West will have to be both cautious and realistic. The economic and political plates between East and West are shifting, and the demographic advantages accruing to the former, while draining from the latter, will shape the way we interact. The world is going to have to accommodate the rise of new economic and regional powers in Asia, Africa, the Middle East, and Latin America alongside the United States, Japan, Europe, and Australasia. Reformed and strengthened international institutions that give the developing countries additional weight and influence will be needed. This would be not only to show proper respect to globalization but also to recognize their rising share of world trade and world GDP. The West needs to engage them in dialogue and collective action over everything from geopolitical shifts to climate change issues.

We must also pay closer attention to immigration and refugee movements—especially to management of the debilitating effects on large numbers of people and the places they are leaving, and the congestion and social effects on the receiving regions. Ethnic tensions may again be significant when economic and social veneers wear thin. Finally, the global economy needs to be managed so that low inflation and high levels of employment can be sustained and so that flaws in the structure of the global monetary and exchange rate system can be addressed continuously. This applies especially as the American and other Western economies face the fiscal and economic burdens of aging, while China and developing countries

make the shift they are resisting currently toward more consumer-oriented (as opposed to export-led) growth.

It is a big agenda, which will almost certainly falter from time
to time and may occasionally fail. The main point to emphasize, though, is that while the demographic contrast between
East and West stands as a potential dark cloud over our future,
together we have the means to prevent it from undermining
global security and to use it to the world's advantage.

Endnotes

1 See notably Francis Fukuyama, *The End of History and the Last Man* (New York: Free Press, 1992).
2 FT/Harris Poll, "Religious views and beliefs vary greatly by country." (December 20, 2006). http://www.harrisinteractive.com/NEWS/all-newsbydate.asp?NewsID=1130.
3 According to Nabil Shaath, Palistinian Foreign Minister, in a three-part series, *Elusive Peace: Israel and The Arabs* shown by the BBC (October 2005).
4 Christopher D. Bader, F. Carson Mencken, and Paul Froese, "American Piety in the 21st Century: New Insights to the Depths and Complexity of Religion in the US," Baylor University Institute for Studies of Religion in Texas (September 2006).
5 Phillip Longman, "The Return of Patriarchy." *Foreign Policy* (March/April 2006).
6 Angus Maddison, *The World Economy: A Millennial Perspective* (Groningen Growth and Development Centre: Groningen, 2001).
7 Eric Kaufmann, "A Dying Creed? The demographic contradictions of liberal capitalism," Birkbeck College, London (March 2007).
8 Kaufmann, op. cit. p. 2.
9 *Washington Post*, "Americans May Be More Religious Than They Realize," September 12, 2006.
10 Charles F. Westoff and Tomas Frejka, "Religiousness and Fertility Among European Muslims," Population and Development Review 33 No:4 (2007)
11 Pew Forum on Religion and Public Life, "US Religious Landscape Survey 2008," Washington, DC (2008).
12 Richard Cincotta, #2: *State of the World 2005* Global Security Brief "Youth Bulge, Underemployment Raise Risk of Civil Conflict." Worldwatch Institute, Washington, DC (March 2005).
13 Gunnar Heinsohn, *Söhne und Weltmacht: Terror in Aufsteig und Fall der Nationen* [Sons and World Power: The Rise in Terror and the Fall of Nations] (Zürich: Orell Fussli Verlag, 2003).
14 Frederick W. Kagan, "The US Military's Manpower Crisis," Foreign Affairs (July/August 2006).

Epilogue

The Boomerangst *generation*

> *Methuselah lived to be 969 years old. You boys and girls will see more in the next 50 years than Methuselah saw in his whole lifetime.* —Attributed to Mark Twain.

We have looked at many facets of demographic change and population aging as they affect our world today. More important, we have looked at the unprecedented ways in which they may shape our future. As I have emphasized, both richer and poorer countries will confront aging in varying degrees sooner or later. Young people in emerging and developing countries should ideally be able to look forward to the economic benefits that follow from reaping their demographic dividend. As I have argued, however, these benefits cannot be taken for granted in the absence of robust institutions and sound policies, especially regarding employment and education.

The more pressing issues and more urgent policy timetable, are in Western societies, where the baby boomers are now leading a charge into retirement over the next 10 to 20 years. In the process, as we have seen, the age structure of society will change in a unique way. In many countries, the numbers of old, and very old, people will increase sharply—both relatively and absolutely compared with toddlers and children. The baby boomers are of course central to the topic of population aging, and while I have referred at various points to the boomers' progeny and the burdens and challenges they will face, it seems appropriate to conclude with some observations specifically about them.

Former US president Bill Clinton told an audience in Little Rock, Arkansas, in October 1991, when he declared his candidacy for the office of president: "I refuse to stand by and let our children become part of the first generation to do worse than their parents. I don't want my child or your child to be part of a country that's coming apart instead of coming together."[1] Clinton wasn't talking about the implications of demographic change but about preserving the American Dream, about restoring the hopes of what he called the "forgotten middle class" and about "reclaiming the future for our children." For a moment, it is worth reflecting on a further extract from the speech: "Middle class people are spending more hours on the job, spending less time with their children, bringing home a smaller paycheck to pay more for healthcare and housing and education. Our streets are meaner, our families are broken, our healthcare is the costliest in the world and we get less for it. The country is headed in the wrong direction fast, slipping behind, losing our way...and all we have out of Washington is status quo paralysis. No vision, no action. Just neglect, selfishness, and division."

You have to consider these words in the context of the time, but it is rather disappointing to reflect that they apply today with as much, if not more, force as they did almost 20 years ago, and not only in the United States. The gathering impact of global demographic change and population aging will undoubtedly exacerbate many of the economic and social issues mentioned, especially what Clinton said about today's children doing worse than their parents.

Today, overlaid on the pressures we face over standards of living and the skewed distribution of wealth and income is the challenge of demographic change. To borrow Clinton's words at the time, the task before us is to "reinvent government to help solve the real problems of real people." So it is against this backdrop that I conclude with some thoughts, not about the baby boomers' world, but about the one they are bequeathing to their children.

As we have noted before, *Boomerangst* is a term that is often applied with tongue in cheek to the angst and insecurity felt by middle-aged baby boomers as they march in legions toward retirement, but the term can also apply to their descendants. They warrant a special focus for two reasons. The first is because of the financial and other concerns with which they are likely to grow up compared with their parents at similar ages. The second is because this generation seems to have developed an unusual tendency to float in and out of parental homes and in and out of employment. It comprises people aged roughly 20–30 years old—the kids of the 1980s, born and raised when the political and economic philosophies of the likes of Margaret Thatcher and Ronald Reagan were in the ascendant. By 2025–2030, they'll be in their economic prime, that is, in their late thirties to early fifties. For many as individuals, the prospect of increased longevity will still be far off and of little immediate relevance. For them collectively, though, the economic and social implications of population aging are becoming all too apparent and will influence how they live—in ways that are sometimes apparent but in other respects, barely imaginable.

You don't have to look too far back to see how aging has already changed our societies. There are organized lobby groups throughout the developed world, many in the voluntary sector, that campaign for the interests of older citizens. One of the most powerful is AARP, the influential American lobby, formerly known as the American Association of Retired Persons. There has been a rapid expansion of leisure activities, products, and services geared largely–if not exclusively—for older people. These include cruise ship, spa and city break holidays, golf, cosmetic surgery, magazines, radio and television stations, organizations for the over-50s, adult education and post-retirement education, physical training facilities for the middle-aged and the elderly, and Viagra. This is a world that no one could have imagined, let alone planned in 1960, and shows how rising life expectancy and aging have already transformed the way we live—mostly in unequivocally positive ways.

Increased longevity—meaning not just higher average life expectancy but also continued increases in the maximum age to which people might live—could bring to the fore unprecedented social and economic issues. Some might wonder whether there will be generational conflict over the distribution of wealth, income and tax burdens, and feuds between families over access to income and wealth. Consider the relatively innocuous, but in some ways, poignant tale of Anna Nicole Smith, who died in 2007 at the age of 39. She had been a Playboy Playmate, model, and reality TV star, but what really brought her into the public eye was her marriage in 1994, aged 26, to one J. Howard Marshall II, a Texan oil magnate aged 89. He died a year later, leaving an estate of more than US$1.5 billion, half of which she claimed he had promised her.

She waged a 12-year feud with one of Marshall's sons over the inheritance and the Supreme Court ruled in 2005 that though she was not to be given a share of the estate, she had the right to pursue a share of it in a federal court. She died, however, after being found unconscious in a hotel room in Florida in February 2007 (the cause of death was not specified at the autopsy). This made-for-tabloids story may have shocked or amused you, or it may even have bypassed you completely. The marriage of young, attractive women to older and wealthy men is hardly seen as unusual, and the motives are mostly self-evident. In aging societies, however, this story raises a rather interesting question, namely how far people may be prepared to go to get access to or lay claim to wealth and financial resources that the elderly may want to hang on to for longer. After all, the elderly usually have financial concerns such as meeting the costs of medical care, longevity treatment, and old-age homes, not to mention good old-fashioned hedonism. The young, however, may have strong financial incentives to persuade them not to do so.

The kiss of debt and other sources of angst

In the immediate future, there are at least three issues that the boomerangst generation will have to confront. First is rising personal debt, incurred as a result of longer periods in, or higher costs of, education, ease of access to credit, and, possibly, the cost of buying a home. This is not to say that younger people cannot or will not reboot their ideas about personal debt and financial behavior. Some sources of personal financial pressure, such as running up cell phone bills and the use of credit and store cards, may be excessive, but these would be the easier ones to adjust to compared, say, with buying an apartment or a house, financing higher education, and providing, for adequate retirement savings. Although it is widely believed that younger people regard as necessities things that their parents see as luxuries or options, it is undoubtedly true that they face a far more financially challenging environment than their parents did.

In the United States, it is estimated that about two-thirds of people in their twenties have some kind of debt, and those who do have been accumulating it more rapidly in the last five years. The average amount of debt for 22- to 29-year-olds was US$16,120 in August 2006, and the fastest growing volume of debt was for those carrying more than US$20,000.[2] The demographic significance of large debt is that it can act to defer marriage, family formation, and parenthood, and it can negate the impact of education (for example, if a trained doctor or engineer opts to go for fast money in different trades or occupations or simply packs up to work abroad or open a bar somewhere).

As a further indicator of the financial challenge facing this generation, in the United Kingdom the building society (mortgage lender) Nationwide has estimated that for the first-time home buyer, aged 29 typically and rising, house prices have gone from about 2.25 times average earnings in 1997 to 5.25 times today without providing any additional (sometimes less) space for the money. The contrast could not be starker between, on the one hand, debt-burdened young adults who find it hard to get onto the property ladder and face insecure pension rights and, on the other, boomers who enjoy considerable wealth tied up in housing and funded retirement schemes and exchange their jobs for comfortable retirement incomes.

In the United Kingdom, a national money education charity, Credit Action, compiles a monthly report outlining the extent of personal debt. It noted that as many as 7.5 million people— or 40 percent of parents—have had to help adult children pay off debts (£2,450, or nearly US$5,000, on average) made up of cell phone bills, car finance, and credit cards, while one in 10 parents help their children to keep up with mortgage payments.³ The report said that 54 percent of graduates leave university with debts of more than £10,000, average consumer debt for 24-year-olds was £13,651, and homebuyers under 25 years owe an average £20,290 on unsecured credit. At the bottom rungs of adulthood, more than half of English teenagers have been or are in debt by the time they are 17 years old.

What is frightening is that about 15 percent of 18- to 24-year-olds think an ISA (individual tax-free savings account) is an iPod accessory, and 10 percent reckon it's an energy drink, according to the same report. It is possibly comforting to think that by saying "iPod" young people would actually become aware that they were "Insecure, Pressured, Overtaxed, and Debt-Ridden," but somehow, that seems rather fanciful.

What is happening in the United Kingdom is extreme but far from uncommon. Similar concerns about overall debt levels, and especially debts acquired by young people, abound in the United States, Australia, New Zealand, Canada, and even in Europe, where the debt culture is not as intense or as widespread. Germany and Ireland worry about the financial obligations, and lack of savings that characterize their young generations, and France speaks of its *Génération Précaire* (precarious generation), which saves little and borrows much.

The second major issue facing some, but by no means all, the boomerangst generation is that of gender inequality. I have already shown that this is a big topic for young people in eastern Europe, China, the Middle East, and India. While it is also likely to affect people in South Korea, Hong Kong, Singapore, and parts of Latin America in the next 20 years or so, young people in Germany, Italy, Japan, and Russia, and even subpopulations in the United States could soon encounter difficulties finding marriage partners. These may result from the raw demographics of couples who have no children or only one child, but they could arise from migration trends, too.

The most educated and marketable young people in relatively poor countries and regions tend to forsake their communities or countries to find careers and partners in more prosperous ones. In many instances, for example, in the eastern parts of Germany, it is women who are the better educated and more marketable, and when they leave their towns and villages, they leave behind disproportionately large male populations. Leaving to look for a new and better life is certainly no novel migration phenomenon, but it is much more important when the youth population is stagnant or declining. Against this background, gender imbalance becomes more acute.

Finally, the changing structure of the global economy is underscoring the *angst* in *boomerangst*. This is not itself a generational issue in a single society in that it does not involve the young and the old competing for resources and lifestyles. It is a generational issue, however, in the sense of younger, more powerful emerging economies and political powers clashing with older or fading ones. The baby boomers in the West grew up in the aftermath of the Second World War and under the shadow of the Cold War but in a world they could confidently believe belonged to them. It was theirs to influence and change. As they did so, they accumulated wealth and economic privilege on an unprecedented scale, a process their children and grandchildren may not be able to replicate. Even if this was not the boomerangst generation's chief aspiration, however, they will not be able to feel, as their parents did, that the world is theirs alone—or even at all.

British people have had a long time to get used to the idea of not being citizens of an imperial power. The country may still be able to influence global issues, but its capacity to pursue goals and implement solutions alone faded a long time ago. Continental European people have lived for a long time on the fringes of global power politics and have sought to influence only their immediate geography through the organizing force of the European Union. America has been the sole global power and democratic country with both the will and the ability to continue to shape the world through its economics, politics, military, culture, and philosophy. Young people especially, the world over, have identified with American movements in music, the media and entertainment, business methods, and general attitudes. But for how long will this continue?

This is not to suggest that on a global level attention to youth culture or the cult of young celebrities will not survive; we still prize the energy, innovation, and fresh ideas that younger people bring to political and corporate leadership. Nevertheless, the old, familiar domination of Western culture seems to be in slow decline, or at best, less potent now—courtesy of changes in the global order and the balance of financial and political power. Instead, the future belongs increasingly to Asia, specifically China and India, and to other young, dynamic emerging markets.

Insecurity, inequality, and changing family structures

The sequential order of adolescence, adulthood, marriage, parenthood, and retirement is already changing as longevity rises and as globalization transforms work, industry, education, family, and income security. The boomerangst generation seems in many ways to have a falsely optimistic view about the future—one for which it seems increasingly unprepared, especially financially. Some people wonder whether it has itself to blame for these exaggerated expectations. The baby boomers, however, are not blameless. While their intentions were and are no doubt the best, some have overprotected their children to the extent that many lack the means or capacity to pursue personal development and to use initiative. In short, childhood bonds haven't really been allowed to break as they should.[4]

Blame and responsibility aside, it is undoubtedly true that children are having a tougher time growing up than their parents. Aging societies are already characterized by more insecurity and inequality than the boomers experienced as they made their way through young adulthood. Former US Secretary of Labor, Robert Reich, has argued that the economic slowdown in the United States is only part of the reason for the plight of the middle class.[5] He noted that a male in his thirties today earns 12 percent less than a similarly aged predecessor in the 1970s and that America's middle classes have now exhausted the means they employed during the last decades to sustain or increase consumption. The first was the sharp rise in the numbers of women joining the labor force. The proportion of working women with school-age children rose from less than 40 percent in 1970 to about 70 percent over the next 30 years. This tap has now run dry. The second was the rise in the number of hours people work, now about two weeks longer on average than in 1970. The third was the boom in credit demand and in the practice of using housing wealth to consume and borrow more ("home equity withdrawal," as it is known)—a phenomenon now in sharp decline, as we saw earlier in this book.

These demographically driven coping mechanisms, as Reich called them, have become exhausted. In the immediate future, Americans will have to trim their lifestyles and consumption. But the implication over the longer term is that demographic change could intensify the pressure on all citizens, not just the middle classes. If economic insecurity is already widespread and it is not possible to increase female labor force participation or total hours worked, other methods will have to be found to avert a demographically induced economic malaise for the boomers' children.

Increased longevity, moreover, means that healthcare costs and medical insurance premiums are going to be higher. This will almost certainly favor the more affluent, who will be better able to afford old age, while the less well off may simply have to confront longevity with greater financial trepidation and die younger than their more affluent compatriots. It means bigger financial burdens and sacrifices—both to pay for the coming wave of retirees and to meet the increasing costs of retirement. It means working longer because of a higher mandatory retirement age or because more people want or need to be useful for longer. It means that there will be more of a focus on wealth inequalities as the boomers take their wealth with them into old age and leave to their children little by way of inheritance. It could involve a greater incidence of marital breakdown later in life, and thus an even greater proliferation of small or single-adult households and fewer financial resources and time for parenthood.

The whole character, look, and feel of cities and neighborhoods, towns and rural villages is likely to change, reflecting both youth depopulation and growing numbers of older people and the shifts in social and family structures toward smaller units. In the past, there seemed to be a certain order to the way we grew up and to the way families evolved. Typically, children grew up in families with at least one sibling and had a network of relatives, including two sets of grandparents as well as aunts, uncles, and cousins. They would go to university and or go to work and eventually have their own families and, with luck, inherit worldly goods and property from their parents. In the decades following the Second World War especially, this sequential order became a bedrock of aspiration and well-being. It was reinforced and supported by a generally benign economic and social backdrop, including sustained economic growth, the acceptability of wider income redistribution by government, continuous career employment in settled industries, and greater access to high-quality secondary and university education.

Gradually this is all changing. In the first place, children are being born into families that are more "long" than "wide." In other words, they may have no siblings, cousins, aunts, or uncles, but they could expect, as a norm, to have not only parents but also living grandparents and great-grandparents. It is quite possible to imagine this but much harder to know what it might mean.

Think about how family structures are changing even today. In the United States in 2006, for example, there were 92 million people who were unmarried or single, equivalent to 42 percent of all people over the age of 18 years. Of these, 60 percent had never married, 25 percent were divorced, and 15 percent were widowed. At the household level, a quarter of people were living alone, and an unmarried person headed nearly half of households. Only a third of households had children aged less than 18 years (compared with a half in 1960), and by 2025–30, this proportion may be no more than a quarter. In a nutshell, childless single people will continue to grow as a group.

What will become of the role of the family in preparing young people for interaction in society if the family is comprised mainly of older relatives? Without siblings and peer age group relatives, how will children learn to offer and receive help and comfort as they do in bigger or extended families? Facebook may be fun and a great way to stay in touch with or make new friends, but it is no substitute for the extended family. Family units without biological peers and comprising three, or possibly even four, generations create different demands from more traditional ones. These include young and middle-age parents having to bear more responsibility for dependent children as well as their parents and grandparents, while more family members require care and financial support in old age. Furthermore, if older people work for longer, employment possibilities for younger people could be compromised. At the same time, financial opportunities may be limited by lower economic growth generally, reduced retirement benefits, higher taxes, and the costs associated with retirement provision. None of this is to say that families will not adapt, but life will be different. New family structures and relationships will evolve in the process, and for many, financial and lifestyle aspirations may have to be revised in line with changing economic circumstances.

Conclusion

The boomerangst generation, then, faces a quartet of life-changing developments. First, it may find that parental wealth slips away into the financing of longevity and old-age care instead of into an inheritance pot. While this ensures that wealth is transferred to the rest of society by way of purchases of goods and services and through taxes, it isn't the same thing as inheritance. This may cause conflict between individuals of different generations, if the younger ones think it fair or proper still to inherit.

Second, it will almost certainly become directly involved in wider generational policy issues. These include the financing of age-related spending for parents and grandparents, a less generous pension and tax environment, bigger pressures for self-provision in retirement, and possibly higher inflation and less buoyant property markets.

Third, they and their children in turn will mature with different types of family structures and support networks in which grandparents and great grandparents may play much more important roles. Some couples may spend the best part of 40 years together after their child or children have left home, but some will divorce and or remarry, establishing new and sometimes complex household structures and relationships. Many will have to get used to living alone in older age. Well over half of women aged over 75 do already, largely because they live longer than men and also because older widows have much lower remarriage rates than older widowers.

Finally, the boomerangst generation will have to address how their aging world will adapt to new patterns of globalization and continued high levels of immigration, but in a different and unfamiliar context. The dominance of the West that they might naturally have assumed to be their cultural inheritance may turn out to be hollow, as younger societies in the developing world grow in stature and size to fill the gaps being created by aging societies elsewhere.

Some things will doubtless favor the boomerangst generation. It will grow up and advance toward prime working age at a time when incomes, consumption, and savings will be higher. There will be fewer of them, compared with their parents, so there will be markedly less competition for university places, jobs, and financial resources. Because of tightening labor markets, low unemployment rates may become the norm. Housing could become significantly more affordable if the long-run trend in real house prices weakens after the current housing bust has passed. Last but not least, it has grown accustomed to the effects of deindustrialization, certainly compared with the time of Clinton's speech in 1991. More to the point, the information economy continues to throw up new opportunities for work and leisure, which it is sure to exploit.

From a big picture standpoint, the boomerangst generation will have to find its own solutions and ways of adjusting to population aging. It is likely to involve an expansion of government responsibility and authority for the management of change, specifically with regard to population aging but doubtless other important issues. Preparation for population aging is, like other matters that concern us today, a priceless public good, the benefits of which are indivisible.

In saying this, I am not arguing that private provision and self-interest cannot come up with solutions, but the likelihood is that people may not care for the repercussions, which would almost certainly include wider societal divisions and inequalities. As more and more people want to live a dignified and satisfying old age, with more of it active or at work, changes in social attitudes and public policy will become necessary, especially in the work, education, health, and care sectors. This will be a major task.

The Spanish film director, Luis Buñuel, who lived until he was 83, was once believed to have quipped that "age is not important unless you're a cheese." Those who are sitting back in poolside chairs at a retirement condominium in Miami or Malaga, may understand what he meant. Collectively, though, we are about to find out just how important this point is going to become in societies that are poorly prepared for the Age of Aging.

Endnotes

1 Available at http://www.4president.org/speeches/billclinton1992
   announcement.htm.
2 *USA Today*, November 27, 2006.
3 Credit Action, "In Debt Facts and Figures," (October 1, 2007).
4 For an interesting opinion on this, see Will Hutton, "Why too much care for your child can harm society," *The Observer*, February 3, 2008.
5 *Financial Times*, "America's middle classes are no longer coping," January 30, 2008.

Population forecasting

Unless otherwise noted, most global population data come from the United Nations Population Division (UNPD), which has a user-friendly website (http://www.un.org/esa/population/unpop.htm) where it is possible to download or consult a myriad of population data from 1950 all the way out to 2050. The UNPD website also carries up-to-date information on reports, newsletters, and conferences that it has commissioned, sponsored, or written on topics including general population issues, migration, urbanization, fertility and mortality, contraception use, HIV/AIDS, and living arrangements for older people. The UNPD's forecasts are produced using a central case and a high and a low variant. I have used the central case projections throughout the book.

Although population variables are widely assumed to be among the more predictable, they are also liable to error and revision. The oft-stated warning that any forecast is only as good as the assumptions made by the forecaster is as true for demographers as it is for scientists, economists, and professionals in other social disciplines. When we talk about birth rates and life expectancy over the next 20, 30, or 50 years, and deduce what a society's age structure will look like and what the implications might be, while we can be reasonably confident, there is always a risk that things will not evolve as we expect.

Low or falling fertility in many societies is generally assumed to be a permanent phenomenon. The UNPD predicts that by 2050, fertility rates in developed economies will rise a little, but not enough to make a material difference to the overall outlook for age structure. The decline in global fertility has been explained in terms of advances in adult education, female literacy, and cheap and readily available methods of birth control. There may be other social, economic, and cultural factors, however, that influence the decision as to how many children women have. These factors may be rooted in changes in living standards and modernity, and they are apt to change for various reasons over time.

The more substantial economic and social problems in aging societies are expected to come not so much from living longer but from low fertility and the stagnation in the number of young and working-age members of society. It is important, therefore, that aging societies try to understand better what it is that depresses fertility rates and, should they chose to do something about it, what social and economic policies might work to bring fertility rates back to the replacement rate.

Rising life expectancy is widely assumed to be a likely prospect for most of us, but there is no unanimity about how long we may expect to live now, let alone what might occur in the future. In North America and most of western Europe, males can expect to live to about 75–76 and females to about 81. By 2050 life expectancy will have risen to about 80–81 for men and 85 for women. In Asia and Africa, increases in life expectancy are forecast to be even sharper. Asian males and females today have life expectancy of 67 and 71 years respectively, but by 2050, it is expected to have risen to 77 and almost 80 respectively. In Africa, male and female life expectancy is forecast to rise from 49 and 50 years to almost 64 and 67, respectively.

Some demographers believe scientific advances and behavioral changes involving smoking, alcohol, diet, and exercise will continue to push the bounds of longevity toward 95–100 years. As a result of changes that have already occurred, a significant part of rising life expectancy comes from falling mortality in the over-50s age group. However, some say the rising life expectancy in the past has been the result of dramatic, but one-off, improvements in reducing infant and child mortality. Other demographers say there might be a sudden or significant reversal in life expectancy in the future from big shocks such as a bird flu pandemic, a more intensive spread of HIV/AIDS, and the outbreak of larger wars. More mundane causes, such as the disturbing increase in obesity, diabetes, and other chronic diseases, lie within our own capacity to address. A report by the Milken Institute, a California-based global policy think tank, said that more than half of Americans suffer from one or more chronic diseases, the most common of which cost the American economy more than US$1 trillion a year in treatment and medicines.[1] To this one would have to add other costs in respect of time off work, under-par performance, and other forms of lost output and income. The institute argued that the cost could rise sixfold by 2050 but is entirely avoidable. Apart from the cost, the demographic significance is to do with whether obesity-related disease might actually halt or reverse rising life expectancy.

According to the World Health Organization, there are now about 1.6 billion adults (people aged over 15) classified as overweight and 400 million as obese. That is about 25 percent and 7 percent of the world's population respectively. It is expected that by 2015 these numbers will have risen to 2.3 billion and 700 million respectively, at which point they will account for more than 31 percent and roughly 10 percent of the world's population. The highest prevalence of overweight and obese people exists on the islands in the Pacific, but generally Asian countries enjoy exceptionally low occurrences of both. Surprisingly perhaps, countries in the Middle East, including Saudi Arabia, Bahrain, Egypt, and Iran, and some in Latin America have far higher rates of obesity and overweight people than many countries in western Europe. In western Europe the lowest rates are in France, Italy, and Spain, the highest in the United Kingdom and Germany. About 40 percent of America's adults and 25 percent of those in the United Kingdom, Canada, and Australia are classified as obese.

Since death rates arising from different forms of obesity are anything from 10 percent to 80 percent higher than for the nonobese, the implications for life expectancy seem to be serious in the very long run if these conditions are not checked and reversed. Where the number of people classified as obese represent a significant fraction of the adult population over the next 10–15 years, overall life expectancy trends could be affected adversely. While we can all acknowledge the individual health risks from poor diet and lack of exercise as self-evident, the risks to life expectancy for the population as a whole are by no means agreed among doctors and scientists. Many health and safety issues that are in the fore-front of public campaigns hide from view direct funding inter-ests (in the case of obesity, from the weight-loss industry), genetic predispositions toward particular types of chronic dis-ease, and arbitrary definitions of terms, such as *overweight* and *obese*. For the purposes of this book, I have assumed that while obesity clearly is a serious health problem, lifestyle and dietary changes will continue to exert downward pressure on its prevalence in the long run.

There are many factors relevant to the evolution of aging societies about which we have insufficient knowledge or understanding. These could affect long-term trends for fertility and longevity directly, as well as indirectly, via the ways in which we will cope with aging. Genetic research, cloning, and antiaging technologies might all have positive effects on life expectancy, our ability to absorb and use information, and remain stronger for longer as we age. Robotics may comprise a part of the solutions to aging populations, neutralizing some of the adverse economic and personal effects of aging.

Japan, for example, is the number one world producer of robots, accounting for almost half the world's robotic work-force. In the last few years, partly in response to aging and partly to the country's hostility to immigration, Japanese robotic manufacturers have developed, among other things, a feeding machine that deploys a joystick-controlled swivel arm that scoops food off a plate and brings it to the mouth; a furry, therapeutic seal that has sensors that make the animal respond to petting; robotic canine companions; voice-activated wheel-chairs; an automatic vacuum cleaner on wheels that uses lifts to travel up and down floors; and robot receptionists, security guards, and visitor information staff.

You may consider some of these to be rather outlandish as ways in which life for the elderly could change in the future—but maybe no more so than the functions of the Internet might have seemed to our parents and grandparents. It is certainly not far-fetched to imagine that technology will produce a range of voice-activated devices and androids to perform care and household functions. These may enable elderly people to enjoy an improved quality of life while allowing more of our working-age people to undertake more productive work instead of being diverted into care-related functions.

Last, the effects of rapid population aging rely on population and age structure predictions, which may be as fallible as any other forecasts. Aging is a slow-moving phenomenon, however, and even if some of our assumptions prove to be off the mark in the long run, the implications of aging and the policy issues raised in this book describe more than sufficiently a picture of aging for the foreseeable future.

Endnote

1   Ross DeVol and Armen Bedroussian, "An Unhealthy America: The Economic Burden of Chronic Disease," The Milken Institute (October 2007).

Index